1971

Windows of the Morning

A Critical Study of William Blake's

Poetical Sketches, 1783

BY

MARGARET RUTH LOWERY, Ph.D.

ARCHON BOOKS
1970

[*Yale Studies in English, Vol. 93*]

SBN: 208 00918 3
Library of Congress Catalog Card Number: 73-91183
Printed in the United States of America

To the Memory
of my Mother

PREFACE

THE scholarly studies of William Blake through the years since Gilchrist's *Life* was published have been extensive. Yet there have been on the part of most scholars such a curious neglect of the *Poetical Sketches,* published in 1783, and such a failure to credit Blake with the full significance to which that performance entitled him that a fresh evaluation of the *Poetical Sketches* was needed.

The investigation incident to such an appraisal required, first of all, a re-examination of the sources of information about William Blake's youth. This has made it possible to separate authentic biographical material from much that is apocryphal which has until now been unquestioned. Consequently, some environmental forces have been given a different emphasis, and new significance has been observed in relationships previously slighted.

This study of the *Poetical Sketches* sets forth a complete description of the book, corrections of errors in information about its production, new circumstantial evidence as to its printing and as to the personal relationships with which it allied Blake.

That the *Poetical Sketches* was imitative work has long been taken for granted. This book is an examination of the full extent of Blake's indebtedness to others, a critical analysis of how his creative imagination acted upon what he derived from his early reading, and an appraisal of the *Poetical Sketches* in the light of these circumstances.

Research has not justified the unsupported general assertions of critics either that the Elizabethan influence was more extensive than any other or that the influence of Blake's own century was negligible. This study specifically points out that the Bible and Milton were significant influences upon Blake in his youthful poetry; that the influence of Spenser was the most subtle and essentially poetic; that Shakespeare's influence, although great and less definable, was largely confined to *King Edward the Third* and to a deepening of Blake's per-

sonal convictions; that there is little demonstrable influence
from Ben Jonson and others of Jonson's time; and that the
eighteenth century exerted the most extensive influence both
in the number of poems affected and in the number of authors
who were Blake's sources.

The work of James Thomson was found to have directly
inspired Blake's art before 1783, and to have influenced a
larger number of poems than anyone has previously made
known. Misconceptions about the impossibility of Blake's
knowing Chatterton's work before 1778 have been corrected.
That Chatterton was the medium through which Ossian's
greatest early influence acted, and that Chatterton served to
sustain the lyrical qualities of Blake's poetry against the
counteracting power of Ossian have been demonstrated.
Blake's adherence to certain other literary fashions of his day
has been pointed out, as well as the ways in which he departed
from the prevailing contemporary styles in poetry and anticipated the later romanticists.

The specific parallels which have justified these conclusions
have furnished a basis and a perspective for a critical sum-
mary of the nature of Blake's creative powers and of the
originality of his achievement in the *Poetical Sketches*.

This book in another form was offered at Yale University
in partial fulfillment of the requirements for the degree of
Doctor of Philosophy. Whatever merit there may be in this
study—first and last—must be ascribed to Professor Chaun-
cey Brewster Tinker who directed my work and put at my
disposal his Blake collection, including the Gaisford copy of
the *Poetical Sketches*. His stimulating suggestions and con-
stant interest can never be adequately acknowledged. To
many Blake scholars who have preceded me, gratitude is expressed in the notes for various kinds of aid. Apart from the
indebtedness I share with all scholars to the unfailing courtesy
of the staffs of libraries, particularly the British Museum, the
University of London Library, the Fitzwilliam Museum, the
Henry E. Huntington Library, the Library of Congress,
the Wellesley College Library, the Fogg Museum, and the university libraries of Harvard and Yale, I am especially grateful to Mr. Oliver R. Barrett for the use of his Blake manu-

script, to Mrs. William Emerson and to Mr. A. E. Newton
for the privilege of seeing their Blake collections, and to Mr.
A. Bone of the Nash Mills for his aid in dating the paper
Blake used.

Another bestowal of kindness I shall not readily forget.
Without the invaluable criticism of the manuscript by Dr.
Blanche H. Dow, Dr. Anna M. Painter, and Mrs. Emory H.
Wright, and without the labor of proofreading by Miss Ethel
Hester and Mr. Kenneth Harper, this book could not have
reached completion.

April 6, 1940.

CONTENTS

ILLUSTRATIONS

WINDOWS OF THE MORNING

CHAPTER I

THE YOUTHFUL BLAKE

THE anecdotes of William Blake's childhood have an apocryphal air, as do those of children in whom normal inquisitiveness is closely allied to a flashing imagination. One suspects that they have acquired authority more from their repetition than from indisputable evidences of their authenticity. They savor of too much telling; they have the relish of the marvelous and the astonishing. Childhood seldom leaves an adequate or authentic record of itself. Details of childish behavior fade from memory as new activities engage attention, and, consequently, when they are recited later, episodes of childhood receive new lustre and meaning according to the skill of the narrator and the need to account for what the child eventually became. The result is often a distortion of the normal play of fancy. This was particularly true of Blake. There are singularly few details known of any period of his life, and those that have been recorded of his childhood and youth, more meager still and more marvelous, arouse in one a certain skepticism with respect to the significance that later-day critics have read into them.

The documentary sources of information about the first period of Blake's life are few. Of the five principal sources only two were written by men who knew Blake during his earlier years. A third was unacquainted with him until his last years, and the other two, invariably drawing upon one of these three, added facts received from living witnesses who knew Blake at one time or another but for the most part in his declining years. Those who record impressions of his last days, such as Crabb Robinson, John Varley, John Linnell, or Joseph Farington, are not trustworthy testimony for Blake's youth. The host who have written about Blake since his death have added almost nothing new about his childhood; all have drawn from these five first sources. If the unreliability of anecdotes of childhood as well as the strangely uncommunicative nature of the members of the Blake family are considered, these sources are likely to continue to be the canon of authority for this period of Blake's life.

The first printed account is a brief sketch by Benjamin Heath Malkin, embedded within a dedicatory epistle, dated Hackney, January 4, 1806, to Thomas Johnes of Hafod, M.P., Lord Lieutenant of the County of Cardigan, which accompanies *A Father's Memoirs of His Child*.[1] Malkin had spent several months with Thomas Johnes at Hafod in the summer of 1805, when the latter persuaded him to furnish the public with facts of the life of his precocious son, Thomas Williams Malkin, who had died July 31, 1802, lacking about three months of being seven years old. Malkin was temporarily deterred from publishing the memoirs by what he called "the prevailing folly of the time," his explanation of which has considerable pertinency to an understanding of the environment into which William Blake came. His explanation was: "The passion for infantine and puerile exhibitions, . . . had almost weighed upon my mind, to defer or abandon the project. . . . This town has of late been in a fever of precocious admiration; ready to catch at whatever might administer food to the rage for novelty and the surprising. The most approved models of just recitation, of impressive eloquence, of passionate expression, have been laid on the shelf for inarticulate lispings, or at best for a parrot-taught monotony, the effect of premature and master-ridden study. The powers of music have been called in, to inspire the fatuity of childhood. Memory has been loaded with all the lumber of misplaced erudition. But these are not instances of a powerful and overtopping mind. They may be evidences of parts, but not of genius."[2] At the same time that he disapproved of this prevailing "fever of precocious admiration," Malkin printed several of Blake's earliest poems and dealt critically with them. As contemporary judgment, therefore, his appraisal increases in value as Blake's work stands in contrast with the popular accomplishments which Malkin condemned.

Whether Malkin first heard of Blake and approached him, or whether Blake heard of Thomas Malkin, whose mind showed such kinship with his own, and sought him out, is not known and perhaps matters little. In either case it would have been merely an example of the strange affinity that exists between minds similarly endowed. Casual as he said their connection was, Malkin wrote the first account of Blake's childhood to illustrate his convictions about genius: "It rarely happens, that the world affords even the ordinary allowance of happiness to men of transcendent faculties. Their merits are too frequently denied the protection and encouragement, to which they feel themselves entitled, from the private intimations of their own scrutinizing spirit. . . . They necessarily have but few companions; few, who are capable of appreciating their high endowments, and entering into the grandeur of their conceptions. Of these few, those who come the nearest to their own rank and standard, those who might be the associates of their inmost thoughts, and the partners of their dearest interests, are too often envious of their fame. It is a common remark, that great men are not gregarious. This is but too just; and so much of man's happiness depends upon society, that the comparative solitude, to which a commanding genius condemns its possessor, detracts considerably from the sum of his personal enjoyment."[3]

These remarks were provoked either by discussion with Blake or by a close observation of him. The emphasis placed upon happiness signifies that Malkin, at the same time that he acknowledged the inability of gregarious people to understand the happiness of the "commanding genius" who prefers solitude to society, concluded that Blake was unhappy. There lurk in this same passage hints that such spirits as Blake's are desirous of the approval of others and of the attainment of a fame that shows "appreciation of their transcendent faculties." With the phrase, "grandeur of conceptions," Malkin revealed either that he was acquainted with the products of Blake's pen and brush, or that he was uniquely "an associate of his inmost thought."

Malkin's understanding of Blake appears in these general remarks, but his words immediately preliminary to his mention of Blake's name are more illuminating of how real was his acquaintance with Blake's nature: "Hitherto, it has confirmed the observation just hazarded, on the probable fate of

stubborn originality in human life. There seems now indeed
some prospect, that the current will turn. . . . In the mean
time, I am confident that you, and my other readers of taste
and feeling, will readily forgive my travelling a little out of
the record, for the purpose of descanting on merit, which
ought to be more conspicuous, and which must have become
so long since, but for opinions and habits of an eccentric
kind."[4] Herein appears one of the most significant traits of
Blake's character which alone can account for much of his
lifelong behavior. Malkin called it "stubborn originality" and
then softened it to "opinions and habits of an eccentric kind."
It was his well-intentioned tribute to Blake's conspicuous
merit; it was at the same time discriminating insight into one
of Blake's unfortunate characteristics.

There are other reasons for considering Malkin's report of
Blake accurate. Malkin was a fellow of the Society of Antiquaries, and could have become well acquainted with Blake
through James Basire, the official engraver for the Society of
Antiquaries, between the years 1771 and 1778, when Blake
was apprenticed to Basire. Malkin must have invited Blake to
design the frontispiece for the *Memoirs* because he liked
Blake's work, or because Blake admired his child's head. Malkin said that its shape and character had often been admired
by artists,[5] and Blake was doubtless one of these artists. Malkin expressed satisfaction with Blake's work when he said
that the designer's testimony was that "the idea of beauty in
the human frame can never be disjoined, at least not justly,
from that of healthy and normal conformation."[6] The design
is a very Blakean one. There is the appearance of the rays of
sun or heavenly light in a perfectly symmetrical pattern, often
present in Blake's pictures, with the clusters of clouds that
separate in part the sphere mundane from the sphere divine.
There is the angel with the long, flowing draperies which, together with the upraised arm beckoning the child away from
the kneeling mother's arms, give the graceful, long-curving
line so distinguishing in Blake's pictures. There is, besides, in
the cast-aside book, compass, and pens the appearance of an
obvious symbolism. This ornament forms a frame to a charm-

ing child's face, a trifle smug but perfectly eighteenth-century in style and sentiment.[7]

At some time Malkin must have asked Blake's judgment on the child's sketches, for he preserved, with excusable pride, the very words which Blake wrote in commendation of them. They express one idea to which Blake held with stubborn, or, should one say, "eccentric" tenacity all his life: "They are all firm, determinate outline, or identical form. Had the hand which executed these little ideas been that of a plagiary, who works only from memory, we should have seen blots, called masses; blots without form, and therefore without meaning. These blots of light and dark, as being the result of labour, are always clumsy and indefinite; the effect of rubbing out and putting in, like the progress of a blind man, or of one in the dark, who feels his way, but does not see it. These are not so. . . . All his efforts prove this little boy to have had that greatest of all blessings, a strong imagination, a clear idea, and a determinate vision of things in his own mind."[8] Blake's approval of the child reveals much about himself in that it forecasts the belief concisely stated in *Milton:* "The Imagination is not a State; it is the Human Existence itself."[9] It may have been Malkin's gratitude for this commendation from Blake that led him to procure a copy of the *Songs of Innocence,* dated 1802,[10] and to interest a pupil, Edward Fitzgerald, in owning both a copy of the *Songs*[11] and of Malkin's *Memoirs.*[12]

These details suffice to show that there was a sufficient connection between Malkin and Blake for Malkin's information to have been accurately acquired. His taste in writing with enthusiasm about his extraordinary child has been criticized,[13] but the honesty of his information about William Blake has never been questioned. Since this is the only account of Blake written within his lifetime and the only one written without interest in coloring the subject to suit some personal motive, it is a primary authority.

The second printed source of information about Blake's early life is that written by J. T. Smith, Keeper of Prints and Drawings in the British Museum, and published in London a year after Blake's death. It appeared in the second volume of

Nollekens and His Times, published by Henry Colburn of
New Burlington Street. In a book published as late as 1845,
Smith made an entry under the date 1784, which has consid-
erable significance if it can be relied upon. It is the only evidence of Smith's early personal acquaintance with Blake. In
1784, the year following the printing of the *Poetical Sketches,*
John Flaxman introduced Smith to the Reverend Henry
Mathew of Percy Chapel, Charlotte Street. Smith said: "At
that gentleman's house, in Rathbone Place, I became acquainted with Mrs. Mathew and her son. . . . At Mrs.
Mathew's most agreeable conversaziones I first met the late
William Blake, the artist, to whom she and Mr. Flaxman had
been truly kind."[14] Smith would have had to learn the facts of
Blake's childhood from random hearsay rather than from intimate personal acquaintance. The date when he met Blake is
not specified, although it probably was during 1784, or else he
would have made a separate entry or referred to an earlier
date. Besides, it was by no means certain that Blake was a
guest at Rathbone Place later than 1784. The evidence is too
inconclusive to convince one that Smith's record can be entirely trusted for this event. Here is the first appearance of
one of the much-repeated anecdotes whose authenticity may
be questioned.

The third source of information about Blake's boyhood
was the last to be printed. The next one in order is the one
by Allan Cunningham whose biographical sketch,[15] almost entirely dependent upon Smith's account, appeared in 1830,
three years after Blake's death. Cunningham wrote to Mr.
Ritchie of the *Scotsman,* October 28, 1828: "I have some no-
tion of writing the Lives of the British Painters, on the plan
of Johnson's 'Lives of the Poets.' I am full of information on
the subject, have notions of my own in keeping with the nature of the art, and I think a couple of volumes would not be
unwelcome from one who has no theory to support, and who
will write with full freedom and spirit."[16] Nor is the third
source the one printed after Cunningham, for that is the account given by Alexander Gilchrist, who characterized Cunningham's work as "pleasant mannered generalities, easy to
read, hard to verify."[17] The *Life of William Blake* by Gil-

christ was the first real biography. It was published posthumously in 1863, having been brought safely through the press by Mrs. Gilchrist with the assistance of Dante Gabriel and William Rossetti.

The third primary source was the *Life* by Frederick Tatham, first published in 1906, sharing a volume with letters of William Blake, edited by A. G. B. Russell. Until 1906 this account existed in manuscript bound with a unique copy of *Jerusalem,* unknown apparently to Gilchrist, for he seems to have derived information directly from Tatham himself, but referred to (although not with Tatham's name) by Swinburne as the source of his authority about the cause of Blake's death.[18] The earliest possible date of its writing is determined by the fact that it concludes with the story of Mrs. Blake's death. It cannot be determined exactly how early Frederick Tatham knew Blake. Russell (on what authority is not known) said that Tatham was "about twenty"[19] years of age (1825) when he met Blake. It is altogether possible that he knew him much earlier, for Blake had some relationship with Tatham's father, Charles Heathcote Tatham, which was sufficiently personal in nature to prompt Blake to make him a gift; the "A" copy of Blake's *America* is inscribed "From the author to C. H. Tatham October 7 1799."[20] In that case Blake knew the elder Tatham six years before Frederick was born and even two years before C. H. Tatham's marriage. If this relationship had anything of friendship about it, and if due allowances are made for the infrequency with which Frederick Tatham through his youth could have been with Blake, he may still have held him as his boyhood ideal and been able through his father to know details of Blake's own youth. The date, 1799, also reveals an error Laurence Binyon made in saying: "He [Linnell] introduced Blake to Charles Heathcote Tatham, a well-known architect, and it was at Tatham's house that George Richmond first met Blake, and the same evening accompanied him home. A boy of sixteen, he was thrilled with awe and delight as the old man told him of his visions."[21] Linnell did not meet Blake until 1818, when he was twenty-six. He could hardly have introduced Blake to C. H. Tatham whom Blake knew by 1799. If Tatham's *Life*

errs, it is on account of the credence his almost idolatrous affection for Blake caused him to give to the material which he
secured either at second hand or from the memory of Blake in
his declining years. Some shadow has been cast upon his reliability by the cloud of suspicion that gathered around his head
because of his appropriation of Blake's worldly effects and his
reputed destruction of many of them. Russell alone defended
him. One cannot see that either selfish interest or his fanati-
cal religious prejudices would have led him to alter greatly
the facts of Blake's early life. His difficulty was rather in
having a chance to know correctly the events of the years so
far behind him.

Of these five documents, Malkin, Smith, and Tatham give
independent accounts of Blake's boyhood and early manhood,
although Malkin's sketch is the only one published while
Blake lived. Cunningham and Gilchrist, while able to draw
upon information from living witnesses, relied heavily upon
these three accounts.

Such then is the meager record which is the basis for understanding one of the most arresting personalities in the history of art or poetry. What were the factors of heredity and
environment which enlighten one about this young man?
What can one know of the forces which made him what he
became? Only from the sources sketched above and from
Blake's own work can one derive the answers. Each step will
be followed to see how much it accounts for the interesting
personality that gave expression first to songs and then to
"gigantic conceptions" in his prophetic books. Primarily, this
discussion is limited to a consideration of the material in the
Poetical Sketches.

The meagerness of information about William Blake is
again apparent when Arthur Symons, who previous to 1907
made extensive research through parish registers, began his
report by saying: "The origin of the family of William Blake
has not yet been found; and I can claim no more for the evidence that I have been able to gather than that it settles us
more firmly in our ignorance."[22] The year 1893 saw two new
theories advanced. One was that Blake's family was connected with that of Admiral Blake.[23] The other, entirely fan-

tastic, was that Blake's father was an Irishman, an erstwhile O'Neill.[24] Neither theory has the least documentary support, and both may be dismissed as unfounded.

James Blake, the father of William, made a respectable,[25] and probably more than comfortable,[26] living as a hosier, for fifty years according to Cunningham and twenty according to Gilchrist. This discrepancy in dates is not easily explained. It may be that James Blake's father had conducted the same business so that for thirty years he was connected with his father before he became owner in his own right of the shop at No. 28 Broad Street, Carnaby Market. *The London Directory*[27] for 1780 and again for 1784[28] lists a Stephen Blake, haberdasher, 28 Broad Street, Carnaby Market, and the same person is listed in 1783 in *The New Complete Guide to all Persons who have any Trade or Concern with the City of London*.[29] It is not known who Stephen Blake was. There is an entry, "Blake and Son, Hosiers and Haberdashers, 28 Broad Street, Soho," in the *Post-Office Annual Directory for the Year 1801*.[30] It may be that Cunningham erred here as he did elsewhere. Gilchrist, ambitious to write a comprehensive, reliable life, would have been much more likely to secure accurate information before he gave exact figures than Cunningham would have been, who obviously was chiefly interested in the mere readability of his work. Since Gilchrist drew from Cunningham, it would seem that he was correcting an error. On the other hand, it is likely that James Blake would have been established in his business at least by the time he was married. Gilchrist's date would put the beginning of the hosiery business eleven years after his first child was born. Unless he had other means of livelihood, that is unlikely. No record has been found to set this matter right.

What Tatham meant by describing James Blake as a man of "easy habits" is also uncertain. He evidently did not intend any derogatory implication because in the same sentence he mentioned his "substantial worth," a phrase which strikes one, who sees William Blake's whole life in the perspective of a century's distance, as being especially descriptive of the son. Likewise, thinking of the temperate life of William, one judges that Tatham's mention of James Blake's "moderate desires and moderate enjoyments" shows the son's further likeness to his father.

Malkin made but slight reference to Blake's father, but that reference is significant. He called him "an indulgent parent." Add to this Tatham's further delineation that "his disposition was gentle, . . . his temper amiable," and his nature "lenient and affectionate," and one sees again traits which were those of his gifted son. The importance of these characteristics of the father cannot be too much stressed because they furnish the best knowledge of one of the most formative influences of Blake's childhood. They indicate sympathy with eccentricities, patience with resistance against following the ordinary bent of the family, and encouragement of artistic expression. Cunningham implied that the latter was a question of the father's pride because his son attracted the attention of neighbors and patrons who noticed his drawings on the backs of shop bills,[31] but, universal as such paternal satisfaction is, Malkin furnished a better suggestion. Evidently James Blake was aware very early of his son's natural inclination toward art, and more than that had the prudence and discernment to see that it should not be discouraged. He provided Blake with money to buy prints.[32] A suggestion as to the type of print chosen appears in Blake's remark: "I am happy I cannot say that Rafael Ever was, from my Earliest Childhood, hidden from Me. I Saw & I knew immediately the difference between Rafael & Rubens."[33] Besides this, James Blake bought various casts for him, and more wisely gave his son the pleasure of buying for himself in the auction rooms of Langford and Christie, until he drew even the friendly assistance of the auctioneer.[34] Blake's extensive collection of prints that was sold in 1821 probably was acquired for the most part during these years.[35] Blake's father also gave him money to pay the entrance fees to exhibitions in royal and in private collections. This on first thought may not seem significant, but it proves how extraordinary it was for a child—and Malkin said "very early in life"—to have access to these collections. Exhibitions anywhere were not easy of access. William T. Whitley, in his *Art in England, 1800–1820,* said that the majority of the people in England had never had the opportunity of seeing a good picture before the opening of the nineteenth century. There had been exhibitions in London before 1760, but only a small fraction of the population saw them. Royal collections or private collections were closed to the poor man unless he gained access as a workman or servant. People of the middle class could not afford the expense of visiting the private collections; the cost was so much a public scandal that when Carlo Vanloo, the French king's painter, came to England in 1764 to see the private collections, the English newspapers "warned him of the rapacity of those who had charge of them."[36] Of course, Malkin may have generalized from a single instance, for he may have had in mind the generosity of the Duke of Richmond who opened his gallery of casts from the antique at his house in Whitehall to all students in 1758, under control of the Incorporated Society. There Cipriani and Wilton gave instruction to anyone wishing it, and there pupils of Henry and William Pars were sent to draw. There, too, Blake, as one of those pupils, may have first known Mortimer, whose influence can be noted in Blake's earliest work, for Mortimer attended the gallery for many years.[37]

Blake's father showed much intelligence in the manner in which he was "indulgent," for he seems not to have compelled William to do what he did not want to do. To be sure, that same indulgence may have been the undoing of Blake's brother John,[38] who was said to have been the parents' favorite.[39] What Blake most disliked was attendance at school. Malkin's silence on this subject might indicate that he took this matter for granted. Cunningham's only comment was that Blake "neglected the figures of arithmetic for those of Raphael and Reynolds[40] and his worthy parents often wondered how a child of theirs should have conceived a love for such unsubstantial vanities";[41] but Tatham added an entirely new and important aspect when he said "his father dared not send him to school."[42]

Why did he dare not? In answering this one comes upon a principle which easily marks every decided stage in Blake's life—his strong aversion to rules and restraints. Tatham, knowing Blake only as an old man, yet said that Blake "possessed from a child . . . [a] daring, impetuous, and vigorous temper,"[43] and that his father feared what would happen from the blows he would receive at school. In a fragment of poetry, written sometime between 1808 and 1811, Blake himself recalled the fact that he had not gone to school, and he unwittingly revealed its significance:

> Thank God, I never was sent to school
> To be Flog'd into following the Style of a Fool.
>
> The Errors of a Wise Man make your Rule
> Rather than the Perfections of a Fool.[44]

The imminence of flogging is suggested again in the "cruel eye" and the "fears that annoy" in the very autobiographical poem, *The Schoolboy,* where is added a further reason for wishing to avoid school:

> How can the bird that is born for joy
> Sit in a cage and sing?[45]

However much one may feel that the discipline of education would have served Blake's later work exceedingly well, one still must be grateful that he was not shut in a cage if it would have meant the loss of his songs. His choice was to become an artist, and at ten years of age he entered his first drawing school. "The tender plant" was not "stripped of its joy" in the "springing day."[46]

So far the authorities have stressed his father's part in his life. Was his mother entirely negligible? Malkin does not mention her; Cunningham merely said that the boy was "privately encouraged" by his mother, leaving one to wonder why "privately," since the father's sympathy was plainly shown. Gilchrist, repeating one of the "vision" episodes, represented the mother as shielding the child from the corporeal reprimand his father was about to administer. Tatham said: "Catherine Blake, his wife, and the mother of the artist, has been represented as being possessed of all the endearing sympathies so peculiar to maternal tenderness."[47] This statement is conventionally sentimental enough in its eighteenth-century phrasing to characterize her small part in the record which is due more to the assertive nature of the father than to any real lack of understanding of her son or of her influence upon him. Blake, in turn, may be said to have dominated his own household in the same way. The *Songs of Innocence and Experience* have abundant references to "father" and "mother" which are doubtless autobiographical insofar as they show a child's attitude toward parents and a boy's memory of them. They come from experience and give assurance of their reality, as illustrated in these lines:

> Can a father see his child
> Weep, nor be with sorrow fill'd?

> Can a mother sit and hear
> An infant groan an infant fear?
> No, no! never can it be![48]

There is one more aspect of the elder Blake's character which has much value in the consideration of what the son became. Cunningham alone mentioned that James Blake was "a devout man." Blake's poetry is so permeated by the Bible that he must have come to his first acquaintance with it at his father's knee. Blake was fortunate to belong to a generation that learned the Bible that way. There are two stories current among his later biographers which definitely associate his father with nonconformist religious interests. The first is the statement made in 1915 by H. N. Morris: "Certain it is that he was from a child familiar with the writings of Swedenborg. His father and his brother James were both students and admirers of his writings. We know that both were members of the Swedenborgian or New Jerusalem Church in Hatton Gardens, London, and one at least of the 'Songs of Innocence' was written by William Blake in that Church."[49] Morris cited no authority for this interesting statement, but five years later in an address before the Blake Society on Blake and Swedenborg, he said: ". . . and we have it on the authority of C. A. Tulk, then Member of Parliament from Poole, and an enthusiastic Swedenborg student, that Blake's poem on the Divine Image—beginning with the words, 'To Mercy, Pity, Peace and Love'—was composed by him whilst sitting in the Hatton Garden Church. He was therefore a frequenter of that church up to the year 1799. . . ."[50] Morris also asserted that Blake's father possessed a copy of the *Arcana Caelestia,* the *Divine Love and Wisdom,* and the *Apocalypse Revealed.* C. A. Tulk would, of course, have had authentic information because he must have been personally acquainted with Blake in their association together in the New Church at the time that Blake and his wife became members, April 13, 1789.[51] He was one of the few people who owned a copy both of the *Poetical Sketches* and of the *Songs of Innocence and Experience.* The first bears the inscription, "To Charles Tulk, Esq.—from William Blake."[52] The second is the copy from which James Garth Wilkinson made the first typographical reprint of the *Songs* in 1839, as well as the copy which Coleridge borrowed in 1818.[53] Furthermore, his father, John Augustus Tulk, a man of wealth who "by his zeal, ability, and judgment added strength"[54] to the new church, was one of the first members of the group before it became an organized church, and his was the first name signed, December 7, 1788, to the pamphlet, "Reasons for Separating from the Old Church. . . ."[55] He acted as chairman of the meeting on February 26, 1810, which was held to provide funds for printing Swedenborg's work, one member of the committee to accomplish this being C. A. Tulk. There is no question then of Blake's own later association with the Swedenborgian disciples, nor any question about the authentic character of the testimony of the Tulks. Yet the fact remains that Blake's father is not mentioned by them or anyone else at the time. If Blake's father knew Swedenborgian doctrine, one reason for the depth to which Swedenborgian ideas had permeated Blake's mind would be known.[56]

The second story is one which seems to have originated with William Muir, who was the late Thomas Wright's authority[57] for saying that previous to James Blake's interest in Swedenborg, Blake's parents attended the Moravian Chapel in Fetter Lane. There is one bit of confirmatory evidence not previously noted. The Moravian Peter Böhler arrived in London February 7, 1738, and on that day met John Wesley[58] with whom he drew up the statutes for the first society of

Brethren which met at the house of James Hutton, a book-
seller, until September 7, 1742, when Hutton took out a li-
cense for Fetter Lane Chapel under the designation, "Moravian Brethren, formerly of the English Communion."[59] The
list of members of the Fetter Lane Society in London in 1743
began:

Married Men	Married Women
Bell, William	Bell, ——
Bennett, ——	Bennett, ——
Blake, ——	Blake, ——[60]

Like the Swedenborgians, the Moravians disagreed among
themselves in November, 1742, and in 1766 another organiza-
tion of which Bell was secretary was effected. But no Blake
was on that list. Without knowing the given names at least,
one can only conjecture that the Mr. and Mrs. Blake on the
roll of the Fetter Lane Society were the parents of William.

Slender and only partly convincing as this evidence is that
Blake's father was a member of any dissenting group, the
possibility is there. Which group he favored matters less than
the fact that his association with some group was active and
sincere. The genuine religious feeling that is never absent
from Blake's work—not even his earliest—may take rise in
the fine subtle power of the example which Blake had in his
father. When Cunningham described Blake's father as a "devout man," it carried with it greater implications than at first
thought. James Blake may have been a dissenter—and he was
buried July 4, 1784, in a dissenters' burial ground, Bunhill
Fields—; he yet had his family christened in the parish
church in Westminster, and it was the service of that church
which Blake in turn favored when he, too, was laid to rest in
the same burial ground on August 12, 1827.[61]

So much space has been given to this aspect of Blake's early
environment because it is thought to have outweighed all
other early circumstances. When one comes to estimate the
influence of the other children in the family, it is quite a different matter; and as to the effect of youthful associates,
there is all but complete silence. The membership of the

Blake household is best seen in the parish register of the church of St. James, Westminster, where there are the following entries:

James Blake, the son of James and Catherine Blake, born July 10, christened July 15, 1753
John Blake . . . born May 12 and christened June 1, 1755
William Blake . . . born November 28 and christened December 11, 1757
John Blake . . . born March 20, and christened March 30, 1760
Richard Blake . . . born June 19, and christened July 11, 1762
Catherine Elizabeth Blake . . . born January 27, and christened January 28, 1764[62]

Since this record contains two Johns, it has been surmised that the first died in childhood and his name was given to the fourth son.[63] Tatham must have been unaware of this because he called John an elder brother.[64] Richard, by an error in recording, must have been the beloved Robert who lived with Blake until his death in 1786—the one to whom Blake afterwards attributed so much of the guidance his spirit received. This record not only corrects Tatham's error in the date of Blake's birth, but it throws light on another matter. If the Blakes on the membership roll of the Fetter Lane Society were the parents of William, they were married before 1743, ten years before their first child was born. Mrs. Blake was seventy years old when she died in 1792,[65] and hence she would have been thirty-one when she began to rear her family and twenty-one when she joined the Society. She certainly was not married at twelve years of age which would have been her age if she were married when her husband began the hosiery business in 1734 according to Cunningham.[66]

Blake seems to have had little companionship with his brothers and sister. Not until Robert became a member of the household after his father's death does one ever hear of his congeniality, in spite of Tatham's assertion that "like plants, planted side by side by a stream, they grew together and entwined the luxuriant tendrils of their expanding minds. They associated and excelled together, and, like all true lovers, delighted in and enhanced each other's beauties."[67] James, the

eldest brother, continued in the father's business, and apart
from one recorded letter which Blake wrote to him, there is
no information beyond the strangely critical description of
him by Tatham: "James . . . having a saving, somniferous
mind, lived a yard and a half life, pestered his brother, the
artist, with timid sentences of bread and cheese advice, got
together a little annuity, upon which he supported his only
sister, and vegetating to a moderate age, died about three
years before his brother William."[68] If Tatham's information
were derived from Blake, it must reflect Blake's attitude
toward his brother, although his letter unburdening his mind
about his difficulties with Hayley showed none of this attitude.[69] In it, however, Blake carefully concealed his pecuniary
needs from James. His seeming boastfulness about his profi-
ciency in learning languages may be better understood if one
remembers that he was addressing his more material-minded
brother. One concludes that his brothers and sister seem not
to have made much difference one way or another in his childhood unless one can assume that John aroused a certain stubborn independence in him, and Robert gave him inspiration.
The reason for this may be that Blake spent less and less time
in the family circle after he was ten years old.

Records are again silent about the immediate circumstances
that caused Blake to be sent to an art school. But it is reason-
able to suppose that it was because an appreciative father was
aware not only of the unusual aptitude that his son showed
for artistic things but of the impossibility of bending him in
any direction that ordinary children take. Nor are there signs
that Blake opposed his father's decision to place him, only ten
years of age, at a drawing school in the Strand at No. 101
kept by Henry Pars. If the school had the reputation of fit-
ting its pupils for some useful work,[70] Blake's father may
have hoped to turn his son's talent to account. It was at this
time that Blake's father bought casts of the "Gladiator and
Hercules and Venus of Medicis," and other pieces for study,
and that Blake himself showed his early excellent taste by the
search for examples of Raphael, Michelangelo, Martin Hems-
kerck, Albert Dürer, and Julio Romano;[71] Blake once said:
"Taste & Genius are Not Teachable or Acquirable but are

born with us."[72] Malkin said that "his choice was for the most part contemned by his youthful companions, who were accustomed to laugh at what they called his mechanical taste."[73] But probably the ridicule only fixed more firmly than ever Blake's disposition to continue with his own predilection. At any rate, he selected prints as if an informed and cultivated taste guided him, and he never repudiated his early selections. As a matter of fact, Blake's own work never quite escaped the effect of his early study of the massiveness, the muscular firmness, the solidity, and the "determinate" outlines of Michelangelo. The engravings of the Portland Vase which Blake made for Erasmus Darwin's *The Botanic Garden,* Part I (1791), are said to show a resemblance to Michelangelo's figures on the Medici tombs in Florence.[74] There is in the Huntington Gallery a figure from Michelangelo's "Last Judgment" inscribed: "W. Blake 1776." Blake must have had opportunity to see many examples of the best masters, and he must have studied them intimately enough to formulate his definite notions into a sort of artistic credo to which he adhered through his life.[75] In 1800, he wrote to George Cumberland about the accessibility of good prints: "There are now, I believe, as many Booksellers as there are Butchers & as many Printshops as of any other trade. We remember when a Print shop was a rare bird in London & I myself remember when I thought my pursuits of Art a kind of criminal dissipation & neglect of the main chance, which I hid my face for not being able to abandon as a Passion which is forbidden by Law & Religion, but now it appears to be Law & Gospel too, at least I hear so from the few friends I have dared to visit in my stupid Melancholy."[76] It was eight years later that he recalled an early episode of rage at Moser who criticized him for studying the prints from Raphael and Michelangelo in the Library of the Royal Academy.[77] There had been a cry[78] raised in 1737 against the prints from abroad which was in keeping with the disapproval of his tastes which Blake heard from his companions. But no one's ridicule deterred Blake from championing the masters vigorously thenceforward.

Silent as the four years are in which Blake attended the Pars drawing school, they are significant years. Within this period there was an early association which possibly links Blake to Flaxman and Wedgwood. A sister of William Pars was an expert enamelist and engraver. She was the one of twenty-eight women, employed during 1774 by Wedgwood to produce designs for the famous dinner set for the Empress of Russia, who did the most difficult and important pieces.[79] It surely must be more than coincidence that in 1773 Blake engraved from an old Italian drawing what he called "Joseph of Arimathea among the Rocks of Albion,"[80] and later (*c.* 1790) another known as "Joseph of Arimathea Preaching to the Inhabitants of Britain,"[81] when one of the important pieces of the dinner service mentioned above had a scene of the Chapel of St. Joseph of Arimathea at Glastonbury, "a Gothic fragment of the best Early English."[82] The chapel in Blake's picture is suggestive of the larger work which was surely drawn by Miss Pars. Had Blake known and discussed the story with Miss Pars while at the Pars School?[83]

The biographers who are silent about the period spent with Pars are without exception accurate in marking the next stage of Blake's life, when he left the parental roof and, for the time between his fourteenth and twenty-first years, lived under a new master, subject to a certain discipline and in contact with a different circle of people. Ever alert to significant ideas which would confirm him in his early opinions, his mind during this interval received information and impressions which were to be transmuted by the fire of his own mental energy into poetic imagery, rhythmical thought, and the verbal music of his early poetry—if not the gigantic forms in his later writing. It is the period when his intense curiosity awakened him to the meanings of the forces that control destiny, prompted his aspirations and the testing of his own innate powers, and quickened that first exaltation of spirit which is youth's singular experience. In this period his first adjustments to living, his first art, and his first poetry appear. If one could fully reconstruct Blake's daily life to 1778, one should come near to the secret not only of what Blake became as a personality, but also of the elements that entered into his mind, there to coalesce and to become metamorphosed by the power of his imagination into poetry.

Reports are various about why James Basire of 31 Great Queen Street, Lincoln's Inn Fields, was chosen for his master. Gilchrist is the sole authority for the tale, which is probably an apocryphal one, of Blake's own rejection of William Wynne Ryland because he looked as if he would "live to be hanged"[84]—as it turned out he did.[85] Since this story appeared in the years when a certain body of myths had grown up around Blake because of his eccentric ways of speech and behavior, of his seclusion, and of his mystic experiences, and since it was most certainly derived from hearsay, it may be justly questioned. It has no place in the accounts of those who knew Blake personally, not even in that of the garrulous Smith or the credulous Tatham.

Tatham said, without naming the person, that a "painter of eminence was proposed, and necessary applications were made"; but that Blake objected because of the injustice to his "brothers and sisters" (Blake had but one sister) of having so much money spent on him as the premium demanded. Tatham said that Blake therefore himself "proposed engraving as being less expensive and sufficiently eligible for future avocations."[86] The most interesting thing in these varying, if not apocryphal, versions is that Blake himself did the deciding in every instance. Malkin, the one nearest the whole experience, passed silently over all these preliminary matters, and said that at the age of fourteen "he fixed on the engraver of Stuart's Athens and West's Pylades and Orestes for his master. . . ."[87] There is something very paradoxical in the fact that Blake, who, up to this time and in almost every aspect of his life later, was unwilling to undergo restrictions and dictation from others, should subject himself willingly to the exactitude of engraving, to the monotony of an engraver's life, and to the very idea of being bound to anyone for seven years at any price. (Basire asked fifty guineas.) But when was Blake not paradoxical?

It speaks much for Blake's force of character that he continued to do engraving when painting and poetry provided such enticing means of escape. Yet he said of himself: "Mr. B., having from early Youth cultivated the two Arts, Painting & Engraving, & during a Period of Forty Years never suspended his Labours on Copper for a single day."[88] This would push the beginning of his engraving to 1769, before he went to Basire (could Miss Pars have given him instruction in engraving?), and he confirmed it twice. Once he said: "Mr. B.'s Inventive Powers & his Scientific Knowledge of Drawing . . . acknowledg'd; it only remains to be Certified whether . . . an unbated Study & Practise [*sic*] of forty Years (for I devoted myself to engraving in my Earliest Youth) are sufficient to elevate me above the Mediocrity to which I have hitherto been the victim."[89] The second time, when writing to Hayley, he complained of his lack of employment: "How is it possible that a Man almost 50 years of Age who has not lost any of his life since he was five years old without incessant labour & study, how is it possible that such a one with ordinary common sense can be inferior to a boy of twenty who scarcely has taken or deigns to take a pencil in hand but who rides about the Parks or saunters about the Playhouses who Eats & drinks for business not for need how is it possible that such a fop can be superior to the studious lover of Art can scarcely be imagined."[90] Perhaps Blake would not have become an engraver if Basire had not been a "patient, plodding person" of "good disposition."[91] Blake referred to him always as "my master," and never disrespectfully. When one remembers that all Blake's acquaintances, except Fuseli, had some epigrammatic thrust recorded against them, this is high testimony to the respect, if not the affection, with which Blake regarded his master. It is, likewise, a high testimony to the skill and understanding of Basire that he handled this rather intractable youth with so much success. The result was that Blake attained a serenity of mind and a happiness without which there might never have been the sweet singing quality of his poems. Blake defended Basire against the ridicule with which Woolett, Strange, and Gravelot spoke of Basire's work.[92] This criticism may have been the reason why Blake detested those engravers. Malkin, once more, added just the revealing comment needed when he said: "Basire, whose taste

was like his own, approved of what he did."[93] This may account for Blake's modeling his design for the "Canterbury
Pilgrims" after Basire's "Edward VI's Coronation" which he
drew in 1787, for the Society of Antiquaries from a "coëval
painting at Cowdray."[94] Basire was a thorough teacher. He
had himself learned his art from his father, from Vertue, his
predecessor as official engraver for the Society of Antiquaries,
and from Richard Dalton, keeper of royal drawings under
George III, with whom he lived several years in Italy. Basire's
election as official engraver to the Royal Academy came just
previous to Blake's apprenticeship.[95] Basire engraved in what
is described as a hard and dry way, scoring firm, definite lines
and working up the detail with such exactitude and elaborate
crosshatching that the effect was that of a mechanical and la-
bored execution. Blake was many years developing his own
individuality and freeing himself from the manner of his
master. Gilchrist affirmed that it was the public's distaste for
this outmoded style of engraving that prevented Blake's winning custom from the public.[96] That he finally did achieve his
own style of engraving shows the inspiration of his own talent. How Blake regarded engraving is known from some remarks in his later years. Once he spoke as if engraving were
his true field, for he said: "Engraving is the profession I was
apprenticed to, & I should never have attempted to live by any
thing else. . . ."[97] He found that it was harder to engrave
from other people's designs than his own. On January 10,
1802, he wrote to Thomas Butts that he had always been pursued by the idea that if he did not confine himself to the
"drudgery of business"[98] he should not live. Another time he
said: "Endless work is the true title of engraving."[99] A month
earlier he had written: "Engraving is Eternal work; . . . I
curse & bless Engraving alternately, because it takes so much
time & is so untractable, tho' capable of such beauty & perfection."[100] The seven years with Basire must have been fairly
happy ones. The only rift of which there is a record occurred
after Blake's second year when new apprentices made things
unpleasant with what seemed to be the inevitable treatment
accorded to the impulsive, reticent, and dreaming youth when
he did not conform to others' ways. Basire solved the matter

by sending Blake elsewhere to do drawings for him. This much-repeated tale may have had another side. Basire probably was aware of the worth of Blake's drawings, and he knew that it would be to his profit for Blake to do them. Some scholars[101] believe that many of the plates signed by Basire during 1771–78, and even later, were actually the work of Blake. If that were true, it would account for the modest prices which Basire charged. It makes Blake's kindly feeling toward Basire all the more remarkable, for he never hesitated to speak bitterly about people who "stole from him."[102]

No event in Blake's life was a greater moment than Basire's transfer of him to Westminster Abbey. With his almost idolatrous liking for Michelangelo, and his inbred religious sentiments, if he could have had the good fortune which many another young artist had to spend some years in Italy, quite a different turn of mind might have been his, for he would have seen a new application of his favorite precept of "firm and determinate" outline, and his imagination, by nature so fantastic, might have been made to glow in quite a different direction. But as it was, this most impressionable youth spent days and days, month after month, alone among Gothic monuments in Westminster Abbey, "where Death sits brooding o'er his noblest spoil."[103] All that was romantic in his instinct must have made immediate response to this new atmosphere, and the continued presence of the conceptions of Death and Eternity in both his pictures and his poetry shows how the youth's imagination responded to his solitary brooding there. He was fascinated. Malkin said that in the Gothic monuments he found a treasure he knew how to value.[104] All his religious conceptions, whether derived from his reading of the Bible, from Swedenborgian or Moravian sources, found here something germane to them. They were intensified, and one can well believe that visions of the past and visions of the future came to this sensitive mind in the silent twilight atmosphere of the Abbey. He drew kings and queens, and Malkin specified that ". . . particularly that of King Henry the Third, the beautiful monument and figure of Queen Elinor, Queen Philippa, King Edward the Third, King Richard the Second and his Queen, were among his first studies."[105] One instantly associates this roll of names with those figures he used in *King Edward the Third,* which was forming in his mind in these very days of intense preoccupation among the effigies of York and Lancaster,

> Their idle contest for dominion o'er,
> While Death's strong grasp cements
> each rival rose.[106]

These monuments he drew from every angle and frequently from above. The heads he considered as portraits, and the ornaments he thought of as "miracles of art."[107] There is no question that these ornaments affected the sort of ornamentation Blake put around the borders of his pages, and the draperies of his figures can be traced in the models he had before him. The recumbent effigy-like figure is predominant in Blake's pictures; and the "couch of death" not only is seen in his pictures but is also the title of a prose poem composed in these very years, a phrase that reappears again and again in his prophetic books.[108] However much he endowed the "couch of death" with new, symbolic meanings, the image came from the tombs. His poem, *Holy Thursday,* describes what Blake may have witnessed while he was at work, and the word "beneath" which troubled Wicksteed[109] in his interpretation may suggest that Blake held an elevated position while he viewed the scene, and perhaps composed lines about it, for, since the poem is entirely unlike others in the *Songs of Innocence,* it may have been written as early as the *Poetical Sketches.* When Blake needed a test or pattern by which to judge correctness of costume for his "Canterbury Pilgrims," he referred to the "authentic monuments."[110] Where had he seen such but in the Abbey? Blake made another interesting allusion to these days later when he commented on the monopoly sculpture had in the churches and abbeys, and appealed to the Society for Encouragement of Art to consider placing paintings in Westminster and other cathedrals to "make England what Italy is, an envied storehouse of Intellectual Riches."[111]

When Gilchrist began his research for the *Life,* he received from Samuel Palmer, August 23, 1855, a long account of

Blake whom he had known in 1824 when he and Blake attended an Academy exhibition.[112] One paragraph of that letter tells more of what Westminster Abbey meant to Blake: "He loved to speak of the years spent by Michael Angelo, without earthly reward, and solely for the love of God, in the building of St. Peter's, and of the wondrous architects of our cathedrals. In Westminster Abbey were his earliest and most sacred recollections. I asked him how he would like to paint on glass, for the great west window, his 'Sons of God shouting for Joy,' from his designs in *Job*. He said, after a pause, 'I could do it!' kindling at the thought."[113] Tatham,[114] too, must often have heard from Blake's own lips his treasured memories, showing how long the power of the influence of Westminster Abbey persisted. He said about this experience: "Blake pursued his task, and his absorption gathered to itself impressions that were never forgotten. His imagination ever after wandered as in a cloister, or clothing itself in the dark stole of mural sanctity, it dwelt amidst the Druid terrors. His mind being simplified by Gothic forms, and his fancy imbued with the livid twilight of past days, it chose for its quaint company such sublime but antiquated associates as the fearful Merlin, Arthur and the Knights of his Round Table, the just and wise Alfred, King John, and every other hero of English history and romance. These indigenous abstractions for many of the following years occupied his hand, and ever after tinctured his thoughts and perceptions."[115] It is evident that for Blake Gothic was living form.[116]

Blake's apprenticeship gave a certain amount of lesiure which he spent reading, studying history, or making historical drawings. For his own amusement he selected two of the latter to be engraved from a great number he had made[117] which now have disappeared. These two were "The Penance of Jane Shore in St. Paul's Church"[118] and "King Edward and Queen Eleanor." The latter was seen by Gilchrist,[119] but was not again known until it was found cut in two pieces, upon which had been written a portion of *Vala, or The Four Zoas*.[120] It was listed by Blake as "Edward and Elinor, a Historical Engraving. Size 1 ft. 6½ in. by 1 ft. price 10s. 6 d." in a *Prospectus* of works for sale dated October 10, 1793, a

single copy of which, known to Gilchrist, is unknown today.[121]
The first Blake thought well enough of to exhibit in 1809,
and of it he said in his *Descriptive Catalogue* for the exhibition of his own works: "This Drawing was done above Thirty
Years ago, and proves to the Author, and he thinks will prove
to any discerning eye, that the productions of our youth and
of our maturer age are equal in all essential points."[122] This
would date the drawing before 1779—another indication of
how much earlier than generally thought Blake began his
work.

Malkin and Gilchrist were the only ones who recorded the
attendance of Blake at the Royal Academy schools after his
term of apprenticeship ended, and Malkin barely mentioned
it,[123] while Gilchrist erred in giving the date as 1778. Russell, evidently using Gilchrist as authority, made the same
error.[124] Probably because at that time students could enter
the Royal Academy Schools free,[125] Blake was admitted on
October 8, 1779, when George Moser was Keeper. There is
no record of when he left the Schools.[126] Between 1780 and
1808, he exhibited twelve pictures at the Royal Academy,
"The Death of Earl Godwin," No. 315, being the only one
before 1784.

Blake's other artistic productions previous to 1783 that are
extant are few in number. The one known as "Glad Day" is
significantly related to the early poetry—as will be discussed
in Chapter VI. The only remaining evidence of his use of his
newly acquired profession was the engraving of designs after
Thomas Stothard. This acquaintance must have begun previous to 1780, because in that year Stothard made a drawing
called "A Boating Excursion" which portrays an excursion
taken up the Medway by Stothard, Mr. Ogleby, and Mr.
Blake, "that amiable, eccentric, and greatly gifted artist,"[127]
for the purpose of sketching. This picture has erroneously
been attributed to Blake.[128] Russell, in his catalogue of Blake's
art works, lists thirty-three plates engraved by Blake after
Stothard between 1779 and 1784.[129] There were probably
many other drawings and engravings which have been destroyed. Blake suggested as much in describing No. VI, "the
Spirit vaulting from a cloud," and No. IX, "Satan calling up

his Legions," in the *Descriptive Catalogue*. Of the first he said it was a picture done "many years ago, and was one of the first Mr. B. ever did in Fresco."[130] Of the second he said it was among "numerous others painted for experiment."[131] Blake must have done a large amount of experimenting, some of the products of which he very likely destroyed himself. Enough remains to testify to a very productive period, doubtless more remunerative than is known.

With the completion of his term of seven years of training under Basire, and with the return to his own home, Blake must have become suddenly aware that he no longer had a child's place in the home. He had outgrown it. He had reached the legal age of independence from authority; he had become fully aware of the creative powers within him. He was possessed of great energy of far different import than the physical energy of healthful youth for which he was noted.[132] The glowing imagination, the vigorous mental curiosity, the spiritual exaltation must have made Blake restless in his old surroundings, never any too congenial to him. It is not surprising then that he should wish the independence of a home of his own. No evidence one way or another will probably ever be found to verify a much-repeated story, first recorded as a footnote,[133] reporting what "a friend told him," in Smith's biographical account of Blake's bemoaning to Catherine Boucher how badly treated he had been by Polly Wood, and of the instantaneous decision of Blake to reward Catherine for her expressed pity with an offer of marriage. This story bears all the marks of an apocryphal tale. In the first place, Smith's testimony always needs strong confirmation, and the fact that Tatham did confirm[134] it does not necessarily add weight to it, because Tatham, like Smith, had an ear for a good story and took much from hearsay. In the second place, Smith admitted receiving it by the route of gossip, never reliable where eccentric persons are involved. But, principally, this story is altogether out of key with everything known of Blake's life and character. His uncommunicative nature, his reticence, his independence of friend or of foe would surely not have permitted him to reveal to anyone, much less to a strange maiden, his rejection by another girl. Catherine, doubtless, had all the ingenuousness of her homely simplicity and untaught mind, but never did she in later records appear in this light. Much as the later Freudian interpreters of Blake like to exaggerate every tiny intimacy of his personal life, the plain truth probably is that Blake's courtship was a perfectly natural, boyish one, full of tenderness and genuine devotion. We may reasonably suppose that Blake's works were, as already set forth, much more numerous and remunerative than the surviving examples indicate, because by August 18, 1782, he had saved enough to warrant his beginning housekeeping with Catherine at 23 Green Street, Leicester Fields.[135]

It does not lie within the scope of this study to take account of Blake's married life, although any interpretation of his later poetry would require it. As Blake said in his closing hours, Catherine proved to be "an angel to him."[136] As early as 1800, he described her as being "like a flame of many colours of precious jewels."[137] Whatever tribulations life held for the two of them,[138] the period up to the *Songs* is best reported in Blake's own language in *Jerusalem,* where Vala speaks:

> "Wherefore hast thou shut me into the
>   winter of human life,
> "And clos'd up the sweet regions of
>   youth and virgin innocence
> "Where we live forgetting error, not
>   pondering on evil,
> "Among my lambs & brooks of water,
>   among my warbling birds:
> "Where we delight in innocence before
>   the face of the Lamb,
> "Going in and out before him in his love
>   and sweet affection?"[139]

Blake's youth and early manhood may be truly summed up in the terms by which he referred to the period: "Inspiration & Vision was [*sic*] then, & now is, & I hope will ever Remain, my Element, my Eternal Dwelling place."[140]

CHAPTER II

"THE PRODUCTION OF UNTUTORED YOUTH"

THE *Poetical Sketches,* unlike any later accomplishment, marks the termination of a unique period in Blake's literary life. It cannot be said to have been published, as there is no evidence that within his life it was ever offered for sale by him or by any agent, authorized or unauthorized. There is no publisher's imprint on the title-page. It came from the printer's hands in loose sheets with a blue-gray wrapper. There are two copies extant in the original condition: one (the Butts copy) in the library of the late Mr. T. J. Wise, and one in the library of Dr. A. S. W. Rosenbach. The first of these is stitched, and the second is unstitched. If Blake stitched one copy before giving it to his friend, Thomas Butts, it was the first time that he ever attempted any phase of bookmaking, an accomplishment which thereafter he was fully to attain, with Catherine's aid; for all his books except the *French Revolution* were entirely the product of his brain and of his hands. The copy of the *Songs of Innocence* owned by Mrs. William Emerson of Cambridge, Massachusetts, is a unique copy, the only one remaining in the original gray-blue, plain-paper wrappers and stitched by Blake's hand much as the *Poetical Sketches* may have been. It is interesting that when Blake turned to the making of books independently, he should have clothed his second book in the garment of the first.

The *Poetical Sketches* bore the following title-page: POETICAL / SKETCHES ./ [short rule] / By W. B. / [short rule] / LONDON : / Printed in the Year mdcclxxxiii.

Proportion in the general appearance of the page was gained by printing *Sketches* in a larger size of Roman capital than *Poetical.* Modesty, or some reticence made popular by wide contemporary practice, concealed the author's identity by the

initials *W. B.* A pleasing balance was gained by the arrangement of *By W. B.* in one line rather than in two as was the
more usual practice. There was no complexity of matter so frequently found in long titles that commented on contents, in expository information about the author, in intricate vignettes,
or in lists of shops and addresses. All was simplicity itself,
reserved, austere. In taste, the title-page showed that Blake did
not observe the accepted conventions of his time, or that those
who dictated in the matter (if Blake did not) accurately understood what best suited him and his little volume of verse.

The *Poetical Sketches* is a demy octavo printed in half-
sheets. There is no half-title; neither is there a table of contents. The first nineteen selections are grouped under the head-
ing, *Miscellaneous Poems,* which is displayed on the first page
attractively spaced between a series of three unequal short
rules and another long rule of uneven thickness. No similar
caption serves to group the three following dramatic fragments: *King Edward the Third; Prologue, Intended for a
Dramatic Piece of King Edward the Fourth;* and *Prologue
to King John.* Isolated from the other songs, *A War Song to
Englishmen* is placed between the dramatic pieces and the
prose selections, so located probably because it fits into the
general theme of the dramatic pieces. The prose selections,
which close the book, *The Couch of Death, Contemplation,*
and *Samson,* also lack a title corresponding to *Miscellaneous
Poems.* There are running titles on only a few of the pages
which have a continuation of the selection from one page to
another. Lack of uniformity in this respect gives an unbal-
anced appearance. There is no uniformity in the margins, even
on pages where there is exactly the same amount of letterpress. On page 24 the poem, *An Imitation of Spencer,* allows
a wider top margin than usual, and the space so allowed is
sufficient to have included the final five lines which run on to
page 26 and impair the symmetry of that page. There, in contradiction to the practice in a similar situation on page 2, the
running title is dropped. The letterpress is not always carefully managed; the pagination is very erratic as is the bracket-
ing. There are such irregularities in the type used that one
concludes the printer may not have had a full font of any one

kind and resorted to using odds and ends. These details are all evidences of imperfect preparation either by careless or by inexperienced workmen.

In matters of mechanical workmanship, the book lacks uniformity and consistency, and certainly would have displeased the artist-author. This state of affairs further suggests that Blake probably had no hand in preparing it for the press or in seeing it through the press. The *Advertisement* says that the author "was deprived of the leisure requisite to such a revisal of these sheets, as might have rendered them less unfit to meet the public eye." Whether the author of the *Advertisement* had in mind the special preparation of the manuscript for the press, the mechanical details of the format already cited, or whether he referred to inaccuracies in the text, one cannot say, but his phrase, "irregularities and defects," could easily cover all sorts of errors. That there are errors of a textual nature would be expected. They are surprisingly few if one considers Blake's youth and education and the generally haphazard way the text was handled. Gilchrist was the first, after the author of the *Advertisement,* to point out that the *Poetical Sketches* lacked mechanical perfection: "The author's absence of leisure is pleaded, 'requisite to such a revisal of these sheets as might have rendered them less unfit to meet the public eye.' Little revisal certainly they had, not even correction of the press, apparently. The pamphlet, which has no printer's name to be discredited by it, is as carelessly printed as an old English play, evidently at an establishment which did not boast a 'reader.' Semicolons and fullstops where commas should be, misprints, such as 'beds of dawn' for 'birds,' by no means help out the meaning."[1]

How far is this criticism justified? It seems likely that the printer exercised some authority in correcting spellings and capitalization, since in these details the book is more conservative and regular than Blake's later work where no one altered his engraved letterpress. A confirming side light on this matter occurs in a letter of W. M. Rossetti to Mrs. Gilchrist, September 13, 1880, in which he said: "Along with this B[lake]. M.S. I found another scrap of same handwriting, giving a few details about names of Gods in different mythologies. It is a mere memorandum, but, if you like to see it, I will send it to you. The spelling is very bad, & must belong to B's youth."[2]

The only passage in which Blake used capitals for common nouns when there was no apparent personification was in *King Edward the Third* where he capitalized, probably for emphasis, all the names of the creatures he introduced into Sir Thomas Dagworth's speech asking the king to allow him to return to England.[3] R. H. Shepherd, in the first reprinted text, reduced these to small letters.

Gilchrist's criticism of Blake's punctuation may be well taken, especially if one holds to the more rigid standard of better printing houses. But if one remembers the circumstances, again one is surprised that there are not more errors. Barring examples where one may equally well take either of two choices, there are several places where semicolons are used wrongly in that they isolate a dependent clause from the main sentence without which its meaning is not clear. In *Fair Elenor* there are two examples:

> (*a*)   As the deer wounded Ellen flew over
>   The pathless plain; as the arrows that fly
>   By night; destruction flies, and strikes in darkness,
>   She fled from fear, till at her house arriv'd.
>   (p. 8, ll. 13–16.)
> (*b*)   "He seeks thy love; who, coward, in the night,
>   "Hired a villain to bereave my life."
>   (p. 10, ll. 1–2.)

This second example, although punctuated contrary to convention, has yet a certain rhetorical forcefulness because of the abrupt separation gained. In "Memory, hither come," the last two lines are separated from the preceding lines by a semicolon, although they are not a complete sentence:

> Walking along the darken'd valley,
> With silent Melancholy. (p. 14, ll. 15–16.)

The whole first stanza of "When early morn walks forth" has this same use of the semicolon:

> When early morn walks forth in sober grey;
> Then to my black ey'd maid I haste away,
> When evening sits beneath her dusky bow'r,
> And gently sighs away the silent hour;
> And village bell alarms, away I go;
> And the vale darkens at my pensive woe.
>
> (p. 17, ll. 1–6.)

In this example there is justification in that the first and third
lines are in strong adversative force to the second and fourth,
and the semicolon, by its very strength in separation, contributes effectively to this contrast. There is besides a kind of
enumerative purpose in the subordinate clauses, all accumu-
lating to a climax in the last line. The punctuation, if errone-
ous according to rule, seems to serve a real purpose. There is
an example that appears less purposeful in the misuse of the
semicolon in *Gwin, King of Norway:*

> The King is seen raging afar,
>   With all his men of might;
> Like blazing comets, scattering death
>   Thro' the red fev'rous night.
>
> (p. 22, ll. 13–16.)

To be sure, this has something of the ellipsis that has been
granted since time immemorial to poetry, especially to ballads.

As for Blake's use of full stops where they should not be,
which annoyed Gilchrist, there are two conspicuous examples.
The first example, from *Blind-man's Buff,* has ambiguity of
meaning:

> And those who play should stop the same
> By wholesome laws; such as all those
> Who on the blinded man impose.
> Stand in his stead as long a-gone
> When men were first a nation grown;
>
> (p. 28, ll. 12–16.)

The irregularity seen in the second example imitates the ejaculatory character of the words in the impassioned speech in
Samson when Dalila counterfeits her despair before Samson:

"My days are covered with sorrow! Shut up; darkened: By
night I am deceived!" (p. 66, ll. 5–6.) This variety of punctuation marks seems only to strengthen the mood of the speech,
for where there is ellipsis there is suggested a temporary sus-
pension of breath on the part of the agitated narrator. The
lines in *Blind-man's Buff* are confusing because of punctuation and capitalization:

> "Now, Kitty, now; what chance hast thou,
> "Roger so near thee, Trips; I vow!"
> (p. 27, ll. 9–10.)

If one omits what may be legitimate elliptical sentences (p.
25, l. 11; p. 28, l. 3; p. 28, l. 19; p. 54, l. 7), there is but one
example in which a full stop is needed where there is none.
That is in *Fair Elenor:*

> . . . as the arrows that fly
> By night; destruction flies, and strikes in darkness,
> She fled from fear, till at her house arriv'd.
> (p. 8, ll. 13–16.)

Mr. Geoffrey Keynes, in his Nonesuch edition, emended this
to read

> . . . as the arrows that fly
> By night, destruction flies, and strikes in darkness.
> She fled from fear, till at her house arriv'd.[4]

He followed here the arrangement previously made by Rossetti. Shepherd, however, compromised, using partly the original and partly the modern scheme:

> . . . as the arrows that fly
> By night; destruction flies, and strikes in darkness.[5]

He remained truer to Blake's usage, and yet secured greater
lucidity of meaning. Shepherd, and later Keynes, altered
Blake's lines in *To Winter:*

> . . . his storms are unchain'd; sheathed
> In ribbed steel, I dare not lift mine eyes;
> (p. 4, ll. 6–7.)

to read

> . . . his storms are unchain'd, sheathed
> In ribbed steel; I dare not lift mine eyes.

The words *antient, chace, chrystal, cloathes, croud, faulter-est, vallies,* and *withs* have the justification of current usage, even of the Great Lexicographer himself,[6] and excellent antecedent authority.[7] *Phlosophic* (p. 32, l. 11) and *greeen* (p. 18, l. 6) can be nothing but typographical errors. The long *s* could easily have been mistaken for an *f* and given *fell* for *sell* (p. 65, l. 25). *Ly* for *lie* (p. 65, l. 8) and *wou'd* for *would* (p. 25, l. 15) are errors of the same sort. There is no wish not to credit Blake with errors when he is at fault, and there are many instances in Blake's later work of similar errors; but in the *Poetical Sketches* the gravity of error has been overemphasized.

More important, too, than the presence of various mechanical errors in the *Poetical Sketches* is the attitude Blake took toward such inaccuracies. In none of the technical details already cited did he make any alterations in copies extant; but in details which changed the meaning of the text, there are several corrections made in Blake's own hand.

The one that called forth the most discussion among scholars is in *Mad Song.* The original first stanza reads:

> But lo! the morning peeps
> > Over the eastern steeps,
> And the rustling beds of dawn
> The earth do scorn. (p. 15, ll. 5–8.)

When Dante Gabriel Rossetti edited the selections to be included in Gilchrist's *Life* (1863), he altered *beds* to *birds.* What his reason was will never be known, although he could have seen a copy wherein the alteration had been made, or he could have followed the example set by Robert Southey, who in *The Doctor* (1847) printed *Mad Song* so emended.[8] Southey had known Blake personally, having visited him July 11, 1811, when Crabb Robinson recorded the event in his diary.[9] It may have been the interest Charles Lamb had in Blake's *Descriptive Catalogue,* furnished him by Crabb Rob-

inson, that caused Southey to attend Blake's exhibition in
1809, which he recalled as late as May 8, 1830, in a letter to
Caroline Bowles, Keswick.[10] Since Southey quoted only *Mad
Song* from the *Poetical Sketches,* he probably took it from
Blake's own copy for the provenance of no extant copy shows
Southey's ownership. Furthermore, Southey stated in the letter cited above : "I have nothing of Blake's but his designs for
Blair's *Grave,* which were published with the poem. His still
stranger designs for his own compositions in verse were not
ready for sale when I saw him, nor did I ever hear that they
were so."

When Shepherd edited the first reprint of the *Poetical
Sketches* in 1868, he objected to the tampering with the text
which Dante Gabriel Rossetti had done, giving that as his
justification for reprinting the original faithfully from a "copy
which had luckily fallen"[11] into his hands. The copy belonged
to Ann Flaxman. It would seem from the fact that Shepherd
restored *beds* that this copy had not been emended by Blake.
When, in 1874, William Michael Rossetti published his edition of Blake's poems, he followed Shepherd rather than his
brother, although he questioned in a footnote whether or not
beds should be *birds.*[12] Saintsbury, reviewing this new edition
of Blake's poems, was delighted with the restoration of the
original reading. He said : " 'Beds,' however, appears to us
much better ; nor is 'rustling beds of dawn' too far-fetched an
expression for the loose texture and shaken ragged outline of
the clouds whence the sun rises, while it should be observed
that the whole imagery of the poem is atmospheric and dae-
monic, ordinary living things being nowhere introduced."[13]
As late as 1910 Saintsbury again reiterated his earlier statement, ". . . the entire imagery of the poem is *atmospheric,*
and the phrase '*beds* of dawn' for the clouds whence sun and
wind issue is infinitely fine."[14] Nine years later Professor
H. J. C. Grierson resumed the discussion of what he called a
"textual crux in English poetry" because it involved a principle ; namely, that aesthetic preferences should be a last re-
sort in textual emendations. He cited the appearance in Blake's
later poems of similar lines where "birds rustle," and concluded that, such a rendering giving an equally definite mean-

ing, Dante Gabriel Rossetti's alteration of *beds* and *birds* was to be desired.[15] Professor Grierson's communication had been prompted by the appearance of Sampson's two editions and Ellis and Yeats' edition in which the original reading had once more been restored. There the matter stood, each editor free to choose his own rendering, until Mr. Geoffrey Keynes responded to Professor Grierson's *Times* letter by complimenting him upon his common-sense defense of the alteration of *beds* to *birds;* he had seen a copy in which Blake himself had corrected the word with India ink. The copy was one which Thomas Butts acquired, now in the Ashley Library.[16] Three other copies contain the same emendation. The first is now owned by Mr. W. Graham Robertson;[17] the second is the Kemble–Devonshire copy in the Huntington Library;[18] the third is in the library of the University of London.[19] A fourth, Ann Flaxman's copy (not now located), is known to have contained "various MS. alterations";[20] but, again, since it was the copy Shepherd reprinted, it must not have had this correction.

The other alterations in the text made by Blake vary in the copies, and may be best seen by observing the changes made in each one.

There are three manuscript corrections besides the one in *Mad Song* in the Tulk copy in the Huntington Library:

(*a*) In *To Winter,* *in* before *his* is crossed through with ink:

> He withers all in silence, and in his hand
> Unclothes the earth, and freezes up frail life.
> (p. 4, St. 3, l. 3.)

(*b*) In *Fair Elenor,* the *s* in *cheeks* is crossed through with ink:

> She shriek'd aloud, and sunk upon the steps
> On the cold stone her pale cheeks.
> (p. 7, St. 2, l. 2.)

(*c*) In the song "Love and harmony combine," *her* is altered to *his:*

And thy lovely leaves among,
There is love: I hear her tongue.
(p. 12, St. 4, l. 4.)

The Kemble–Devonshire copy lacks the correction in the *Song,* and the error in *Fair Elenor* is erased and not crossed through. Mr. Graham Robertson's copy has the same emendations as the Tulk copy except the one in *Fair Elenor*. Besides, it adds two more. The first is in *Fair Elenor* where *I am* is "rubbed out with care and 'behold' printed in ink in imitation of type"[21] in the line, "O Elenor, I am thy husband's head" (p. 9, St. 16, l. 1.) The second is in *To the Evening Star,* where *whilst* is altered to *while* in: "Now whilst the sun rests on the mountains," (p. 5, l. 2.) The last alteration in *Fair Elenor* is the only correction that is specified in the auction record of Ann Flaxman's copy. This copy is further interesting because it contains on the two front flyleaves three manuscript Songs by Blake, entitled: Song 1st by a Shepherd; Song 2nd by a young Shepherd; Song 3rd by an old Shepherd—written not in Blake's hand, as Sampson assumed,[22] but in Catherine's writing.

The emendations which Blake made affected only six passages in all, and were primarily concerned with the sense of the passage. One other instance in which an alteration might have been expected occurs in the line in *An Imitation of Spencer* where later editions read *ears* for *cares:* "Midas the praise hath gain'd of lengthen'd cares. . . ." (p. 24, l. 15.) The old myth, to be sure, gave Midas the ears of an ass by way of punishment, but if it were not for the suggestion the word *lengthened* makes to recall the myth, *cares* would still be appropriate. Surely Midas' new touch gave him cares that lengthened his sorrows as well as his miserable days. Since Blake did not alter this reading in copies where he changed even less noticeable errors, it may be assumed that he meant *cares.*

All in all, whether it is in matters of syntax or typographical errors, there are too few consequential errors to have disturbed Gilchrist so much or to have justified a certain condescension on the part of later writers.[23] The erratic and haphazard matters of format were characteristics of the *Poetical Sketches* which would have disturbed Blake more than misspelled words and may have induced him to seek other ways of producing his books. He would rather have been moved by the beauty of a page, by the artistic unity in the arrangement and appearance of it.[24]

Since all Blake's other books but one were executed by his own hand with no help save that of his devoted wife, no human relationships associated with them are of consequence. The *Poetical Sketches,* on the other hand, is one of the most vital connections between Blake and John Flaxman. Their personal relationship is complex and fraught with lasting and significant influences, the background of which was touched upon by Malkin in his remarks preliminary to introducing Blake.

It is very well to regard a person who becomes eminent as above and ahead of his time. He usually is both; else he would have remained hidden among other mediocre and lesser men. But it is folly to deny the importance of those who do not rise to eminence to the one who does. Fashions of thought as well as habitual actions of people, whether one wills to be independent of them or not, have their coercive effect. Currents of ideas drift in from past times and from other lands. The signs of the times, as read in the contemporary magazines, give evidence that through the decades of 1760 and 1770 there was a rising tide of juvenile verse, and one can only surmise how strongly that wave caught Blake before 1783. The editor of the *Town and Country Magazine* gave hope to the aspiring versemakers of seeing their effusions in print, although he wrote in April, 1772, in a column called the "State of Europe": "Scarce a month passes in London, without giving birth to some poetical performance, which would be justly applauded and admired in any other civilized country, where these essays are not so common. . . ."[25] The second number of the *Town and Country Magazine* alone had four selections[26] by young folk, one of whom proved to be Chatterton, who continued contributions under different pen names. The *Town and Country Magazine* was only one magazine receptive to youthful poetry. The *Monthly Magazine* published Thomas

Dermody's *Monody on Chatterton,*[27] which he wrote in his twelfth year (1787). This is excellent evidence that one youth was affected by another. Thomas Dermody's collection of poems, 1792, stated on the title-page, as a sort of bid for attention, that it was written between the thirteenth and sixteenth years of his age. The *Monthly Ledger* for January, 1774, had an *Ode on Spring,*[28] written by a youth at the age of fifteen. This had the "smiling fields," "the feather'd choir," and "the vocal offerings" of all its kind and kin. The *Lady's Magazine* for February, 1771, printed *Verses spoken at the Juvenile Society in Bristol.*[29] A group of young men, apprentices mainly, formed the Juvenile Society which met once a fortnight in a room hired for the purpose with their three-penny contributions, where they became "disciples of Melpomene," gave full scope to their free sentiments, cursed their masters, or in some way sought to immortalize their own names. In 1771 Blake, too, was an apprentice in London. Among the members of this Bristol group were some of the youthful contributors to the London magazines, James Fowler, J. Thistlewaite, Thomas Cary, Alcibiades, Juvenis, and Chatterton himself. Who knows that it was not the force of this group which impelled Chatterton to subterfuges, directed his pen toward satire, encouraged his restiveness under the restraints of his apprenticeship, and made him unduly ambitious for fame? Its influence reached beyond the provincial town and drew attention of youths in the metropolis. There is no doubt that Blake knew the *Town and Country Magazine* which, new and well advertised, would have been accessible at Basire's if not at his own home. Chatterton's work which most greatly influenced Blake appeared in the first numbers of the *Town and Country Magazine* (1769). Of course, it is not new that many poets have written at a very early age, lisped in numbers, as Pope said he did. It is to be expected. The lyric impulse is strongest then and most urgent to be freed. The stranger thing is that so many youthful aspirants to verse had their work widely accepted.[30] These environmental forces may have accounted not so much for Blake's early attempts at poetry as for his willingness to present them to the public.

This introduces one of the most perplexing questions con-

nected with the *Poetical Sketches*. Who were the actual spon-
sors of the book? Who were the friends who believed it had
"poetical originality which merited some respite from oblivion"? Who were the ones who wished to confirm their opinions by the judgment of a "less partial public"?

Accounts are at such variance that it is difficult to arrive at
the truth. Malkin, the most reliable of authorities, passed over
the subject in silence. Smith was the first to state the circumstances. His statement was: "After leaving his instructor
[Basire], in whose house he had conducted himself with the
strictest propriety, he became acquainted with Flaxman, the
Sculptor, through his friend Stothard, and was also honoured
by an introduction to the accomplished Mrs. Mathew, whose
house, No. 27, in Rathbone-place, was then frequented by
most of the literary and talented people of the day. This lady,
to whom I also had the honour of being known, and whose
door and purse were constantly open and ready to cherish
persons of genius who stood in need of assistance in their
learned and arduous pursuits, wordly concerns, or inconven-
iences—was so extremely zealous in promoting the celebrity
of Blake, that upon hearing him read some of his early efforts
in poetry, she thought so well of them, as to request the Rev.
Henry Mathew, her husband, to join Mr. Flaxman in his truly
kind offer of defraying the expense of printing them; in which
he not only acquiesced, but, with his usual urbanity, wrote the
following advertisement, which precedes the poems."[31] This
story has been accepted without question by later writers, although some have played variations upon it. Tatham, for instance, said: "Between the age of twelve and twenty he wrote
several poems, afterwards published by the advice and with
the assistance of Flaxman, Mrs. Matthews, and others of his
friends."[32] Because Tatham missed the exact name of the
patroness and included more patrons than Smith when he certainly had a better chance of being informed, it is possible
that he relied upon hearsay and that Smith had not reported
correctly. Yeats merely said (probably reporting from Smith)
that the book was produced by Flaxman and some dilettanti
friends.[33] Professor Allardyce Nicoll named Mathew and Fuseli as patrons when he commented on Blake's singing to "an

enraptured company."[34] Since Smith is the only one who ever
reported about Blake's singing his early songs, he must have
been the principal source for this statement. He said: "Much
about this time [1784] Blake wrote many other songs, to
which he also composed tunes. These he would occasionally
sing to his friends; and though, according to his confession,
he was entirely unacquainted with the science of music, his
ear was so good, that his tunes were sometimes most singularly beautiful, and were noted down by musical professors."[35]
He recurred to this in *A Book for a Rainy Day:* "There [at
Mrs. Mathew's conversaziones] I have often heard him read
and sing several of his poems. He was listened to by the company with profound silence and allowed by most of the visi-
tors to possess original and extraordinary merit."[36] It must
be remembered that it was not until a year after the *Poetical
Sketches* was printed that Smith met either Blake or the Reverend Mr. Mathew.

Several things somewhat color the credence one may be
willing to give to Smith's story. The first is the very obvious
manner of flattery toward both the Reverend Henry Mathew
and Mrs. Mathew. He felt his importance at being noticed by
the "accomplished Mrs. Mathew" who was so ready to "cherish persons of genius." Gilchrist, as if half-amused at Mrs.
Mathew's pretensions, wrote: ". . . The 'celebrated Mrs.
Mathews?' Alas! for tenure of mortal Fame! This lady
ranked among the distinguished blue-stockings of her day;
was once known to half the Town, the polite and lettered part
thereof, as the agreeable, fascinating, *spirituelle* Mrs. Mathew,
as, in brief, one of the most 'gifted and elegant' of women."[37]
Then, as if not satisfied with this half-ironical description, he
drew upon his imagination to people the drawing room with
the well-known women who by their actual social position or
by their individual capacities held a considerable place in society. He playfully, and obviously, used his imagination to
gather around Mrs. Mathew the well-known coterie of "blue-
stockings." His account has been faithfully repeated ever
since.

While there is no definite evidence to discredit completely
Gilchrist's and Smith's accounts, there are some grave doubts

about them. In the first place it is unbelievable that Mrs. Mathew could have been so "celebrated," so "accomplished," so generous to all youthful geniuses, so charming in personality that no record of it got tucked away in contemporary documents, when there were James Boswell, Horace Walpole, Hannah More, and Fanny Burney freely jotting down their candid impressions of every sort of folk. Yet the pages of their diaries, memoirs, biographies, and letters are altogether silent on this "agreeable and fascinating" woman. So are the records made by members of the various literary clubs. So silent are the letters and memoirs of all the estimable women whom Gilchrist named that one can be certain Mrs. Mathew was not the "intimate friend or companion" of any of them. Gilchrist, as good as confessing the flight his imagination took, made finally a similar admission when he said: "As she does not, like her fair comrades, still flutter about the bookstalls among the half-remembered all-unread, and as no lettered contemporary has handed down her portrait, she has disappeared from us."[38] This final and more sober statement of Gilchrist contains another implication to refute Smith's account. She, with all her pretensions to learning and all her eagerness to encourage aspiring poets, never, so far as extensive searching through volumes of eighteenth-century publications has revealed, put her name on any subscription list, whereas other less "celebrated" people were frequent subscribers. As just one example, the subscription list which Hannah More solicited for her protégée, Ann Yearsley, lacks the name of Mrs. Mathew; yet there are the names of Dr. Burney, Miss Burney, Mrs. Ord, Sir Joshua Reynolds, Mrs. Vesey, the Hon. Horace Walpole, Miss E. Carter, and, most interesting of all, William Blake, Esq.

There is yet another pertinent circumstance which discredits Mrs. Mathew's share in the *Poetical Sketches*. If she had sponsored the printing of the *Poetical Sketches,* as sure as it was to have been considered important by such competent critics as most of these learned women were, just so surely would Mrs. Mathew have expected them to take copies, and even more surely would they have requested copies. Yet the provenance of all the extant copies of the *Poetical Sketches*

shows not the slightest trace of a copy once in the possession
of one of them. If they had heard Blake read and sing his
songs, they would have wanted at least a *Songs of Innocence.*
Yet, again, none belonged to them. It is curious, too, that no
one else mentioned Blake's singing; though his poetry and art
have survived, there are extant none of his songs "noted down
by musical professors."

One fact, of no such circumstantial nature, refutes the statements of Smith. In the *Builder* for January 17, 1863, Peter
Cunningham, son of Allan Cunningham, whose life of Blake,
full of inaccuracies, has already been shown to come from
that of Smith, gave some new material for a life of Flaxman.
In connection with this he printed for the first time some correspondence from Maria Denman relative to many errors of
fact in Cunningham's *Life of Flaxman,* and relative also to a
breach of faith in Cunningham's use of information given to
him confidentially before the *Life* appeared. Maria Denman,
Mrs. Flaxman's sister, lived with John and Ann Flaxman, for
she had been adopted by them in her early life; and upon her
devolved the duties and cares of the family both before and
after Mrs. Flaxman's death. She alone attended John Flaxman in his last illness. She would have given truly trustworthy
information, and the facts she offered to refute numerous
misstatements in Cunningham's *Life of Flaxman* furnish the
most ample new material there is about Flaxman, regarding
whom, all in all, there is about as meager information as there
is about Blake. She made two statements that directly pertain
to Mrs. Mathew's part in the *Poetical Sketches.* The first is:
"Page 277 [referring to the original edition]. Mr. Flaxman
befriended Blake, as well as many others, but without being
assisted by anyone, besides recommending him to many of his
friends."[39] That this is understood to apply to the occasion
just named is not a fancy conjured up to support a general
theory of this study, for another person noting the existence
of this record, William T. Whitley, specified the Reverend
Mr. Mathew: "Although Miss Denman must have been well
acquainted with William Blake she does not mention him in
her annotations, except to say that Flaxman assisted him

alone, and not with the help of the Rev. Henry Mathew as Cunningham states."[40]

The second statement of Miss Denman refers to page 292 of Cunningham's *Life,* and clearly states the implication, from the various circumstances already related, felt about Smith's reliability: *"You must be careful how you quote* [Nollekens] *Smith;*—he had too coarse a mind to understand Mr. Flaxman's ways, and knew very, very little of Mr. Flaxman's affairs."[41] In the light of these observations, it seems that the story of Mrs. Mathew's part in the *Poetical Sketches* must be another of the apocryphal anecdotes which has achieved its place by mere repetition. Blake may have attended meetings with Mrs. Mathew's friends for a time, but after 1784 these people drop completely out of the record so far as Blake is concerned except as one may consider the satirical *An Island in the Moon* his effort to show his disregard for them and their social aspirations; but it is exceedingly doubtful that Mrs. Mathew shared the expense of the *Poetical Sketches,* as it is also very certain that Blake did not have as wide acquaintance with prominent club members, either men[42] or women, as Smith and Gilchrist said.

Probably Blake had no human relationship, outside his marital one, which meant as much to him for so long a time as his friendship with John Flaxman. It was not one-sided. Although Flaxman may be said to have gone the Greek way and Blake the Gothic, both showed dependence upon and influence from the other for many years. The whole story of their association will never be known, but piecing together the many stray fragments, one sees something of its pattern and how it involved the *Poetical Sketches.*

It has generally been believed that Blake met Flaxman about 1780, through Stothard. They may have been introduced earlier. Smith put the date "after leaving his instructor [Basire]" (1778),[43] and Cunningham said "while yet with Basire," adding that Blake studied occasionally under Flaxman and Fuseli.[44] Constable points to an earlier date of meeting: "An early friendship with Stothard had brought Flaxman into touch with Blake, and before 1780 the two had become fairly inti-

mate. Blake's youthful passion for medieval art joined Stothard's more tepid enthusiasm to stimulate the same tastes in
Flaxman. The chessmen were an early consequence. The cos-
tumes of the figures are those of the kings, queens, soldiers,
and prelates in medieval sculpture and illuminated manuscripts. . . ."[45] Another set the date as early as 1775.[46] Dif-
fering also as to the date of Flaxman's marriage (1781 or
1782), the records agree that on that occasion Flaxman went to
live near Blake at 27 Wardour Street. John Flaxman was one
of the original group of the New Jerusalem Church, meeting
in New Court, Middle Temple, and it may be that it was Flaxman who was most responsible for Blake's interest in joining
the New Church. The spirituality of each man is a marked
characteristic, and, although their piety was very differently
expressed, each was definitely religious in the whole tenor and
aim of his life. Flaxman very often expressed his piety in his
letters.[47] Blake's manner of address revealed the vital tie between them; as, for example, "Friend & Companion from
Eternity," "Sublime Archangel," "Dear Sculptor of Eternity."[48] A further hint of the beginning of their friendship is
found in the so-called *Rossetti MS.* where, about 1810, Blake
asserted: "Flaxman cannot deny that one of the very first
Monuments he did, I gratuitously design'd for him. . . ."[49]
Taking Blake's remark literally would push the acquaintance
earlier than 1780,[50] for Flaxman's first works were done before his fifteenth year,[51] and he was winning silver medals
with his models at the Royal Academy by 1770.[52] Blake could
have alluded to the marble figure of "Alexander the Great"
modeled in 1784 for Mr. Edward Knight,[53] to the sketch of
a monument for Chatterton exhibited in 1780, or to the monument to Mrs. Sarah Morley in 1784.[54] No evidence has come
to light to identify the right one.

    When in 1787 Flaxman and his wife went to Italy, Blake
turned to their mutual friend, Fuseli, as he reported in a poem
within a letter to Flaxman September 12, 1800, which began:
"MY DEAREST FRIEND. It is to you I owe All my present Happiness. It is to you I owe perhaps the Principal Happiness of my life."[55] The concluding lines to this enclosed
poem tell one of the qualities of Flaxman which endeared him

to Blake. After mentioning the terrors of the wars in America and in France, he said:

> And My Angels have told me that seeing such
>   visions I could not subsist on the Earth,
> But by my conjunction with Flaxman,
>   who knows to forgive Nervous Fear.[56]

Blake must have appreciated one friend who understood him and had patience with him, and with whom he had some spiritual kinship. Flaxman, tolerant and amiable, was of even temperament and of great purity and simplicity of character. Mrs. Flaxman said of him: "Flaxman is my Hope his presence chears me, his good will's my anchor."[57] Blake's estimate of Flaxman was as generous as it was high. To William Hayley in three different letters he expressed this admiration:

(*a*) [November 26, 1800] Our dear friend Flaxman is the theme of my emulation in this industry, as well as in other virtues and merits.[58]

(*b*) [September 19, 1803] My admiration of Flaxman's genius is more and more—his industry is equal to his other great powers.[59]

(*c*) [April 25, 1805] . . . I conceive Flaxman stands without a competitor in sculpture.[60]

Blake's regard for Flaxman included a fine appreciation of Mrs. Flaxman whom he referred to at times as "Nancy,"[61] Flaxman's own name for her,[62] and whom he called "a connoisseur in engraving."[63] To her, "the flower of Flaxman's joy,"[64] he sent with the pleasing verses of appreciation[65] the copy of Gray's *Poems* which he illustrated, one may believe, especially for her.[66] Blake's attempt to express his feeling for Mr. and Mrs. Flaxman may be seen in Flaxman's letter to Hayley August 12, 1805: "The day after I received your last letter Blake brought a present of two copies of the Songs, it is a beautiful work, Nancy and I are equally thankful for the present, and equally delighted with your bounty to the Poet-Artist."[67] Both Mr. and Mrs. Flaxman had copies of the

Poetical Sketches, although Mrs. Flaxman gave hers away in 1784.[68]

Flaxman's beneficences to Blake will probably never be fully known. The three most conspicuous ones that were entirely due to Flaxman's interest were the printing of the *Poetical Sketches,* the expenses of which Flaxman bore, the employment by Wedgwood, and the sojourn at Felpham while employed by William Hayley. After Blake went to Sussex, Flaxman wrote to Hayley: "You may naturally suppose that I am highly pleased with the exertion of your usual Benevolence in favour of my friend Blake . . ., indeed I hope that Blake's residence at Felpham will be a mutual comfort to you & him & I see no reason why he should not make as good a livelihood there as in London, if he engraves and teaches drawing, by which he may gain considerably as also by making neat drawings of different kinds but if he places any dependence on painting large pictures, for which he is not qualified, either by habit or study, he will be miserably deceived."[69] After Blake returned to London, disillusioned about how "golden" his sojourn was "beneath the thatched roof of rusted gold,"[70] he wrote to Hayley about Flaxman, saying: "I have seen Flaxman already, as I took to him, early this morning, your present to his scholars. He and his are all well and in high spirits, and welcomed me with kind affection and generous exultation in my escape from the arrows of darkness."[71]

A time came when the feeling between the two men was altered. It is not surprising. Blake's inability to take criticism may have contributed to the estrangement, or he may have resented not only criticism[72] from Flaxman but his attempt to suggest what he should do. That Flaxman did make suggestions appears in two letters. The first is one Blake wrote to Hayley December 4, 1804: "PROOFS of my plates will wait on you in a few days. I have mentioned your proposals to our noble Flaxman, whose high & generous spirit relinquishes the whole to me—but that he will overlook and advise."[73] The second is from Flaxman to Hayley August 12, 1805: ". . . concerning the Edward the first, I have sent two or three noble sketches by Blake which might be drawn in outline by him in a manner highly creditable to your book & I would

overlook them so far as to see that they should be suitable to
the other designs."[74] Blake's deference to Flaxman's opinion
is strongly shown in an unpublished letter to Hayley on March
21, 1804: "I have been to look at the Drawings and Picture.
but Flaxman has not yet been able to go with me. Am sorry
to inform you that one of the drawings which Mr. Romney
destined for you is Lost or at least cannot now be found it is
that of the Witch raising the Storm. Mr. Romney says that in
lieu of the last Drawing you shall have choice of either of the
remaining ones of which Sanders says there are Several. but
I only saw one more because I would not give much trouble
as Flaxman was not with me."[75]

Flaxman's abundance of work, his ample financial recom-
pense for it, and his successful association with the Royal
Academy circle of artists may have caused Blake to withdraw
little by little from him. Blake wrote Hayley February 23,
1804: ". . . he [Flaxman] is so busy that I believe I shall
never see him again but when I call on him, for he has never
yet, since my return to London, had the time or grace to call
on me."[76] Blake's letter to George Cumberland on July 2,
1800, serves as a commentary on this situation: "I begin to
Emerge from a deep pit of Melancholy, Melancholy without
any real reason for it, a Disease which God keep you from &
all good men. . . . I have been too little among friends which
I fear they will not Excuse & I know not how to apologize
for. . . . I feel very strongly that I neglect my Duty to my
Friends but It is not want of Gratitude or Friendship but
perhaps an Excess of both."[77] Flaxman gives another clue to
a possible source of ill feeling. Writing to Hayley December
10, 1806, about some sketches he was doing for Hayley's
Triumphs of Temper, he said: "I must beg my name may not
appear in it for two reasons, first, because I have refused to
design for the works of several distinguished modern writers,
and secondly, because, designs for books are in the practice of
a distinct branch of artists who live almost entirely upon it;
and therefore for a Sculptor who has abundant employment,
to intrude on that province would evince a little vanity and
greediness which could not fail of being injurious to himself
and offensive to others."[78]

Whatever the cause of the strained relations, Flaxman showed in his letter to Hayley on May 4, 1808, that it had reached a serious phase, and Flaxman's unadorned statement is very telling: ". . . concerning the engravings Mr. Raimbach thought very modestly that Mr. Blake would execute the *outlines* better than himself but it was not possible to take the commission from the person that brought it to town, besides at present I have no intercourse with Mr. Blake."[79] Blake's "barberous stillettos" Flaxman no longer regarded as "poetic *jeu d'esprit*,"[80] but it is to Flaxman's credit that he refrained from explaining to anyone why he no longer saw Blake. At some point in this relationship between Flaxman and Blake there fits a small piece of manuscript, unpublished and unrecorded, which is in Blake's handwriting. The writing is upon what appears to be a portion only of a sheet of note paper, on the back of which are some penciled drawings such as are to be seen in the *Rossetti MS.,* and remnants of sealing wax. The paper has been so cut that the date which is a part of the watermark, G. Jones, is lacking. G. Jones is Griffith Jones[81] of Hertfordshire who between 1804 and 1810 made paper at the Nash Mills, now owned by John Dickinson and Company, Ltd. Preserved there are the original moulds upon which G. Jones made paper, and a minute comparison and measurement of the watermark[82] identified 1806 as the date when this sheet of paper was made upon which Blake wrote the brief but significant message:

Mr. Blake with Compls. sends Mr. Flaxman a Dra[f]t for £100. & begs to have a Receipt

Essex Street
9 Mch[83]

One is instantly struck by two or three significant things. In the first place, for what did Blake owe Flaxman £100, and when did Blake have £100? Secondly, what did Essex Street —a street on which William Blake never lived—have to do with it? It has already been surmised that Blake's early art work was more remunerative than people have known, for he delayed his marriage only one year. At his father's death in 1784, he should have received a portion of the estate if his

Mr. Blake will take the

of ... on a ... for the

hope to time a Receipt

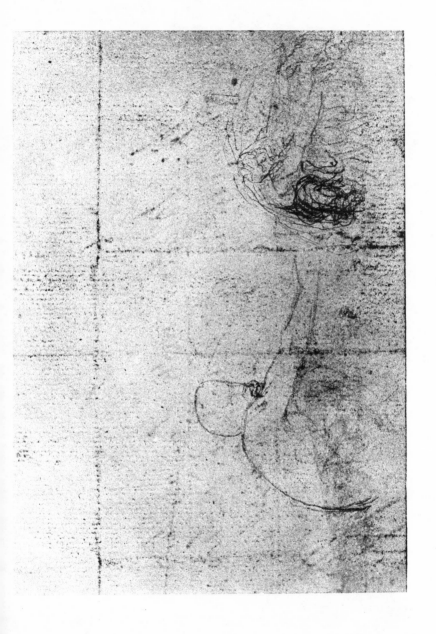

father had been as prosperous as he was supposed to be. On October 4, 1803, after his arrest for treason, Blake was admitted to bail at £100, while Hayley and the printer Seagrave were each bound for him at £50. This indicates only a judge's assumption of ability to pay. One hundred pounds was thought to be a sufficiently restrictive amount. The account between Butts and Blake in 1805[84] says a good bit about a possible income, for Butts was only one customer. Too, as shown in the price list to Dawson Turner,[85] Blake could have had a fair return on prints which he issued apart from the poems.

The opinion that Flaxman alone bore the expenses of printing the *Poetical Sketches* has been advanced. It is certain that Blake would not have been pleased with this aid, for he was not one to accept patronage, especially when it was given with the apologetic and condescending spirit in which the *Advertisement* was written. There is a striking resemblance between the language of the *Advertisement* and that of a letter which Flaxman wrote Hayley April 23, 1783, when he sent Hayley "a pamphlet of poems" (unquestionably the *Poetical Sketches*), in which he said: "I have left a pamphlet of poems with Mr. Long which you will transmit to Eartham; they are the writings of a Mr. Blake you have heard me mention: his education will plead sufficient excuse to your liberal mind for the defects of his work, and there are few so able to distinguish and set a right value on the beauties as yourself."[86] Blake, also, never accepted anything in the way of charity. The splendid works he did for Thomas Butts, who, as is supposed, magnanimously disguised his charity, are but an instance of his giving value received for generosity. It is unlikely that he would have allowed a debt which Flaxman incurred by having the *Poetical Sketches* printed to remain unpaid, especially if anything had happened to sever their friendship. One cannot believe that the actual cost of the printing amounted to £100, but that cost could have been a part of it, and expenses of Robert Blake's last illness could have been another. It is not known how many copies of the *Poetical Sketches* were printed. Surely the issue was not large; only a possible twenty-five copies are extant.[87] If Blake had been displeased enough to destroy the books, the few surviving copies give no fair clue to the original number. It is difficult, therefore, to estimate the cost. Three years later the Kilmarnock edition of Burns's *Poems,* at three shillings each and with 612 copies in the first issue, cost about £70, for Burns said he pocketed "(all expenses deducted) near twenty pounds."[88] But the price for job printing in a provincial town in Scotland might not be a correct standard for judging prices in the great publishing center, London. Blake's note has a formality not expected in a communication between friends, a formality of semilegal character. Could, then, the estrangement between the two men have arisen over money matters, and be allied to this small manuscript? It is quite possible. But why Essex Street? Blake lived in seven places in London, but never on Essex Street.

Here enters a new person, never before mentioned in the numerous discussions of Blake. Exactly what relationship he had to Blake is unknown. There are records to show that a John Blake, an attorney, did business in Essex Street between 1770 and 1783.[89] There are wills on file in Somerset House of a John Blake of Clement's Inn, Carey Street, a cousin of John Day Blake, who died July 8, 1828; of Robert Blake of 14 Essex Street, father of John Goble Blake and law partner of Richard White from 1798 or earlier to his death March 5, 1823; of Robert Blake of Cook's Court, father of Robert Blake and John Day Blake, who died November 24, 1826. It appears that both John and Robert Blake conducted a law business in Essex Street. If one or both were related to William Blake, Blake could have secured money through them to discharge the debt to Flaxman if it were pressing either from Blake's sense of pride and independence or from Flaxman himself. Blake refers to a cousin, unnamed, in a letter to John Linnell dated February 1, 1826: "For I am again laid up by a cold in my stomach; the Hampstead Air, as it always did, so I fear it always will do this, Except it be the Morning air; & That, in my Cousin's time, I found I could bear with safety & perhaps benefit."[90] Proof of these conjectures cannot be offered without the aid of supplementary documents or official records, which are unlikely to be promptly forthcoming. These surmises are based credibly upon what is known of

Blake's peculiar temperament and positive independence from
his earliest youth; upon his high sense of honor toward Flaxman who is known to have obligated Blake to him in the
printing of the *Poetical Sketches,* and, finally, upon a mysteri-
ously estranged relationship known to have come to a crisis
by 1808.

The manuscript is thought to be involved with conditions
arising before 1808, rather than later, because, in the dissen-
sions between Blake and other people in the latter part of his
life, Flaxman remained friendly to him personally and to the
character of his art, recognizing, as few did, that genius was
at work. Flaxman never relaxed his efforts to recommend
Blake to others. An inquisitive person tried to make Flaxman
commit himself that Blake was not mentally balanced: " 'But
Blake is a wild enthusiast, isn't he?' Ever loyal to his friend,
the sculptor drew himself up, half offended, saying, 'Some
think me an enthusiast.' "[91] When Blake wrote the epigram
To Nancy Flaxman:

> How can I help thy Husband's copying Me?
> Should that make difference 'twixt me & Thee?[92]

he touched upon what may have contributed to his ill feeling
toward Flaxman, as well as upon the direction of the influence between the two men. Unquestionably, Blake's doctrine
of "firm and determinate outline" was strengthened by Flaxman's skill in drawing; but Blake's visionary manner is visible
in Flaxman's series of forty drawings made to illustrate *The
Knight of the Burning Cross,* a poetical allegory, which Flaxman made for a birthday gift to Mrs. Flaxman on October 2,
1796. The originals in the Fitzwilliam Museum were reproduced in H. N. Morris's *Men of Genius* in 1915. Blake's influence upon these drawings is seen, first, in the language of
the dedication: "After the hero is exalted to the Spiritual
World and blessed with a Celestial Union," and in the angelic
figures used decoratively on the dedication page. Some figures
in the pictures are poised in air or float in graceful lines characteristic of Blake's work; others are muscular figures, often
with large heads and staring square faces, struggling as in
torture or grouped closely together bending heads over knees

—all reminiscent of the figures in Blake's prophetic works. Still others are portrayed as falling headlong as Blake's often are. The many-coiled serpent, loved by Blake and so beautifully represented that one never forgets it, is utilized by Flaxman. Just the year before these drawings were presented, Mrs. Flaxman, describing to Hayley a monument to Sir William Jones which Flaxman was at work upon, used the phrase: ". . . treated with the same visionary manner with the well known bas relief of Love and Pity."[93] Therein she acknowledged a quality Flaxman caught from Blake. The beauty and technical mastery of the human form, the grace, clarity, and harmony of Flaxman's best work are in contrast with the mystic, tremendous, and disproportionate extravagance of much of Blake's work. But in spiritual conception and aspiration there is a kinship—a tie that bound them from their first acquaintance, enduring in the character each achieved for himself.

There is still a certain mystery about Blake's attitude toward the *Poetical Sketches*.[94] Had he been overpersuaded to have the book printed; had he been disappointed in the beauty of his own lines when they confronted him in ordinary, colorless type; had he unpleasant associations with the book because of the sort of patronage bestowed by well-meaning friends; had he thereby become too greatly indebted to Flaxman for his pride; had his "unbending deportment" made strained relations with his associates? To these questions there is only one sure answer: Something had happened to cause him neither to publish it nor to bestow it as a gift upon many persons.

In 1921, when Mr. Keynes compiled his handsome bibliography of Blake, he recorded fourteen extant copies. Five more copies have been traced to their certain owners, while there are records of a possible six others. There was no copy in the British Museum when Gilchrist wrote his *Life*[95] so that he had to borrow one of the dozen extant copies known to him. One of the untraced copies, however, is described in the auction catalogue as Alexander Gilchrist's copy.[96] Copies which have within them inscriptions to indicate early owners belonged to Thomas Butts, Charles Tulk, George Cumberland, John Flaxman, Ann Flaxman, Samuel Palmer, John Linnell, and William Hayley, all personal acquaintances of Blake. It is a striking commentary on Blake's feeling toward the book that no manuscript of it has ever come to light. Even if Tatham did destroy some of Blake's work, it is inconceivable that the manuscript of the *Poetical Sketches* could have been offensive. Blake's notebooks show how he kept every scrap of verse he wrote—even when it served for nothing more than to relieve his anger—and even when it was on miscellaneous pieces of paper. Yet such a sentiment as causes people to keep their first schoolday essays was not strong enough in him to overbalance an aversion he seems to have had.

The extent of the popularity of a work can under ordinary circumstances be partly told by the number and distribution of the reprints from it. Malkin was the first to reproduce (1806) anything from the *Poetical Sketches*. He printed the songs, "How sweet I roam'd from field to field," which he stated was written before Blake was fourteen years old, and "I love the jocund dance." Crabb Robinson reprinted *To the Muses,* which was translated into German (1811). "How sweet I roam'd" was the one Smith chose for *Nollekens and His Times* (1828). Cunningham's first edition contained *To the Muses* and the following lines from *King Edward the Third:* p. 44, ll. 2–12; p. 51, ll. 10–27. His second edition (1830) added "I love the jocund dance" and "several stanzas" from *Gwin, King of Norway,* beginning: "The husbandman now leaves the plough." Southey chose *Mad Song* for *The Doctor.* D. G. Rossetti gave a much more generous selection in Gilchrist's *Life.* There he reprinted: *To Spring, To Summer, To the Evening Star,* "How sweet I roam'd," "My silks and fine array," "Love and harmony combine," "I love the jocund dance," "Memory, hither come," *Mad Song, To the Muses, Blind-man's Buff,* and *King Edward the Third* in the following selections: p. 30, l. 15 to the end of p. 31; p. 39, l. 13 to p. 42, l. 19; p. 44, l. 2 to the end of p. 46; all of Scene 5; all of Scene 6 except p. 53, ll. 3–6, p. 54, ll. 13–15, p. 55, ll. 1–4 and 9–11. Rossetti altered the order of the selections and put *King Edward the Third* into verse form of his own, besides making many alterations in the text. The text of Gilchrist's *Life* used as illustrations "How sweet I roam'd" (all

but the last stanza), "When early morn walks forth," and all
but the first stanza of "Fresh from the dewy hill." Swinburne
reprinted within the text of his essay (1868) the following:
the second and third stanzas of "Love and harmony combine"; ll. 41–42, 45–51 from *Fair Elenor;* ll. 5–10 from *To
the Evening Star* (in which he changed "Blue curtains of the
sky" to "The sky's blue curtains"); ll. 2–4 of *To the Muses*
—very few selections in all compared with the amount of
quotation from Blake's later writings. Of the *Poetical
Sketches* Swinburne thought very well, saying that it was
". . . work . . . not simply better than any man could do
then; better than all except the greatest have done since; better too than some still ranked among the greatest ever managed to do."[97]

In America as early as 1848 there appeared *To the Evening
Star, To Morning,* "How sweet I roam'd," "My silks and fine
array," and "Love and harmony combine."[98] After Gilchrist's
Life (1863) and Swinburne's essay (1868) had made Blake
more widely known, new interest was manifest in many
studies and editions. The same year in which Swinburne's
essay appeared, the exact reprint of the entire book was published by Basil Montagu Pickering, edited by Richard Herne
Shepherd. Following this were many reproductions now listed
in chronological order in Keynes's *Bibliography.*

The lack of recorded contemporary opinion regarding the
Poetical Sketches provides another reason for the belief that
few copies were distributed. No review of the book appeared.
There were two brief references in reviews of Malkin's *A
Father's Memoirs of His Child* (1806). One stated: "The
poetry of Mr. Blake, inserted in the dedication, does not rise
above mediocrity; as an artist he appears to more advan-
tage."[99] The second is equally brief and much more scornful:
"In the long dedication to Mr. Johnes of Hafod, a biographical notice is inserted of Mr. William Blake the artist, with
some selections from his poems, which are highly extolled:
but if 'Watts seldom rose above the level of a mere versifer,'
in what class must we place Mr. Blake, who is certainly very
inferior to Dr. Watts?"[100]

The answer to the question raised by the reviewer in 1806

about the evaluation of William Blake in comparison with other poets must be based upon an examination of the poems themselves, upon a discussion of the sources whence they derived their substance and their spirit as involved in the background of Blake's youth, and upon the circumstances attendant upon the production of his poetry. The final answer to the question will effect a conclusion which is at sharp variance with opinion that has prevailed and which, also, will show that from Blake's inscrutable and sovereign imaginative mind there was evoked a "poetical originality which merited some respite from oblivion."

CHAPTER III

THE INFLUENCE OF MILTON AND
THE BIBLE

A PSYCHOANALYST may feel capable in his own
mind of analyzing Blake's behavior and of charting
the unconscious processes of his mind. He may also
greatly err. It is impossible to see into the depths far enough
to know exactly how Blake's creative powers refashioned
every experience, or to know what his emotions, his dreams,
his visions added to the final artistic product. Such processes
may be what is most worth knowing about the *Poetical
Sketches,* but to attempt to penetrate the secret mysteries of
the creative processes leads to uncontrollable and hazardous
conjectures unless possible conclusions grow logically out of
strong objective circumstances not subject to imaginative explanation. The observation is not new that Blake's early
poetry is reflective of his reading. During his boyhood and
early manhood he doubtless became acquainted with a great
many more books than have survived with his mark of ownership. These books would have been an important phase of his
experience. He took them to himself imaginatively with varying degrees of assimilation, and, combining them with all
other possessions of his alert and restless mind, he reshaped
much from them into his early poems.

The first work of any poet must be in a sense experimental.
As any experimenter must do, Blake began with what was at
hand. If his attention had been absorbed in Milton or Chatterton, it is only natural that, when his creative mind sought a
means of expression, it followed the mode which was most
ready to give its thoughts and fancies shape and substance, be
that mode the one of Milton, Chatterton, or another. It is
very unlikely that he was aware of most of his imitation or that
he deliberately borrowed from anyone. His pronouncement of
1808, which seems to contradict this assertion, applies to quite
another subject: ". . . no one can ever Design till he has

learn'd the Language of Art by making many Finish'd Copies
both of Nature & Art & of whatever comes in his way from
Earliest Childhood. The difference between a bad Artist & a
Good One Is: the Bad Artist Seems to copy a Great deal. The
Good one Really does Copy a Great deal."[1] If the assimilation
of all that his mind magnetically drew to itself had been perfect, there would have been so much less trace of his sources
that he would have been considered "entirely original."[2]
That his imitation was sometimes very obvious and often
rather misshapen need not mean that he strove to copy what he
admired. His natural independence of mind, as well as his inherent integrity of character, would have forbidden that. The
manner, almost secretive, in which he produced his books
throughout his life shows furthermore that he did not write
primarily to be read. This does not imply that he did not have
something of moment to communicate, nor that the communication may not have had even more value to others than if it
had been composed with a view to wide circulation. It does
signify that Blake gave shape to something that was beautiful
to himself, something which satisfied him because it expressed
the emotional and spiritual experience with all these associated elements. To be relevant to his readers, what he found
lovely for himself had to be adequately embodied and rendered anew, and if in doing this he extracted something from
other writers, even that imitativeness may be a part of his individuality and a part of the human value of the work. In fact,
if Blake's mind had not had the power to draw to itself stray
bits wherever he found them, there would have been no medium through which the lyrical impulse could have found release. If his mind had not been adventurous and had not
sought something which held meaning for him, he would never
have created the songs which live and give pleasure today.
They testify afresh to the immortality of those masters whence
they drew certain elements of their being. Thus does the time-
lessness of the old help one to understand and to appreciate
the new.

One can hardly speak of a "first" influence upon the *Poetical Sketches* because it is impossible to know which influence
was earliest. The selections composing the *Poetical Sketches*

are much of a piece; all to some extent are reflective of every recognizable influence. One cannot say that upon this poem alone Spenser put his mark, on another, Ossian. The influences crisscross within and emerge from each one. It is doubtful even that whoever arranged the poems in the book put them in the order in which they were written. That the first cluster of poems should have a title, and that prose pieces follow the dramatic ones, say rather that similarity of form determined the arrangement. The ·order, therefore, in which Blake's sources are here discussed is merely a matter of convenience. It is not the order of time nor of importance although it has been discovered that, contrary to all previous comment on Blake, the influence of the eighteenth century is more extensive than that of the Elizabethan period.

Living in a time when John Wesley, George Whitefield, Swedenborg, and many leaders of dissenting sects revived among people of Blake's class a desire for intimate and personal knowledge of the Bible, and having a father whose religious interests were zealous and sincere, Blake would have come naturally to know the Bible among the earliest books read. At no time in any document that has come from his pen is there an allusion to a reading during childhood of fairy tales, Newbery romances, or chap-books. He did know old ballads, which children have somehow always regarded as their own. The Old Testament, to which in all his work he made the greatest number of allusions, was ample store of dramatic incident, of legend, of romance, of allegory, and of poetry, to satisfy his need, and it was probably appreciated as such long before he began to see any doctrinal meaning in it. Its figurative character and symbolism caught his attention and at some time gave direction to his thinking. Characters in it became living characters before him. This can be seen in the anecdotes about his childhood visions, so strangely unrecorded by Malkin whose sympathy with such experiences would have been expected, and by Smith and Cunningham who reveled in things out of the ordinary. The silence of these witnesses implies that the early visionary episodes were not regarded as particularly startling. Tatham referred to Blake's seeing the prophet Ezekiel under a tree.[3] He had visions besides of another "tree filled with angels, bright angelic wings bespangling every bough like stars";[4] of angels among haymakers;[5] and of Christ and the Apostles in Westminster Abbey[6] where, also, another time he saw in vision a great procession of priests, choristers, and censer-bearers who made the vaulted roof tremble with chant of plain-song and organ music.[7]

Rather than having any specially mystical implications, these anecdotes illustrate how very real and companionable the characters created in imaginative play can become and how they are so actual in existence that some never fade away from one's intimate circle of invisible friends. These characters from the biblical story were Blake's companions in a much truer sense than were his brothers and sister or their acquaintances. Many children in their make-believe are on intimate terms with angels; Blake's seeing angels was not an abnormal thing. His ability to continue to see them shows again how slender is the dividing line between the imaginative life, or make-believe, of children and the poetic vision of a poet. Except insofar as poets reveal it in their work, it is past finding out how closely akin children and poets are, especially with respect to intuition and the sharpness of sense impressions.

The Bible was one of the greatest influences upon the entire body of Blake's poetry, and was of no less importance in his art, as seen in the numerous biblical subjects, apart from his magnificent series of "Job," that he chose for representation. As he said relative to his picture, "The Last Judgment," ". . . the Imaginative Image returns by the seed of Contemplative Thought."[8] The imaginative images from his early knowledge of the Bible stored his mind richly and abundantly and returned through contemplation all his life.

One of the first points at which one detects the presence of the Bible in Blake's memory is in the language of his poetry. Scores of passages from his complete works could be cited; but the *Poetical Sketches* alone well illustrates the extent of this influence. Another quality of the Bible which lingered as a tune in his memory was its rhythm and cadence. Its parallelism or the antithetical character of style can be detected in the *Poetical Sketches*. Its imagery and figurative nature, particularly the dramatic and pictorial personification, were rendered again in the poems.

S. Foster Damon[9] has called attention to the verbal likeness between these lines from *Fair Elenor:*

> . . . as the arrows that fly
> By night; destruction flies, and strikes in darkness,
> She fled from fear, till at her house arriv'd.

and the following from Psalm 91.5–6:

> Thou shalt not be afraid for the terror by night; nor the arrow that flieth by day;
> Nor for the pestilence that walketh in darkness; nor for the destruction that wasteth at noonday.

Not only is there a verbal likeness in "arrows that fly," "destruction," and "darkness," but there is a close likeness in cadence as well between the first part of the Blake passage and the psalm. Blake gathered up all the ideas of terror and horror which are repeated in the psalm and let "she fled from fear" render them. Blake's rearrangement, in which he expressed ideas more figuratively than the psalm did, and in which he introduced earlier the picture of the darkness of night, gives to his lines dramatic forcefulness.

In *King Edward the Third,* Sir Walter Manny says:

> I know this breathing flesh must lie and rot,
> Cover'd with silence and forgetfulness.
> (p. 50, Sc. V, ll. 4–5.)

Here Blake's use of "flesh" is that of Genesis 6.17: "To destroy all flesh wherein is the breath of life." The same association between "flesh" and the "breath of life" which Blake reduced to the single phrase, "breathing flesh," appears in Genesis 7.15: "And they went in unto Noah into the ark, two and two of all flesh, wherein is the breath of life." The fatalistic touch of Blake in "everything that is in the earth must die" is elsewhere often recorded, as in I Peter 1.24: "For all flesh is as grass, and all the glory of man as the flower of the grass. The grass withereth, and the flower thereof falleth away." The idea of being covered with silence and forgetfulness is a vivid presentation of the picture of a grave. The use of "covered" here as well as in *Samson* ("My days are covered with sorrow," p. 66, l. 5) is like that in Psalm 139.11: "Surely the darkness shall cover me; . . ." and Psalm 140.7: "O God the Lord, the strength of my salvation, thou hast covered my head in the day of battle." When Blake used the same phrase similarly in *The Couch of Death,* "sin covers me as a cloak!" (p. 61, l. 18), the picture in his mind was the metaphorical one that he could have seen in such biblical passages as "the cloke of maliciousness" of I Peter 2.16 or "the cloke of covetousness" of I Thessalonians 2.5. This figurative meaning appears in Ecclesiasticus 50.11: "When he put on the robe of honour, and was clothed with the perfection of glory, when he went up to the high altar, he made the garment of holiness honourable." Blake was probably acquainted with the Apocrypha but, if not, he would have read this passage in Burke's *A Philosophical Inquiry into the Origin of our Ideas of the Sublime and Beautiful* (second edition) where it is used with one from *Henry the Fourth* to illustrate magnificence as a source of the beautiful. It is from the latter illustration, or its original, that Blake chose the line, "To turn and wind a fiery Pegasus," for his motto for Number VI in his *Descriptive Catalogue:* "A Spirit vaulting from a cloud to turn and wind a fiery Pegasus— Shakespeare."[10] These two definite ideas from the same book become significant when it is remembered that Blake said (1808) that he read Burke's *Treatise on the Sublime and Beautiful* "when very young."[11]

Sometimes it is the figure of speech from the Bible that lingered in Blake's memory to reappear in his poem with new associations, retaining only a part of the original. For example, he remembered the familiar act of binding sandals upon the feet and throwing a robe about one in preparation for departure of Acts 12.8 when he wrote in *King Edward the Third:*

> Bind ardent Hope upon your feet like shoes,
> Put on the robe of preparation,
> > (p. 51, Sc. V, ll. 22–23.)[12]

The more figurative meaning of the "garment," as Blake's is, will be seen in Isaiah 61.10: "For he hath clothed me with the garments of salvation, he hath covered me with a robe of righteousness." Blake's passage occurs in the speech of Sir Thomas Dagworth who has overcome his desire to leave the battle, and stands staunchly to combat fear in others. Instead of the usual phraseology of battle, the language is more poetical, more imbued with the spiritual as if remembered from the passage in Ephesians 6.14–18, done likewise in terms of battle array, except that at one point it transcends such terms, as Blake's lines do:

> Stand therefore, having your loins girt about with truth, and having on the breastplate of righteousness;
> And your feet shod with the preparation of the gospel of peace;
> Above all, taking the shield of faith, wherewith ye shall be able to quench all the fiery darts of the wicked.
> And take the helmet of salvation, and the sword of the Spirit, which is the word of God:

The idea of peace and salvation in this passage was the meaning when Sir Thomas Dagworth closed his speech with: "And those that fall shall rise in victory."

In the Old Testament the theme of desolation caused by the wrath of God is very frequent. The prophetic books, to which Blake's own prophetic works showed him to be especially partial, contain such descriptions as:

> Behold, the day of the Lord cometh, cruel both with wrath and fierce anger, to lay the land desolate: and he shall destroy the sinners thereof out of it. (Isaiah 13.9.)

> So will I stretch out my hand upon them, and make the land desolate, yes, more desolate than the wilderness toward Diblath, in all their habitations: and they shall know that I am the Lord. (Ezekiel 6.14.)

This idea is expressed in another way in the figures of speech in Isaiah 42.25: "Therefore he hath poured upon him the fury of his anger, and the strength of battle: and it hath set him on fire round about, yet he knew not; and it burned him, yet he laid it not to heart." Isaiah 66.15, likewise, presents the same fury of anger, bringing in another frequent comparison of the whirlwind: "For, behold, the Lord will come with fire, and with his chariots like a whirlwind, to render his anger with fury, and his rebuke with flames of fire." Blake introduced his dramatic fragment, *King Edward the Third,* with phrases reminiscent of the language of these biblical passages, and also with the prophets' feelings toward the desolation and the destructive force of wrath. He begins:

> O THOU, to whose fury the nations are
> But as dust !   (p. 29, ll. 1–2.)

The first ten lines of the play, less close in language, still carry out in other ways this conception of the devastating wrath of God. The sixth chapter of Jeremiah is full of fury, and the idea of "pouring fury" comes again and again in Ezekiel,[13] Jeremiah,[14] and Lamentations.[15] So Blake ends the first scene of the drama with a figure that is reminiscent of these ideas which were surely latent in his memory:

> A country not yet sown with destruction,
> And where the fiery whirlwind of swift war
> Has not yet swept its desolating wing.
>   (p. 31, ll. 9–11.)

The closing phrase in this passage appears again in *Samson:* ". . . and Desolation spreads his wings over the land of Palestine. . . ." (p. 65, ll. 8–9.) Beautifully condensed and sharpened is this expression of the fury, the destruction, the desolation, in language echoing the prophets. Blake, too, was fond of the whirlwind. One finds frequent suggestion of it in the motion of the details of his pictures. In 1805 he painted "The Whirlwind—Ezekiel's Vision of the Cherubim & Eyed Wheels."[16] The whirlwind was Jeremiah's favorite way of expressing his sense of the wrecking power of fury: "Behold, the whirlwind of the Lord goeth forth with fury, a continuing whirlwind: it shall fall with pain upon the head of the wicked." (Jeremiah 30.23.)[17] Thus, when Blake needed an expression to convey the thought of the wickedness and tempestuous fury of war, his mind turned naturally to these passages, as the close likeness in phrasing shows. In the *Prologue* to *King Edward the Fourth* he wrote:

When the whirlwind of fury comes from the
Throne of God, when the frowns of his countenance
Drive the nations together, who can stand?
                    (p. 56, ll. 6–8.)

If one seeks to understand why, in the illustrations Blake made
for his own prophetic books, there is such intense fury expressed in the facial expressions, in the muscular tautness, and
in the spiraled movement, or why there seems such an onrush
of uncontrolled and consuming terror and wrath in the poetry
of these books, he should look to Jeremiah and Isaiah and
other prophets to find the origin of both the image and the
idea.

Quite a different mood is expressed in other passages where
it seems Blake must have had a biblical image in mind. In *An
Imitation of Spencer,* he devoted all but one line of one of his
Spenserian attempts to the description of the eagle and his
flight, to which he likens Mercury. The winged god is almost
forgotten, for Blake so captures one's imagination that one
follows the eagle in its flight instead of the messenger of the
gods.

As the wing'd eagle scorns the tow'ry fence
Of Alpine hills round his high aery,
And searches thro' the corners of the sky,
    Sports in the clouds to hear the thunder's sound,
And see the winged lightnings as they fly,
    Then, bosom'd in an amber cloud, around
Plumes his wide wings, and seeks Sol's palace high.
                    (p. 25, ll. 16–22.)

Since the title names the poem an imitation, Blake here would
have been expected to strive deliberately to catch something of
the classic manner belonging to Mercury. But in it, instead,
there is a reflection of the picture in Blake's beloved Job:

Doth the eagle mount up at thy command, and make her nest on
high?
    She dwelleth and abideth on the rock, upon the crag of the rock,
and the strong place.
    From thence she seeketh the prey, and her eyes behold afar off.
    Her young ones also suck up blood: and where the slain are,
there is she.   (Job 39.27–30.)

He also would have remembered that in Isaiah 40.31, the prophet stated: "But they that wait upon the Lord shall renew their strength; they shall mount up with wings as eagles; they shall run, and not be weary; and they shall walk, and not faint." These biblical reminiscences invest Mercury with a beauty, different but not less effective than that which he would have had if Blake had succeeded in imitating Spenser aright. Blake's use is an echo of the biblical rather than of the classical.[18]

The likeness of Blake's phraseology to that of the Bible is not confined to a few passages. There are numerous other parallels. In *The Couch of Death* occurs: ". . . 'But lo, there is a God, who made the world; stretch out thy hand to Him.' The youth replied, like a voice heard from a sepulchre, 'My hand is feeble, how should I stretch it out?' " (p. 61, ll. 9–12.) There can be no question that the biblical phrase, "stretch forth thy hand," was borrowed by Blake, nor any that the same source gave him "my hand is feeble." From the time that Moses said, "I will stretch out my hand and smite Egypt with my wonders. . . ." (Exodus 3.20) until Christ told his disciples, "but when thou art old, thou shalt stretch forth thy hands" (John 21.18), the phrase has been descriptive of a supplicating gesture. It is of such frequent occurrence[19] in the Scriptures that it would have come easily to mind when Blake wished to show the dying youth in *The Couch of Death* making supplication for his life. The inability to make supplication was described in the Bible as a "feebleness of hands," as in Ezekiel 7.17: "All hands shall be feeble, and all knees shall be weak as water."[20]

Blake wrote one passage comprising the whole of the *Prologue* for *King Edward the Fourth,* which has such antiphonal balance, strophic cadence, and sublimity of tone that one almost expects to find it verbatim in the Bible. One first searches the Psalms, for surely there the elemental feelings find the most elevated rhythmic expression. One seeks in Job, for there are such antithesis of mood set against mood, such supplication, and such yearning of the human spirit as are in Blake's passage. One seeks in Isaiah where there is a sublime ode in Chapter 53, or in II Samuel where David's "Song of Deliverance" is recorded. But read the Bible through, at no place does one find exactly such a passage. Yet verse after verse and phrase after phrase suggest Blake's *Prologue;* and one finishes the reading fully persuaded that it was only the accumulative echo of countless such passages that resounded in Blake's own poem. Thorough familiarity with the Bible wrought the very essence of it into his memory. The "seed of contemplative thought" sprang into a new imaginative image bearing the colors and lineaments of the original whence it came.

To confirm one's belief that the *Prologue* came from the possession of the rhythm of thought and antithesis, the highly wrought imagery and dignified symmetry, the sweep of harmonious sound, and the simplicity of the Bible, one directs attention to a few passages to which Blake's *Prologue* has an indescribable likeness. Blake's *Prologue* is as follows:

> O For a voice like thunder, and a tongue
> To drown the throat of war!—When the senses
> Are shaken, and the soul is driven to madness,
> Who can stand? When the souls of the oppressed
> Fight in the troubled air that rages, who can stand?
> When the whirlwind of fury comes from the
> Throne of God, when the frowns of his countenance
> Drive the nations together, who can stand?
> When Sin claps his broad wings over the battle,
> And sails rejoicing in the flood of Death;
> When souls are torn to everlasting fire,
> And fiends of Hell rejoice upon the slain,
> O who can stand? O who hath caused this?
> O who can answer at the throne of God?
> The Kings and Nobles of the Land have done it!
> Hear it not, Heaven, thy Ministers have done it.
>
> (p. 56.)

In this selection there is the antiphony of Job 40.4: "Behold, I am vile; what shall I answer thee? I will lay mine hand upon my mouth," and of Job 41.10: "None is so fierce that dare stir him up: who then is able to stand before me?" There is the same balance of form in I Samuel 6.20: "And the men of Beth-shemesh said, Who is able to stand before this holy Lord God? and to whom shall he go up from us?" The interrogative refrain, "Who shall stand?" reappears often. In II Kings

10.4 it is: "But they were exceedingly afraid, and said, Behold, two kings stood not before him: how then shall we stand?" Psalm 24.3 reads: "Who shall ascend into the hill of the Lord? or who shall stand in his holy place?" Psalm 76.7 is similar: "Thou, even thou, art to be feared: and who may stand in thy sight when once thou art angry?" Malachi 3.2 is the reverse of the form, but the effect remains much the same: "But who may abide the day of his coming? and who shall stand when he appeareth? for he is like a refiner's fire, and like fullers' soap." Blake's *Prologue* carried the refrain and the cadence of Psalm 130.1–3:

> Out of the depths have I cried unto thee, O Lord.
> Lord, hear my voice: let thine ears be attentive to the voice of my supplications.
> If thou, Lord, shouldst mark iniquities, Lord, who shall stand?

This is a cadence peculiar to the psalmist's many varied utterances,[21] and especially to Psalm 8.3–4:

> When I consider thy heavens, the work of thy fingers, the moon and the stars, which thou hast ordained;
> What is man, that thou art mindful of him? and the son of man, that thou visitest him?

Meditating upon an answer to such a question as the psalmist succinctly phrased in this last verse, Blake might well have been moved to exclaim as he did in *Contemplation:* "O man, how great, how little thou! O man, slave of each moment, lord of eternity! . . ." (p. 63, ll. 7–8.) He could also have remembered Job's querulous speech: "What is man, that thou shouldest magnify him? and that thou shouldest set thine heart upon him?" (Job 7.17.)

A second passage which, like the *Prologue,* is through many successive lines so strongly in the style of the Bible that one believes it is also a part of some half-remembered psalm, is a portion of *The Couch of Death.* Curiously this passage is embedded within a prose piece that is otherwise not at all suggestive of biblical influence. Set against the descriptive narrative of the prose of this selection, it has such a rich quality of oral utterance that it makes a strong emotional appeal. The first part is plainly an echo of the Twenty-third Psalm: ". . . I seem to walk through a deep valley, far from the light of day, alone and comfortless! . . . I walk in regions of Death, where no tree is; without a lantern to direct my steps, without a staff to support me." (p. 60, ll. 20–21.) The mother of the dying youth pleads with him to supplicate God. The youth replies:

> "My hand is feeble, how should I stretch
> "it out? My ways are sinful, how should
> "I raise mine eyes? My voice hath used
> "deceit, how should I call on Him who is Truth?
> "My breath is loathsome, how should he not
> "be offended? If I lay my face in the dust,
> "the grave opens its mouth for me; if I lift
> "up my head, sin covers me as a cloak!
> "O my dear friends, pray ye for me! Stretch
> "forth your hands, that my helper may
> "come! Through the void space I walk
> "between the sinful world and eternity!
> "Beneath me burns eternal fire! O for
> "a hand to pluck me forth!" (p. 61, ll. 12–24.)

This speech is skilfully constructed. Beginning with a sense of the youth's weakness, expressed in biblical terms, it moves on through a confession of sins, both general and specific, to the picture of his prostrate figure before his grave. The speech closes with a plea for rescue even though the youth, feeling the darkness of death upon him, believes he does not merit the succor he longs to have. The climax of the speech is not unlike that in speeches Job made, nor is the confession of sins unlike Job's: "I have sinned; what shall I do unto thee, O thou preserver of men?" (Job 7.20) or his, "If I be wicked, woe unto me: and if I be righteous, yet will I not lift up mine head. . . ." (Job 10.15.) The youth's speech is full of echoes of the Bible. There is strong parallelism both of meaning and phrase between Job's "My breath is corrupt, my days are extinct, the graves are ready for me" (Job 17.1) and the youth's confession, "My breath is loathsome . . . the grave opens its mouth for me." Blake employed the word "way" in exactly the biblical sense of Job in "But he knoweth the way that I take" (Job 23.10), and "Why is light given to man whose way is hid" (Job 3.23), or of the psalmist in "For the Lord knoweth the way of the righteous: but the way of the ungodly shall perish." (Psalm 1.6.) Among simple words no one word has more specific or meaningful connotation than "way" as used alike by Blake and by the Bible.

The phrase, "O for a hand to pluck me forth," employs another word in the same curious sense that Jeremiah meant in "Behold, I will pluck them out of their land, and pluck out the house of Judah from among them" (Jeremiah 12.14), and that the psalmist used with like intent in: "God shall likewise destroy thee for ever, he shall take thee away, and pluck thee out of thy dwelling place, and root thee out of the land of the living. . . ." (Psalm 52.5.)[22] For his phrase, "voice of deceit," Blake not only made a figure of speech from the memory of such common metaphorical phrases as "voice of joy," "voice of supplication," "voice of weeping," "voice of singing," and "voice of thanksgiving," but he had the same association between the ideas within the figure of speech itself found repeatedly in the Psalms,[23] as in "His mouth is full of cursing and deceit and fraud." (Psalm 10.7.) The conception of character in the phrase, "Him who is Truth," is that which appears in John 14.6: "Jesus saith unto him, I am the way, the truth, and the life." The rhetorical pattern of the youth's speech is that of Psalm 139.8–11:

If I ascend up into heaven, thou art there: if I make my bed in hell, behold, thou art there.

If I take the wings of the morning, and dwell in the uttermost parts of the sea;

Even there shall thy hand lead me, and thy right hand shall hold me.

If I say, Surely the darkness shall cover me; even the night shall be light about me.

Beginning in the *Poetical Sketches* and continuing to a fuller burst of exultation in the *Songs* written in Ann Flaxman's copy of the *Poetical Sketches,* and in the *Songs of Innocence,* there is a sense of joyousness and of rhapsody expressed by a particular personification given almost invariably to hills and valleys. Blake says:

> The hills tell each other, and the list'ning
> Vallies hear;   (p. 1, ll. 5–6.)

in describing the full chorus with which Spring announces her coming. This same figure of speech appears in:

> I love the laughing vale,
> I love the echoing hill, (p. 13, ll. 5–6.)

This laughter swells through Blake's *Laughing Song,* and seems to burst into a shower of joy over woods and streams, valleys and hills. One can only believe that the imagery of these lines as well as the enthusiasm expressed in them comes from his having entered imaginatively and emotionally into the psalmist's paeans of praise.[24] Not only had the meaning of the universal praise from nature been retained in Blake's poems, but the rhythm of the joyous, animated life of nature was held in memory to reappear fully charged with the same spirit. His childhood acquaintances saw the fields and meadows as wonderful places for hunting birds' nests or for flying kites; but for Blake, with his mind teeming with ideas and images from the Bible, there was a deeper and more spiritual meaning which gave distinct character to his poetry. This meaning he conveyed with delicacy and charm in his *Songs* and *To Spring.*

One might reasonably expect that the influence of the Bible would be most direct in *Samson* which would be restricted to the story of Samson as told in Judges 13–16. But again Blake's fondness for Job, for Isaiah, and especially for the Psalms is illustrated by their echoes in *Samson.* Whereas Isaiah 9.6 reads "For unto us a child is born, . . . and his name shall be called Wonderful; . . ." Blake wrote: "The Angel answered, My name is wonderful; enquire not after it, seeing it is a secret: but, if thou wilt, offer an offering unto the Lord." (p. 70, ll. 20–21.) Dalila said to Samson in Blake's story," . . . thy bones are brass, thy sinews are iron! . . ." The meaning, imagery, and phrasing of the metaphor must have come straight out of Job and Isaiah.

Thou hast clothed me with skin and flesh, and hast fenced me with bones and sinews.   (Job 10.11.)

Is my strength the strength of stones? or is my flesh of brass?
                                                              (Job 6.12.)

His bones are as strong pieces of brass; his bones are like bars of iron.   (Job 40.18.)

Because I knew that thou art obstinate, and thy neck is an iron sinew, and thy brow brass.   (Isaiah 48.4.)

Job contributes another striking phrase, embodying an unusual metaphor:

O that my words were now written! oh that they were printed in a book!
That they were graven with an iron pen and lead in the rock forever!   (Job 19.23–24.)

Blake wrote: "O white-robed Angel, guide my timorous hand to write as on a lofty rock with iron pens the words of truth, that all who pass may read." (pp. 64–65.) It is interesting to see how Blake kept the thought in its entirety, and how he rendered the idea of permanency. His "that all who pass may read" is his phrasing of the "forever" of Job, and it gives such a personal touch that one sees in it something autobiographical—something reminiscent of the epitaphs which he read in Westminster Abbey. Was it of himself he was thinking when he wrote "timorous hand"? Another autobiographical suggestion lies in the fact that this passage from Job would have attracted Blake through his association of the ideas with his engraving. It is possible that here is his first hint of the method of book production which he was soon to undertake. This idea was phrased by Jeremiah: "The sin of Judah is written with a pen of iron, and with the point of a diamond: it is graven upon the table of their heart, and upon the horns of your altars. . . ." (Jeremiah 17.1.) That this conception was deeply fixed in Blake's mind is seen in the fact that it was to reappear some fifteen or twenty years later in *Vala, or The Four Zoas* where, after he had described the Satanic flight of Urizen, he said:

But still his books he bore in his strong
　　hands, & his iron pen,
For when he died they lay beside his
　　grave, & when he rose
He seiz'd them with a *gloomy* smile;
　　for wrap'd in his death clothes
He hid them when he slept in death,
　　when he reviv'd, the clothes
Were rotted by the winds; the books remain'd
　　still unconsum'd,
Still to be written & interleav'd with brass
　　& iron & gold,
Time after time, for such a journey
　　none but iron pens
Can write And adamantine leaves
　　recieve [*sic*], nor can the man who goes
The journey obstinate refuse to write time
　　after time.

　　　　　(*Poetry and Prose*, p. 359, ll. 3–11.)

It is one thing to retain the actual language from sources as Blake often did. That alone involves no consummate skill, as is illustrated by much eighteenth-century verse that went no farther than the repetition of the language of its predecessors. Blake did go farther, for he invested such seeming repetition with connotations which transcend a mere transference of phrase. It is a more difficult thing to catch the tune as Blake frequently did. But added to both these abilities is the more important one—the power of his eye to see within a statement the concrete object which renders the emotions as well as the idea. It is a characteristic of the biblical manner that emotions, instead of being set forth by the bodily sensations that accompany them, are portrayed indirectly by the concrete presentation of the objects which arouse the emotions. That is the poet's way. That partly explains what Blake meant in *The Rossetti MS.* in several passages:

The Hebrew Bible & the Gospel of Jesus are not Allegory, but Eternal Vision or Imagination of All that Exists.[25]

The Nature of Visionary Fancy, or Imagination, is very little known, & the Eternal nature & permanence of its ever Existent

Images is consider'd as less permanent than the things of Vegetative & Generative Nature; yet the Oak dies as well as the Lettuce, but Its Eternal Image & Individuality never dies, but renews by its seed; just so the Imaginative Image returns by the seed of Contemplative Thought; the Writings of the Prophets illustrate these conceptions of the Visionary Fancy by their various sublime & Divine Images as seen in the Worlds of Vision.[26]

I assert for My Self that I do not behold the outward Creation. . . . "What," it will be Question'd, "When the Sun rises, do you not see a round disk of fire somewhat like a Guinea?" O no, no, I see an Innumerable company of the Heavenly host crying, 'Holy, Holy, Holy is the Lord God Almighty.' I question not my Corporeal or Vegetative Eye any more than I would Question a Window concerning a Sight. I look thro' it & not with it.[27]

> This Life's dim Windows of the Soul
> Distorts the Heavens from Pole to Pole
> And leads you to Believe a Lie
> When you see with, not thro', the Eye[28]

Somewhat earlier than these statements, Blake asked the Reverend Dr. Trusler: "Why is the Bible more Entertaining & Instructive than any other book? Is it not because they are addressed to the Imagination, which is Spiritual Sensation, & but mediately to the Understanding or Reason?"[29]

Thus Blake explained that it is the eye able to penetrate through the abstractions, and to see concretely embodied the emotions or "spiritual sensations," which beholds the eternal vision of anything. That is the poet's eye. That is the eye with which he saw and registered in memory certain other biblical passages. The more difficult the vision was of concrete incorporation, the more primary the simplicity with which it was finally expressed. The psalmist, ever aware of the presence of a divine spirit, yet ever unable to understand its inscrutable nature, frequently expressed his idea by comparing darkness with a great palace-like structure that stretched forth into secret distances from the very threshold of the spirit's presence. All the most elemental forces, as dark waters and clouds, were a part of this great architectural image—by which the psalmist sought to tell not only what he saw but what he felt.

Thus Psalm 18—the great psalm of deliverance—is consonant with the theme of Blake's *Samson*. From it comes: "He made darkness his secret place; his pavilion round about him were dark waters and thick clouds of the skies." (Psalm 18.11.) This same image of the psalmist is found again in II Samuel 22.12: "And he made darkness pavilions round about him, dark waters, and thick clouds."[30] Recurrent in Blake's mind is this image which he reproduced in *Samson:* "Now Night, noon-tide of damned spirits, over the silent earth spreads her pavilion, . . . from side to side the land groans, her prowess lost, and seeks to hide her bruised head under the mists of night. . . ." (p. 65, ll. 11–12.) This image involves an element found in II Peter 2.17: "These are wells without water, clouds that are carried with a tempest; to whom the mist of darkness is reserved for ever." Another example of a transference on the same basis as the instance just given is in Psalm 45.8: "All thy garments smell of myrrh, and aloes, and cassia, out of ivory palaces, whereby they have made thee glad." Out of this came the echo in Samson's speech to Dalila: "Hear, O Dalila! doubt no more of Samson's love; for that fair breast was made the ivory palace of my inmost heart, where it shall lie at rest . . ." (p. 68, ll. 9–10.)[31]

Such are some of the echoes in *Samson* of biblical passages apart from the narrative about Samson in Judges 13–16. The influence of the latter upon Blake's *Samson* is significant; but in certain details Blake remembered Milton's version in *Samson Agonistes* rather than the biblical one. On the one hand, Blake had the very simple, condensed, and direct biblical narrative, whence Milton had taken the episode that formed the main plot of *Samson Agonistes*. On the other hand, he had Milton's poem with its Greek plan, its subtle character portrayal—especially of Samson—, its Aristotelian tragic theme; its forceful dramatic irony.[32] But he forged his own poem' anew, and if at one time it is the Bible and at another Milton's poem that is visible, it only shows the metals out of which he wrought. They were not yet of one amalgam.

Because Blake's *Samson* appears to be merely a fragment of what may have been planned, it is unjust to say what was the purpose or the plan for the whole. But that he meant to do something quite different from either of the earlier narratives is seen in certain innovations he made in the part written. In the first place, he evidently had the scheme of an epic in mind, for he began with the conventional opening of an epic: "SAMSON, the strongest of the children of men, I sing; how he was foiled by woman's arts, by a false wife brought to the gates of death!" (p. 64, ll. 1–3.) Thus he announced his theme. His first experiment was made in a form that continued to challenge his creative powers. Upon the eve of his return to London from Felpham, April 25, 1803, he wrote to Thomas Butts: "I have in these three years composed an immense number of verses on One Grand Theme, Similar to Homer's Iliad or Milton's Paradise Lost, the Persons & Machinery intirely new to the Inhabitants of Earth (some of the Persons Excepted). I have written this Poem from immediate Dictation, twelve or sometimes twenty or thirty lines at a time. . . ."[33] This suggestion of inspiration recalls Milton's belief in his own divine inspiration which Blake again acknowledged in a letter to Dr. Trusler about certain of his designs: "And tho' I call them Mine, I know that they are not Mine, being of the same opinion with Milton when he says That the Muse visits his slumbers & awakens & governs his song when Morn purples the East. . . ."[34] Milton's own early ambition to write an epic and his successful attainment in *Paradise Lost* might well have been Blake's ideal in such an attempt as this opening sentence signified. Why did Blake not complete *Samson?* Was it a mere practice sketch purposely tossed aside? Would its inclusion not imply the possibility that other hands than his had taken the *Poetical Sketches* and printed it without his knowledge?

Following at once upon this epic introduction are two apostrophes to Truth, through which Blake seemed to say that his narrative would contain new truth for all to read. Then without preparation for her, he introduced Dalila. His point of view in narrative is not clear, for he shifted from the third person to the second person in a speech addressed to Dalila which serves the purpose of simple exposition. Who speaks the second speech? It appears to be the author. Dalila then addresses Samson in a speech which is partly soliloquy, compris-

ing about half the selection. Samson's reply completes it.
There is no action. Nothing is concluded. Blake had made
merely a beginning.

This beginning, however, does not coincide with that of
either the biblical narrative or of Milton's. Blake opened his
sketch with the episode of Dalila's final plea to Samson. Her
previous attempts to learn his source of strength are referred
to only in retrospect. In this scene, which is but an episode in
the other narratives, Blake changed the emphasis. In the Bible,
Dalila's part is told straightforwardly, without elaboration. In
Milton's work, Samson is ever before one, and it is from his
point of view that the reader sees Dalila. With him the reader
sympathizes and hopes for his success. In *Samson,* Blake
elaborated the part of Dalila until one suspects that her character was the object of his interest and that it was from her
point of view he would have related the narrative. Her
speeches to Samson are filled with passion, so bitter in accusation of Samson's shortcomings, so desperate in threatenings,
that one becomes more interested in her than in Samson. This
is seen, too, in the strongly sensual appeal Dalila made to
Samson, and in the consequent reason Samson gave for revealing his secret to her. When Samson yielded, Blake said:
". . . he saw and lov'd the beauteous suppliant, nor could
conceal aught that might appease her; then, leaning on her
bosom, thus he spoke: 'Hear, O Dalila! doubt no more of
Samson's love; for that fair breast was made the ivory palace
of my inmost heart, where it shall lie at rest. . . .'" (p. 68.)
The Bible does not give the least hint of this phase of the
story; and Milton only once alluded to such an interpretation:

> Thrice she assay'd with flattering prayers
>   and sighs,
> And amorous reproaches to win from me
> My capital secret,[35]

The narrative in Judges gave no suggestion of Dalila's dress
or appearance. Milton employed his famous comparison with
a ship to describe her approach as she came "bedeckt, ornate,
and gay"[36] to the suffering, blind Samson. There is no earlier
hint of her appearance. Blake elaborated the picture of her,

reclining on a "sumptuous couch, in gorgeous pride," "more lovely in loose attire" of "fair linen that with the lily vies, purple and silver," her "eyes of love decked in mild sorrow" beneath her "honest-seeming brow" and offering a "holy kiss of love." (p. 65, *passim.*) Such a description makes one wonder if Blake had not in mind as he wrote more the picture of Cleopatra than either the biblical or Miltonic Dalila. The record in Judges gives no tears to Dalila. Milton alluded once to her tears: "O'recome with importunity and tears"[37] Blake had Dalila say: "To thee I pour my tears for sacrifice morning and evening. . . ." (p. 66, ll. 3–5.) Another time his narrative read: "Thus, in false tears, she bath'd his feet, and thus she day by day oppressed his soul: . . . his visage was troubled; his soul was distressed." (p. 66, ll. 23–25; 29–30.) This last phrase recalls the biblical version: "And it came to pass, when she pressed him daily with her words, and urged him, so that his soul was vexed unto death. . . ." (Judges 16.16.)

In the short space of Blake's narrative he succeeded in including a surprising number of details that are to be found in the earlier versions. Some of these details are common to all three; some Blake found only in Milton and some only in the Bible. The selection and cohesion are evocative of meaning. The story of the angel appearing twice is in all three, but the Bible nowhere states "twice." Therefore Blake's phrasing follows Milton's. The latter has:

> O wherefore was my birth from Heaven
> foretold
> Twice by an Angel, (*Samson Agonistes,* l. 24.)

and again, "For this did the angel twice descend." (*Samson Agonistes,* l. 361.) Blake's account reads: "Twice was my birth foretold from heaven, and twice a sacred vow enjoined me that I should drink no wine, nor eat of any unclean thing, for holy unto Israel's God I am, a Nazarite even from my mother's womb. Twice was it told, that it might not be broken. . . ." (p. 68.) The first part of this passage follows the phrasing of Milton's narrative above, but for the rest Blake went to the Bible:

Now wherefore beware, I pray thee, and drink not wine nor strong drink, and eat not any unclean thing:

For, lo, thou shalt conceive, and bear a son; and no razor shall come on his head: for the child shall be a Nazarite unto God from the womb: (Judges 13.4–5.)

Milton thus omits the annunciation given by both the Bible and Blake. The latter, however, in his recital of the annunciation had more in mind than the account in Judges 13.3, which reads: "And the angel of the Lord appeared unto the woman, and said unto her, Behold now, thou art barren, and bearest not; but thou shalt conceive, and bear a son." Blake's account of the annunciation reads: "Hail, highly favoured! said he; for lo, thou shalt conceive, and bear a son, and Israel's strength shall be upon his shoulders, and he shall be called Israel's Deliverer!" (p. 69.) This clearly records a memory of the annunciation to Mary in Luke 1.28, 31 or of the prophecy of Isaiah 7.14. Blake's "And he shall be called Israel's Deliverer" is in form like Luke 1.31, but it also suggests that he may have had in mind likewise the prophecy concerning the Christ in Isaiah 7.14.

The scene of the angel's visitations holds further variations in the three records. Milton and Blake have Manoa pray for a son. This is not in the Bible. Both represent Manoa as an aged man. The Bible makes no mention of the age of Samson's parents. In *Samson* and the Bible, the woman goes into the field to summon her husband. Milton omits this detail. When Manoa presses the angel to declare the name of their visitor, the biblical angel says, "Why seekest thou thus after my name, seeing it is secret?" (Judges 13.18.) Blake added a touch: "The Angel answered, My name is wonderful; enquire not after it, seeing it is a secret; but, if thou wilt, offer an offering unto the Lord." (p. 70.) This is similar to Isaiah 9.6 where "the government shall be upon his shoulder" is echoed in Blake's "Israel's strength shall be upon his shoulder."

A striking and significant detail that Blake added to the story of the angel should be mentioned. Judges 13.20 reads: "For it came to pass, when the flame went up toward heaven from off the altar, that the angel of the Lord ascended in the flame of the altar." Milton's version reads:

Send thee the Angel of thy Birth, to stand
Fast by thy side, who from thy Fathers field
Rode up in flames after his message told
Of thy conception, (*Samson Agonistes,* ll. 1431–1434.)

Blake's *Samson* ends with the angel's command to Manoa to make an offering; Blake lacks the definite event related in these two passages. But Blake's description of the angel's coming indicates that he had a different picture in mind: ". . . when lo, an angel from the fields of light entered the house! His form was manhood in the prime, and from his spacious brow shot terrors through the evening shade! . . ." (p. 69, ll. 9–12.) Here at least is the appearance of that idea conveyed so constantly in Blake's later poetry and art of the emanation of light from within, seen then to take a flame-like ascent and to wreathe in curving lines.[38]

Blake's narrative is like the Bible in one other point which Milton omitted. Both record Dalila's words, "the Philistines be upon thee." All three accounts name three trials of strength, but Blake reversed the manner in which they were told. He put the recital into Dalila's mouth; Milton has Samson recite them to Manoa. The Bible states that every one of the lords of the Philistines offered Dalila "eleven hundred pieces of silver." Milton referred once to Dalila's "Spousal embraces, vitiated with Gold" (*Samson Agonistes,* l. 349) and again to her "weakness to resist Philistian gold." (*Ibid.,* ll. 830–831.) Blake closed his curious address to Dalila with the command to "sell thy Lord for gold." (p. 65, l. 25.)

The Bible does not say that Dalila was a Philistine. She was a "woman in the valley of Sorek."[39] (Judges 16.4.) Milton, evidently drawing upon Josephus who said Samson "fell in love with a woman that was a harlot among the Philistines,"[40] made her a countrywoman of those to whom she revealed Samson's secret. Blake, with Milton, represented her as worshiping the Philistine god, Dagon.

In the cases of both Dalila and Manoa, Blake followed the spelling of Milton rather than the biblical spellings, Delilah and Manoah. Blake's emphasis on Dalila as a wicked woman, and his stated theme of how Samson was foiled by a woman's arts and brought to death, may have been indicative of his interest in Milton's attitude toward woman, most bitterly elaborated in *Samson Agonistes,* but plainly asserted in *Paradise Lost.*

Samson is strongly reminiscent of both the Bible and *Samson Agonistes.*[41] In verbal parallels, the Bible was first at Blake's command. In details of action, chiefly retrospective (as Milton's were also), Blake followed Milton where the Bible was silent. With respect to characterization, Blake's analysis of Dalila was more from Milton's sophisticated and psychological point of view than from the simple, direct facts of the Bible which spoke for themselves. That Blake did not achieve Milton's attainment in characterization is not surprising. The latter wrought from a long life of intense personal experiences with people, which in *Samson Agonistes* were brought into synthesis; Blake wrought from what his youthful imagination sifted from another's experience. Besides, as Blake said, "Every Man's Wisdom is peculiar to his own Individuality,"[42] and he had to achieve both attributes after years of living such as Milton had already had when he wrote *Samson Agonistes.*

All in all, the influence of the Bible, while perhaps greater than the influence of Milton, is in *Samson* a more unconscious, unobtrusive kind. It would seem to show that in 1783 the acquaintance with Milton was more recent and less thorough than the familiarity with the Bible. Later, when Blake came to interpret *Job* through his drawings, he did not do it literally as told in the Bible, but with interpretative symbolism. In a sense, Blake began to do the same with *Samson,* although he made no pictures to accompany it. *Samson,* less symbolical than *Job,* suggests that Blake was yet too close to his first knowledge of Milton, and still too much under the spell that Milton cast, to give himself completely to such symbolism as the Bible alone might have stimulated. *Samson* is important as showing how Blake stood midway between two powerful influences that were moving exactly in the opposite direction.

Milton's influence upon Blake was not confined to *Samson.* It was a power that increased through his life until, in 1804, he engaged upon his own *Milton,* within which interval of time he had come more fully to understand the majestic cosmic scheme of *Paradise Lost,* and to comprehend the spiritual truths embodied in it. How early he began his reading of Milton it is impossible to know, except for one statement made in 1800 to John Flaxman, to whom Blake would have reported without exaggeration:

> Now my lot in the Heavens is this, Milton
>   lov'd me in childhood & shew'd me his face.
> Ezra came with Isaiah the Prophet, but
>   Shakespeare in riper years gave me his hand;[43]

It is believed[44] that one of Blake's first acquaintances with Milton was with a boyhood reading of Milton's *History of England* whence he could have taken his conception of the giant Albion[45] and the Druids. When he described his picture, "The Ancient Britons," in 1809, he made allusion to Milton: "In this Picture, believing with Milton the ancient British History, Mr. B. has done as all the ancients did, and as all the moderns who are worthy of fame, given the historical fact in its poetical vigour so as it always happens, and not in that dull way that some Historians pretend, who, being weakly organized themselves, cannot see either miracle or prodigy. . . ."[46]

The echoes of Milton in the *Poetical Sketches* are various and scattered. Sometimes it is a recollection of a vivid picture as in *An Imitation of Spencer* where Blake wrote regarding Mercury:

> Then, laden with eternal fate, dost go
> Down, like a falling star, from autumn sky,
> And o'er the surface of the silent deep dost fly.
>   (p. 25, ll. 3–5.)

that is reminiscent of Milton's description of Uriel in *Paradise Lost* (IV, 555–558):

> Thither came *Uriel,* gliding through the Eeven
> On a Sun beam, swift as a shooting Starr
> In *Autumn* thwarts the night, when vapors fir'd
> Impress the Air,

Another time it is a kinship of ideas. King Edward, in his
opening speech of Blake's play, reasons about the emergence
of obscure persons from their unimportant position into conspicuous places. He speaks of their personal safety with much
the same marshaling of ideas that Mammon followed in his
speech in *Paradise Lost* (II, 249–261) in which he reasoned
about the battle to recover Paradise. Again it is a verbal echo,
as in King Edward's speech, "O sheathe their hearts in triple
steel. . . ." (p. 30, l. 9) which is in *Paradise Lost* (II, 569):
"With stubborn patience as with triple steel." This idea is not
new to Milton, of course, for it is in Chapman's *Iliad,*[47] in
meaning rather than phrasing, which Blake could have read in
the copy he owned, or in Potter's translation of Aeschylus's
Agamemnon,[48] which he also owned. Another sentence in King
Edward's speech: "Their minds are fetter'd; then how can
they be free. . . ." (p. 30, l. 4) seems a refashioning of the
line in *Samson Agonistes:* "My heels are fetter'd, but my fist
is free." (l. 1235) Milton's *Comus* has a very curious phrase
which Blake seems to have utilized in *King Edward the Third*
when the king tells Sir Thomas Dagworth how valuable he is:

> If Philip came arm'd in the ribs of death,
> And shook his mortal dart against my head,
> Thoud'st laugh his fury into nerveless shame!
> (p. 42, ll. 11–12.)

"Ribs of death!" Such a double image lingered in Blake's imagination from *Comus:*

> . . . I was all ears,
> And took in strains that might create a soul
> Under the ribs of Death,   (ll. 560–562.)

One of Milton's favorite personifications was Contemplation. In *Il Penseroso* he speaks of the "Cherub Contemplation" (l. 54), and in *Comus* (ll. 375–382) of Contemplation
as the nurse of Wisdom. It is a memory of the latter scene in
which Contemplation, in spite of dangers in woods and solitary wilds, is safe in the companionship of Wisdom—that
light within one's breast—that lingered with Blake, and from
it his slight prose sketch, *Contemplation,* drew some sugges-

tion: "WHO is this, that with unerring step dares tempt the wilds, where only Nature's foot hath trod? 'Tis Contemplation, daughter of the grey Morning! Majestical she steppeth, and with her pure quill on every flower writeth Wisdom's name." (p. 63, ll. 1–6.) The entire selection, *Contemplation,* while not close in actual verbal analogy to Milton's language, is much in his spirit and expressive of his ideas.[49]

The concluding lines to Milton's *Lycidas* have about them a suggestion of mystery and quietude, phrased so that the cadence clings easily to memory:

> Thus sang the uncouth Swain to th' Okes and rills,
>
> .   .   .   .
>
> At last he rose, and twitched his Mantle blew
> To morrow to fresh Woods, and Pastures new.

Blake remembered the picture conveyed in these closing lines and the melody of the verse when he wished to conclude his *To Autumn:*

> Thus sang the jolly Autumn as he Sat,
> Then rose, girded himself, and o'er the bleak
> Hills fled from sight; but left his golden load.
> (p. 3, ll. 16–18.)[50]

The quiet tone, the action, and the phrasing with which each poem ends cause one to believe Blake was indebted to Milton for these details. But he wrote with a difference. Milton turns from the lament for his friend with a feeling that his Taskmaster still regards him as a means through which his mighty purposes are to be accomplished with dignity and with a consciousness of his own high trust. Blake, on the other hand, had not yet learned from Milton what he did learn later, or had confirmed in him by Milton—the egotism and pride that came with his belief in his own divine inspiration.[51] The lines closing *To Autumn,* then, carry no implication of the meaning in the final lines to *Lycidas.* It is the picture that Blake sees in Autumn, the visualized person of the jolly Autumn who, as an itinerant peddler of stories and songs as well as more material things, has been enticed by expectant children to pause

"beneath the shady roof." He does not identify himself with
Autumn as Milton does with "the uncouth Swain." Autumn
is the kindly, beneficent, and picturesque personage who, after
singing his "lusty song of fruit and flowers," fled leaving his
"golden load." One may well believe that *To Autumn,* for this
reason, was written earlier than *Samson* where the Miltonic
influence is tinged with the philosophical. *To Autumn* is done
in objective terms, and is effective through the personification
that is based on visual imagery rather than on weight of
meaning. How very subtle the correspondence is between the
endings of these two poems becomes manifest when there is
placed beside them the slavish and belabored imitations of
Milton such as filled the magazines.[52] They have nothing of
the beauty inherent in the sustained and harmonious personification and give none of the aesthetic satisfaction of *Lycidas*
and *To Autumn.*

Blake never took words, as the versifiers of his time who
"imitated" the masters did, merely as cold, colorless words,
but because they flashed images of truth and beauty to his
mind. He reflected the image, often heightened and intensified,
and often made more brilliant by the light of his own imagination. Words reveal merely a fine kinship with the poet, Milton, with whom he had so much in common—a kinship which
is reflected not only in his later poetry and pictures but in the
youthful idealistic face seen in Blake's portrait of Milton,
which he drew for Hayley, now owned by the City Art Gallery at Manchester.[53] It was a kinship of spirit which sprang
from the root of the character, even in childhood. Milton's
lines in *Paradise Regained,* with which he has the Saviour relate his "holy meditations," are for this reason strongly autobiographical:

> When I was yet a child, no childish play
> To me was pleasing, all my mind was set
> Serious to learn and know, and thence to do
> What might be publick good; myself I thought
> Born to that end, born to promote all truth,
> All righteous things;
>   (*Paradise Regained,* I, 201–206.)

These lines could well describe the development of Blake to that place where he found himself identifying his own spiritual power with that of Milton, and giving to Milton a symbolical meaning in his poetry.

Raymond D. Havens states in his study of the influences of Milton on English poetry: "As to his [Blake's] knowledge of Milton's poetry and the importance of the part it played in his thoughts, there can be no question. Over ninety of his paintings and engravings deal with the works of the earlier poet, some forty-two with *Paradise Lost,* twelve with *Paradise Regained,* thirteen with *Allegro* and *Penseroso,* seventeen with *Comus,* seven with the *Nativity;* one is a portrait of the poet himself, and one was suggested by a line in the Death of a Fair Infant."[54] These products of Blake's pencil, brush, and graver came years after the *Poetical Sketches,* as did the most marked expression of Milton's influence in his poetry; yet Milton must have been very real to Blake in the years when he first made Milton's acquaintance. It was in those years that the *Poetical Sketches* came into being.

CHAPTER IV

THE INFLUENCE OF SPENSER

THERE is, perhaps, no better way to understand how a true poet surmounts and becomes, to a remarkable degree, independent of his own direct environment than to see how far afield his mind reaches in the quest for congenial companionship. It is a perennial mystery how the poet, as if by some power of divination, ignoring time, space, and all physical limitations, makes contact with those spirits akin to his own, from whom comes an energizing of mind that quickens in him flashes of insight. Only on the basis of this almost mystic—and surely magnetic—kinship can one account for one poet's discovery, in the first place, of his spiritual ancestors, and, in the second place, his preservation in his own work of a rich heritage of rhythm, expression, and thought, when all other poets, with the same opportunity inherited either a slender portion or nothing at all of these same possessions. Some such tie drew Blake to Milton and to the Bible. But Blake in his *Poetical Sketches* showed his contact with other sources of wisdom, loosely described by the term Elizabethan, although embracing chiefly the work of Spenser and Shakespeare.

When Blake introduced *Europe* with a song by a fairy, he related how he caught the little creature, as boys catch butterflies, in his hat, and said, "How know you this . . . small Sir? where did you learn this song?"[1] This is a question which one puts to Blake constantly while reading his early poetry, and it is a question which those who have written about Blake have not fully answered, for with one accord they have been satisfied with an explanation made by the first and most authentic of Blake's biographers, Malkin, who, in describing Blake's "several irregular and unfinished attempts at poetry," said: "He has dared to venture on the ancient simplicity; and feeling it in his own character and manners, has succeeded better than those, who have only seen it through a glass. His genius

in this line assimilates more with the bold and careless freedom, peculiar to our writers at the latter end of the sixteenth,
and the former part of the seventeenth century, than with the
polished phraseology, and just, but subdued thought of the
eighteenth."[2] Malkin's expressions are always revealing. His
later remarks, for example, illuminate the query his phrase,
"dared to venture," suggests, for he continued: "These poems
["Shakespeare's Venus and Adonis, Tarquin and Lucrece, and
his Sonnets"], now little read, were favorite studies of Mr.
Blake's early days. So were Jonson's Underwoods and Miscellanies, and he seems to me to have caught his manner, more
than that of Shakespeare in his trifles."[3] Malkin thus illustrated how Blake's quest for what would satisfy him took him
to those works "little read" by others, provided they were of
his spirit.[4]

With this reliable testimony that Blake had acquaintance
with the poets of the earlier centuries, it is necessary to examine his poetry to discover his indebtedness to them. Since
Blake's poem, *An Imitation of Spencer,* acknowledges one of
the foremost Elizabethan writers as his source, it is well to
consider Blake's effort in the light of the contemporary opinion about imitations of Spenser. One cannot know how familiar Blake would have been with the critical pronouncements
of his time, but one can be sure that such ideas circulated in
strangely wide currents, and that often the critic's judgment
was only a phrasing of his observations of what the currents
of thought were. There had been much discussion earlier
among literary men on the general subject of imitation, ranging from abstract reasoning on the nature of true imitation,
on whether or not one should imitate the classics, to criticisms
of imitations of specific authors. In Blake's later work there is
considerable evidence through the emphasis he gave to originality that he had read, agreed with, and restated the principles which Young uttered in his *Conjectures on Original
Composition,*[5] first published in 1759 but reprinted three times
in connection with the *Works* in the decade of the 'seventies.
But, at the time he wrote the *Poetical Sketches,* one cannot be
sure that he had yet read it, although in practice he conformed
to its theories. Neither can one be sure that he had read John-

son's opinions on the subject set forth in his *Life of West*[6] and in *The Rambler*[7] which regarded the imitations of Spenser as proofs of industry and nicety of observation but otherwise the playthings of fashion marred by disfigurement of lines through the use of obsolete words and a style of which he disapproved. Gray reiterated Johnson's objection to the forced use of Spenser's language.[8] William Thompson, writing in a preface to his *Hymn to May,* explained that the qualities in Spenser which the youthful poet felt impelled to copy were not the antiquated words but the "musically sweet" lines and the descriptions "delicately abundant, e'vn to a wantonness of painting." "It is the Music and Painting of Nature,"[9] he said. Thomas Warton's *Observations on the Faerie Queene of Spenser* analyzed further what attracted imitators of Spenser in the eighteenth century, and he advised imitation as one way to appreciate the images and their various expressions in Spenser's poetry.[10] The point of view of many imitators appears in Shenstone's advertisement to *The School-Mistress* which states the proper particulars for imitation to be Spenser's *"language,* his *simplicity,* his manner of *description,* and a peculiar *tenderness* of sentiment."[11]

One may turn to Blake's *Imitation* to see what he tried to do. First, in respect to the stanzaic form, it is readily observed that, if Blake endeavored to use the Spenserian stanza, he fell far short of attainment. Of the six stanzas, the first, second, and fifth have nine lines, the third and fourth have eight lines, and the sixth has ten lines. In the second, third, and sixth stanzas he achieves an Alexandrine. The rhythmical pattern in only one stanza, the first, accords with the normal Spenserian stanza, and then only if one permits "dight" to rhyme with "wide," as was probably Blake's intention. The second and fifth stanzas miss the normal pattern by having the Alexandrine rhyme with the seventh instead of the eighth line. Other faulty rhymes were "brow" and "throw" in the third stanza; "field" and "beheld" in the sixth. In the range of the six stanzas, "sky" is used three times as a terminal word, and, accordingly, "fly" appears three times. "High" and "move" are twice repeated. This does not indicate much facility with rhymes. In other respects Blake did not have a mastery of the

Spenserian form, for he achieved none of its melody and complex harmony or long swaying rhythm. For Blake's use a stanza had to be flexible and without restriction, and a Spenserian stanza was not flexible except as one made it so by mastery of the form. Sampson's statement that Blake's stanzas were "all different and all wrong" aptly described them.[12]

From the point of view of language, Blake did not attempt to use many Spenserian words, and did not in Johnson's phrase "disfigure his lines with a few obsolete phrases," thinking thereby to "achieve his design." "Dight" and "jocund" in the first stanza give the effect of Spenser's verse where they are frequent,[13] but they appear in the eighteenth century so constantly that they can hardly be regarded as obsolete in Blake's day. A pure Spenserian word is "wons" in *King Edward the Third,* where it has the meaning of "dwells":

> Death wons in cities' smoke, and in still night,
> When men sleep in their beds, walketh about!
>
> (p. 50, l. 16.)

Another one is in the second stanza of *An Imitation of Spencer:* "For ignorance is Folly's leesing nurse." (p. 24, l. 13.) Keynes emended this reading to "leasing,"[14] saying that it was a misprint in the original. He evidently followed the example of Sampson who also said that he read this "with all Blake's editors, leasing nurse, *i.e.* one who holds her charge in a lease or leash."[15] Such an interpretation misses the meaning of the line, and ignores the frequency in Spenser[16] of the word "leasing" in the sense of *lying,* which is the especial meaning of Blake's use. Spenser's use is clearly seen in *The Faerie Queene,* II, ix, 51, 9: "And all that fained is, as leasings, tales, and lies"; or in I, vi, 48, 1: "But that false pilgrim, which that leasing told"; or in *The Shepheardes Calender, September,* l. 150: "Fye on thee, Diggon, and all thy foule leasing!" The spelling *lesings* appears in *The Shepheardes Calender, Maye,* "And tell many lesings of this and that," l. 285. Blake's idea that ignorance is Folly's lying nurse is the conception of the character and activity of ignorance, and as such fits the meaning of the remainder of the stanza. Blake's use of "assay" in the second stanza: "For brutish Pan in vain might thee assay" has the authority of Spenser in *The Faerie Queene*, I, vi, 11, 1: "Such fearefull fitt assaid her trembling hart."[17] The slight use of archaic language in all Blake's poetry shows not only his unscholarly interests but also his kinship with the genuinely poetic character of the work instead of its mechanical details.

It is interesting that *An Imitation of Spencer* is the only poem in which Blake attempted to do anything with classical mythology.[18] Within the range of his six stanzas, he introduced Apollo, Pan, Midas, Mercury, Jove, and Minerva. His slight characterization of them is correct for classical representation, except for two details. The "soft, piteous eyes" of Minerva are not wholly consistent with the classical picture of her as "warrior, maid invincible," "maiden terrible." The picture of Mercury speeding to Jove's court is drawn partly from the scene depicted in *The Faerie Queene*, VII, vi, 14–18, and partly (as shown in the previous chapter) from Blake's memory of Milton. The conventional Apollo in:

> GOLDEN Apollo, that thro' heaven wide
> Scatter'st the rays of light, and truth's beams!
> (p. 24, l. 1.)

is the same one that Spenser portrays in *Virgil's Gnat* (ll. 65–67):

> The fiery Sun was mounted now on hight
> Up to the heavenly towers, and shot each where
> Out of his golden charet glistering light;

One would expect that anyone who attempted to imitate Spenser would have put his narrative into the form of an allegory. Perhaps, as with *Samson,* the fragmentary nature of the poem should preclude criticism of what is not accomplished. There is, however, no hint that allegory would have followed. The allegory of Spenser was at no time well assimilated by Blake for, when he later constructed his symbolical works, it was not Spenser's allegory that was his model. Besides, it is unlikely that, if Blake had really understood the religious aspect of Spenser's allegory, he would not have had more to say about it at some place in his writings. As a matter

of fact, *An Imitation of Spencer* touches chiefly the four preliminary stanzas of *The Faerie Queene*. It would seem as if
he wrote with them before him. Both poems open with addresses to gods and goddesses: Spenser to Clio, Cupid, Mars,
and "Goddesse heavenly bright"; Blake to Apollo, Mercury,
Minerva, and Pan. Spenser's plea to the heavenly goddess to

> Shed thy fair beames into my feeble eyne,
> And raise my thoughts, too humble and too vile,
>   (IV. 5–6.)

finds echo in the mood of humility and hope for divine aid expressed in Blake's first stanza. There is, of course, something
conventional about any invocation to the muse, and yet in no
place may a poet more directly express his personal wishes
than in such introductory stanzas. With Spenser there is a
submerging of the self until there is no flaw in the tone of his
invocation; with Blake there is such an obtrusion of his self-
consciousness that one feels a strong autobiographical import.
Commentators generally deny that there is much that is personal in Blake's early verse; but here the personal element is
unmistakable. There are first the phrases descriptive of his
limited powers—limited only probably as he saw himself at-
tempting to imitate Spenser—, his "darkling verses," his
"earthy mind," "his sleeping brain," "his labouring sense."
How strange to think of Blake's using "earthy" to describe
his mind! It shows how impossible he must have felt it was
for his mind to take flight with Spenser's into the particular
realms of fancy in which Spenser moved at ease. For, after
all, Blake's fancy and Spenser's were very unlike. The difference is partly manifest in Blake's later discussion of his picture, "The Bard, from Gray" in *A Descriptive Catalogue:* "A
Spirit and a Vision are not, as the modern philosophy supposes, a cloudy vapour, or a nothing: they are organized and
minutely articulated beyond all that the mortal and perishing
nature can produce. He who does not imagine in stronger and
better lineaments, and in stronger and better light than his
perishing and mortal eye can see, does not imagine at all."[19]
Blake's imagination corresponded more nearly with the one
that conceived Satan's journey across the Abyss than with the

one that idealized a kingdom of enchantment, decorated with
sets of artificial

> . . . sights
> Of arms and palfries, battels, fields and
>   fights
> And damsels in distress, and courteous
>   knights.[20]

Blake went to Spenser and took some store from him, but in
An Imitation of Spencer he admitted by these personal touches
that he did not quite achieve a sympathetic understanding of
him. Another clue to the reason may be in the lines:

> And wash my earthy mind in thy clear streams,
>   That wisdom may descend in fairy dreams:
> All while the jocund hours in thy train
> Scatter their fancies at thy poet's feet;
>   And when thou yields to night thy wide domain,
> Let rays of truth enlight his sleeping brain.

(p. 24, ll. 4–9.)

The "fairy dreams" and the "scattered fancies" must bring to
Blake wisdom and truth which, if one is to judge the kind of
thought with which his own allegories were laden, were not
exactly Spenser's kind. To Blake, the test of the value of
these fancies was the meaning. There is probably concealed in
these phrases, descriptive of the poet, a yearning for recogni-
tion to which Malkin suggested in his sketch of Blake that
Blake may have felt himself entitled in his youthful years.
The hint of such yearning reappears in *King Edward the
Third,* if one may consider the passage on fame (p. 30, ll.
16 ff.) to have any personal aspects. In a letter to Hayley in
1804, Blake wrote that ". . . if God blesses me with health
[I] doubt not, yet to make a figure in the great dance of life
that shall amuse the spectators in the sky."[21] Another personal
touch is seen in the critical sentiment of the second stanza.
The allusion that Midas sits in judgment of poetry may be an
early reflection of the note that appeared so often later when
Blake resented the power that fashionable, wealthy society
had over the arts.[22] His mention of "tinkling sounds" and

"tinkling rhimes" and "elegances terse" is plainly a reference
to most of the eighteenth-century verse, in contrast with which
the whole force of his poetry came to stand. Disinclined to
rhyme, he would again have left Spenser in favor of Milton
who wrote *Paradise Lost* in blank verse so that he could escape from the "troublesom and modern bondage of Rime-
ing,"[23] a phrase which Blake repeated in his introductory address to *Jerusalem:* "When this Verse was first dictated to
me, I consider'd a Monotonous Cadence, like that used by
Milton & Shakespeare & all writers of English Blank Verse,
derived from the modern bondage of Rhyming, to be a necessary and indispensible part of Verse."[24]

In respect to personification, Blake learned something from
Spenser. His picture of Envy in *An Imitation of Spencer*
could have been drawn from that in *The Faerie Queene.* In
Book I, iv, Envy is the fifth one of the "six sage counsellors,"
who accompanied Duessa and who, with her as Pride, represent the Seven Deadly Sins. He is described as malicious, and
spewing poison from his mouth which "chawed its own maw."
(I, iv, 30–5.) Later in Book V, xii, 31, 4, Envy is an "ill-
favour'd hag" who

> . . . when she wanted other things to eat
> She feedes on her owne maw unnaturall,
>
> (p. 31, ll. 6–7.)

Another example is the "mournful lean Despair" which appears in Blake's song, "My silks and fine array." It is a char-
acteristically condensed picture of Spenser's more elaborate
description of Despair as seen in *The Faerie Queene,* I, ix,
35–42.[25] Mercury's "golden rod"[26] which had the power of
casting charms is described by Spenser, II, xii, 41. The phrase,
"hissing adders," of stanza four appears in *The Faerie
Queene,* I, ii, 9, 8.[27] Meyerstein considers[28] Blake's phrase a
reminiscence of Chatterton's "Soft as the moss where hissing
adders dwell" in *Narva and Modred.* Chatterton's form in the
original was, however, not "hissing adders" but "hooting adders."[29] *The Miscellanies*[30] (1778) and Cottle's edition
(1803)[31] have "hissing adders," but Roberts's edition (1906)

returned to the original "hooting adders." Blake's acquaintance with Chatterton's *Narva and Modred* which would have
affected the *Poetical Sketches* was more likely with the original in the *London Magazine* than with the 1778 edition.

An Imitation of Spencer is one of Blake's least successful
poems in the *Poetical Sketches* in that it is fragmentary, halt-
ing, and irregular in its rhythmical pattern, and not well sustained in thought. It was not, in Johnson's phrase, "a great
achievement of the intellect," scarcely a proof of unusual
"nicety of observation," and it may easily have been "an
amusement of a day." Blake seems not to have been attracted
as William Thompson was to the descriptive, rural elements,
nor as Shenstone was to the "tenderness of sentiment." The
poem has single lines of beauty and poetic imagery; it has
single lines of poetic power. But on the whole, one feels a
stiffness and artificiality and a futile striving for the usual
freedom and felicity of his songs. Blake was not free while
consciously trying to force his poetic fancies into the exact
mould of another, and consequently he fell short of his own
amplitude. When, however, he wrote without the restriction
of a fixed scheme or pattern—and without trying to imitate—
what he did take fully to himself from Spenser was reflected
in a number of his lyrics. This more unconscious reminiscence seen in the retention of phrases which convey a beautiful image, or a figurative representation of truth, is of greater
value than *An Imitation of Spencer.* Imagery was the aspect
of Spenser which attracted Warton; it was one that caught
Blake's attention.

In *To the Evening Star* are the lines:

> . . . and, whilst thou drawest the
> Blue curtains of the sky, scatter thy
> silver dew on every flower (p. 5, ll. 5–7.)

In *The Faerie Queene,* I, i, 39, 7–8, appears the phrase "silver
dew":

> . . . there Tethys his wet bed
> Doth ever wash, and Cynthia still doth steepe
> In silver deaw his ever-drouping hed,

Apollo's steeds are a convention of classical poetry, and from that source Blake could have known them; still it may be Spenser's particular use which is foremost in his recollection. Blake's lines in this instance are more emphatic than Spenser's lines are. In *The Faerie Queene,* I, i, 32, 8–9, is the passage:

> The Sunne, that measures heaven all day long,
> At night doth baite his steedes the ocean
> waves emong.

Blake's passage to be compared with Spenser's is in *To Summer:*

> O THOU, who passeth thro' our vallies in
> Thy strength, curb thy fierce steeds, allay
> the heat
> That flames from their large nostrils!
>
> (p. 2, ll. 1–3.)

Blake's addition of the idea of intense heat to the suggestion from the source is an example of how his imagination worked when it was unrestricted. In Henry Felton's sense of imitation, he imitated by excelling.[32]

There are several examples of definite verbal similarities but these are sufficiently conventional in nature to echo more than one source.[33] But by far the most interesting and surely the most significant reminiscence of Spenser is in *To Morning.* The poem is a mosaic of pieces quarried from Spenser. In its final pattern it is one of Blake's most beautiful compositions, and one generally regarded as most original. The reason is that he has taken each precious bit with such incisive strokes, has polished each with the friction of his own shaping mind, and cemented all with his imagination until there are a lucidity of thought and a clarity of imagery in the whole poem that are almost austere. To separate the component parts seems almost as much a desecration as with chisel to break up the colored mosaic on the walls of some Lady Chapel; but only by so doing can one understand whence the variegated bits all came.

When one reads the *Songs of Innocence and Experience,* one becomes aware that perplexing questions concerned with marriage are involved in the symbolism of the poems. In the later symbolical books, this theme became so pronounced as to dominate Blake's thinking. It has never before been observed that as early as the *Poetical Sketches* Blake's thought was so much upon the same topic. It is a long distance from adolescent idealizing and questioning of mysteries to the most mature convictions. The purity and beauty of the first are in *To Morning* and *To the Evening Star.*

To the youthful Blake, confronting one of the age-old problems of existence, Spenser's *Epithalamion* and *Prothalamion,* to say nothing of the *Amoretti,* would have come with something of a revelation. That he read them again and again until the jubilant music, the joyousness of spirit, and the exuberance of personal emotion were a part of the texture of his mind is not surprising. That he reproduced something from them in one form or another is the natural consequence.

To Morning reads in its entirety:

> O HOLY virgin! clad in purest white,
> Unlock heav'n's golden gates, and issue forth;
> Awake the dawn that sleeps in heaven; let light
> Rise from the chambers of the east, and bring
> The honied dew that comes on waking day.
> O radiant morning, salute the sun,
> Rouz'd like a huntsman to the chace; and, with
> Thy buskin'd feet, appear upon our hills. (p. 6.)

Spenser in the *Epithalamion* (ll. 148–151) wrote:

> Loe! where she comes along with portly pace,
> Lyke Phoebe, from her chamber of the east,
> Arysing forth to run her mighty race,
> Clad all in white, that seems a virgin best.

The picture is that of the virgin, so named by both Spenser and Blake, clad all in white, coming forth from her chamber of the east on her wedding morning. These lines correspond to the conventional praise of the bride in the bridal hymns. Unlike the classical epithalamic tradition, Spenser's *Epithalamion* is celebrated in the morning. Hence, too, Blake's *To Morning.* Line 110 of Spenser's poem has, "Now is my love

all ready forth to come," an expression which is echoed from
The Faerie Queene, I, iv, 16, 3–6:

> As faire Aurora, in her purple pall
> Out of the east the dawning day doth call,
> So forth she comes. . . .

and again from *The Faerie Queene,* I, xii, 21, 4–6:

> Who forth proceeding with sober cheare
> As bright as doth the morning starre appeare
> Out of the east, with flaming locks bedight,
> To tell that dawning day is drawing neare,
> And to the world does bring long wished light;
> So faire and fresh that lady shewd her
>   selfe in sight.[34]

The virgin goes forth to meet the groom, according to the
convention of the bridal song. Blake's presentation of this
part of the scene is condensed to the suggestion in, "O radiant
morning, salute the sun." Then with a stroke such as only an
artist could give, Blake transformed the whole scene from the
more classic plan of Spenser's *Epithalamion* to one of his own.
The bridegroom was roused like a hunter to a chase. By the
attribute, "buskin'd feet," in the last line, he suggested that
the "holy virgin" was also a huntress. For this representation,
Blake may have had the "chaste Diana," the huntress of classical mythology in mind, or an echo of Shakespeare's "Your
buskin'd mistress and your warrior love"[35] of *A Midsummer
Night's Dream,* II, i, 71. For the comparison of the groom
with a huntsman, Blake may have recollected Spenser's
Amoretti, LXVII, i, "Lyke as a huntsman, after weary
chace."[36] This figure Blake liked well enough to use it a second time. In *Contemplation* one reads: "The youthful sun
joys like a hunter rouzed to the chace." (p. 64, ll. 1–2.)[37]
There is another reminiscence involved in this idea of the
bridegroom which appears in Blake's *To Spring,* although
there the word, "bridegroom," is not used. *To Spring* begins:

> O THOU, with dewy locks, who lookest down
> Thro' the clear windows of the morning;
>
>   (p. 1, l. 1.)

Spenser in *The Faerie Queene,* I, v, 2, 4, wrote:

> And Phoebus, fresh as brydegrome to his mate,
> Came daūcing forth, shaking his deawie hayre,[38]

Blake's picture of Spring is done in the same tones and spirit as his picture of Morning, except in the representation of Morning as a virgin. This may suggest merely that they were fashioned either at the same time or out of the same general fund of reminiscences.

To return to the new interpretation of the character of the bride which Blake gave in his epithalamic song by the use of the phrase, "buskin'd feet," one recalls another possible source for Blake's idea. In Michael Drayton's *Endimion and Phoebe* appear the lines:

> The stars on which her heavenly eyes were bent,
> And fixed still with lovely blandishment,
> For whom so oft disguised shee was seene,
> As shee Celestiall *Phoebe* had not beene:
> Her dainty Buskins lac'd unto the knee,
> Her pleyted Frock, tuck'd up accordingly:
> A Nymph-like huntresse, arm'd with bow & dart
> About the woods she scours the long-hu'd[39] Hart.[40]

That Drayton shared with Spenser in Blake's memory of this scene is considered possible because again in the same play appears another phrase that Blake used in *To Morning:*

> And *Cynthia* sitting in her Christall chayre,
> In all her pompe now rid along her Spheare,
> The honnied dewe descended in soft showers,
> Drizled in Pearle upon the tendre flowers;[41]

Blake says for the light to bring "The honied dew that cometh on waking day." (p. 6, l. 5.)

It is thought that Blake wrote *To the Evening Star* and *To Morning* about the same time; for, while *To the Evening Star* is more than an epithalamium, the first part of it very clearly supplements *To Morning.* For it, Blake doubtless had the memory of the lines from Spenser's *Epithalamion* (285–295):

Long though it be, at last I see it gloome,
And the bright evening star with golden creast
Appeare out of the east.
Fayre childe of beauty, glorious lampe of love,
That all the host of heaven in rankes doost lead,
And guydest lovers through the nightes dread,
How cheerfully thou lookest from above,
And seemst to laugh atweene thy twinkling light,
As joying in the sight
Of these glad many, which for joy doe sing,
That all the woods them answer, and their echo ring!

The picture of the evening star wearing a golden crest or crown, appearing as a lamp (or torch) of love, and seeming to laugh at the sight of lovers is all reproduced in Blake's lines:

THOU fair-hair'd angel of the evening,
Now, whilst the sun rests on the mountains, light
Thy bright torch of love; thy radiant crown
Put on, and smile upon our evening bed!
Smile on our loves; and, while thou drawest the
Blue curtains of the sky, scatter thy silver dew
On every flower that shuts its sweet eyes
In timely sleep. (p. 5, ll. 1–8.)

Thus in *To the Evening Star,* Blake carried on the idea of the epithalamium to the conventional conclusion of entering the bridal chamber; and Spenser's own poem moves to the same customary scene (ll. 298–299):

Now day is doen, and night is nighing fast:
Now bring the bryde into the brydall boures.[42]

Blake's youthful reading of the wedding hymns of Spenser may not have conveyed to him the full meaning of the Platonic conception of love and spirituality in Spenser's hymns, but one can feel that he was moved by their beauty. His utterance of an imagined experience, which, even in youth, he doubtless contemplated, lacks all the self-consciousness and artificiality of *An Imitation of Spencer.* He made no effort to imitate the verse form of the *Epithalamion.* He had the freedom of his

own lyrical voice. Insofar as one may call a simple lyric poem
an epithalamium, Blake achieved in *To Morning* and *To the
Evening Star* songs of epithalamic meaning and imagery.[43]

Mona Wilson in her *Life of Blake* objects—and quite
rightly—to the tendency on the part of critics of Blake's symbolic works to impose too definite a meaning upon the lyrics
which contain a picture seen in the flash of the imagination.
If the interpretation were just that the fourteen-year-old
Blake symbolized marriage by the golden cage in the song,
"How sweet I roam'd," she adds: "This would mean the su-
perfluous insertion of a second little bird sulking in the corner
of the cage or trilling unheeded songs from an importunate
throat."[44] Blake's symbolism here was surely a flash of the
imagination, and Blake cared to record only what was seen in
that flash. He would not, therefore, have added such superflu-
ous details as Miss Wilson suggests are lacking. The use he
made of Spenser's *Epithalamion* and *The Faerie Queene*
shows that, even though he may have been but fourteen, his
imagination still caught the salient resemblances. Poetry must
be symbolistic to some degree, for only as the imagination
proceeds from the sensuous knowledge of the naturalistic to
seize upon a higher truth can there be any intuitive apprehen-
sion of the universal and lasting verities. That Blake intended
to write an elaborate symbolic poem in "How sweet I roam'd"
is doubtful, but the idea in it so corresponds with ideas found
in the symbolism he intentionally constructed later that it is
unquestionable that his first use of it was only a symbol to
him—a symbol that one may believe came by way of "a flash
of the imagination." Besides, the source of his idea has the
meaning he symbolized. Blake wrote:

> With sweet May dews my wings are wet,
>   And Phoebus fir'd my vocal rage;
> He caught me in his silken net,
>   And shut me in his golden cage.
>
> He loves to sit and hear me sing,
>   Then, laughing, sports and plays with me;
> Then stretches out my golden wing,
>   And mocks my loss of liberty. (p. 10, ll. 9–16.)[45]

Where, one asks, is the idea of marriage? All seems a simple picture in objective terms.

About 1808, Blake wrote a poem called *The Golden Net* in which it is plain that more was meant about the relationship of the sexes than was expressed in the earlier lyric. Yet he preserved in "golden net" the same meaning of the "cage" in "How sweet I roam'd." In *An Island in the Moon* which was composed before *The Golden Net,* and possibly very soon after 1783, Blake inserted into a lyric that Quid sang, beginning, "Hail Matrimony, made of Love," the lines:

> "Come & be cured of all thy pains
> In Matrimony's Golden cage." (p. 881.)

In the third edition of Davidson's *Poetical Rhapsody* (1621), which Blake could well have seen, was quoted *A Contention betwixt a Wife, a Widow, and a Maid* by John Davies, the first line of which is: *"Wid.* Wiues are as birds in golden cages kept."[46] Blake could hardly have missed an idea which must have been almost proverbial, as is shown by its recurrence.[47]

Malkin's report that Blake read Jonson's *Underwoods* and *Miscellanies* and caught his manner may well be accepted if one is satisfied to generalize on one point, which Malkin phrased as "ancient simplicity" and "bold and careless freedom." Malkin stated:

The following song ["How sweet I roam'd"] is a good deal in the spirit of the Hue and Cry after Cupid, in the Masque on Lord Haddington's marriage. It was written before the age of fourteen, in the heat of youthful fancy, unchastised by judgment. The poet, as such, takes the very strong liberty of equipping himself with wings, and thus appropriates his metaphorical costume to his corporeal fashion and seeming. The conceit is not unclassical; but Pindar and the ancient lyrics arrogated to themselves the bodies of swans for their august residence. Our Gothic songster is content to be encaged by Cupid; and submits, like a young lady's favorite, to all the vagaries of giddy curiosity and tormenting fondness.

. . . .

The playful character ascribed to the prince of love, and especially his wanton and fantastic action while sporting with his captive, in the two last stanzas, render it probable that the author had read the Hue and Cry after Cupid. If so, it had made its impression; but the lines could scarcely have been remembered at the time of writing, or the resemblance would have been closer.[48]

In the light of other parallels for the idea in "How sweet I roam'd" this one from Jonson seems as doubtful as Malkin himself admits by his last sentence. He fancied a resemblance where the "ancient simplicity" and "bold and careless freedom" suggested it ought to be. Jonson's work has been carefully searched for contributions to Blake's imagery, language, or ideas, but, except for one phrase,[49] there is nothing in Jonson's work which resembles Blake's early poems any more closely than the selection which Malkin quoted. Blake probably did read Jonson. He was one of the few early writers whose works were available in Blake's day. Ben Jonson (1716), Beaumont and Fletcher (1711, 1750, 1778), and Massinger (1759, 1761, 1779) would have been Blake's best chance outside of miscellanies to become acquainted with the poets of the late sixteenth and early seventeenth centuries. It is doubtful that Blake would have had much opportunity to see the collections of Elizabethan poetry, for there were no contemporary reprints of most of them. He seems not to have made any use of the selections in Bysshe's *Art of Poetry,* which he owned but could have acquired later than 1783. Sometime before the end of 1757, Gray wrote a friend, L. Brockett, asking him to secure for him from the library of Trinity College the following books: *"Paradise of Dainty Devices, England's Helicon,* W. Webbe's *Discourse of English Poetrie,* Fr. Mere's *Wit's Commonwealth,* Sam. Daniel's *Musa,* or *Defence of Rhyme,* Stephen Hawes' *Pastime of Pleasure,* Gawen Douglas' *Palace of Honour,* Earl of Surrey's *Ecclesiastes* and second and fourth books of the *Aeneid,* and Gascoign's *Works."*[50] If these books were not available to Gray outside the university libraries, one may be sure they were not available to the youthful Blake. Blake makes reference to Jonson in his description of the illustration to Milton's *L'Allegro* written about 1816; but this is, of course, merely a paraphrase of the text of *L'Allegro.* Jonson's *Underwoods* contained first devotional poetry, of which Blake has nothing; love songs and conceits which celebrate aspects of love not found in Blake's early poetry; epistles to people with names of people, places, and personal qualities localized or specified; and elegies. By none of these Blake seems to have been the least affected.

In Percy's *Reliques of Ancient English Poetry,* a copy of which Blake owned,[51] he could have read Raleigh's *Nymph's Reply,*[52] which may have been a part of the associations that entered into the song, "My silks and fine array." The stress upon the note of true love passing or coming to an end is not only the keynote of Raleigh's poem, but of much Elizabethan poetry.

> His breast is love's all-worship'd tomb,
> Where all love's pilgrims come. (p. 11, ll. 11–12.)

is a conceit (and one of the few in Blake's poetry) not unworthy or unlike the best of the metaphysical images, and in itself sums up the Elizabethan emphasis on love, although it lacks the element of wit that belonged to the earlier poets. Beyond that restraint, to the real amorousness of either Elizabethan or Restoration verse, Blake's youthful poetry did not go. There is no suggestion of the catalogues of love's virtues, features, or allurements, and nothing of the bolder conventional comparisons of "my love is like. . . ." Rather it is the condensation and the intensity of feeling, such as Raleigh's *Nymph's Reply* illustrates, that were traits of Blake's "My silks and fine array." Of the pastoral in the Elizabethan sense there is nothing in Blake, and even though the shepherd and sheep become stock figures in the *Songs,* still they are not in the pastoral tradition as found, for example, in *England's Helicon.* "The joyful shepherd [who] stops his grateful song" (p. 16, l. 11) in "Fresh from the dewy hill" is not the conventional shepherd of Arcadia.

Of the writers of the sixteenth and seventeenth centuries other than Spenser and Shakespeare there is little demonstrable influence[53] upon Blake. The fact that his free imagination and the pure lyrical quality of his poetry found rare correspondence in his own day has caused critics to turn to the earlier times, when more careless rapture and sensuous beauty were the characteristic manner of poetry, to find the fountain source of his inspiration. Then, without investigation, they have enlarged upon Malkin's assumption, until there has become incorporated in all the discussions about Blake the assertion that the Elizabethan influence was the most important and the strongest. If Blake's way of seeing and his ecstatic musical expression of what he saw and felt remind one of the Elizabethan poets or the Jacobean, it only testifies anew to the fact that a true poet's eye has flashes of vision, and he sings about them freely because he must release the lyric response to his visions—the essence of poetic truth.

One way to know that the influence of Spenser upon Blake was not so far-reaching as the influence of Milton is to see what use Blake made of Spenser in his pictures. Apart from quoting a few lines from Spenser[54] on one of the pages in the *Rossetti MS.,* there is record of only one subject done from Spenser. That is a large "water-colour drawing"[55] called "The Characters in Spenser's *Faerie Queene"* which showed the figures from the poem brought together in a procession, as if designed as a companion piece to Chaucer's "Canterbury Pilgrimage." Gilchrist mentioned it, and William Rossetti described it in his *List of Works* as: " . . . not so elaborate, correct or exhaustive; fine, nevertheless, though archaic and singular. The Red-cross Knight with the dragon, Una with the lion, Talus, can be readily identified. In the sky are some allegorical figures, and in the background a Gothic cathedral and other buildings. Eighty guineas, a large sum in Blake's case, was given Mrs. Blake by Lord Egremont for this picture, now considerably clouded over by its varnish."[56] At the time Rossetti compiled the *List of Works* for Gilchrist's *Life of Blake,* this drawing was in the possession of Lord Leconfield.

Sir Philip Sidney wrote: "Nature never set foorth the earth in so rich Tapistry as diverse Poets have done, neither with so pleasaunt rivers, fruitfull trees, sweete smelling flowers, nor whatsoever els may make the too much loved earth more lovely: her world more brasen, the Poets only deliver a golden."[57] But the sensuous extravagance of these poets was evidently not the sort to inspire either Blake's pencil or his brush. The images which were reproduced by his pen were retained in his mind because of an association with certain experiences in his youth that were distinctly personal. The imagery of his poetry crystallized experience that was vibrant with poetic meaning. It was the echo of the invisible master utterances retained in memory, and to that imagery, through his imaginative response, he gave new vitality and organic unity.

CHAPTER V

KING EDWARD THE THIRD

IT is, as a rule, an unwise practice to read backward from adult years to determine what transpired in youth. But with Blake it is safe to believe that in matters of convictions he altered his principles very little as he became older. There is even some evidence that he later preferred to be in error than to change an opinion.[1] "Always did and now do,"[2] "was then and now is,"[3] "I read . . . when very Young. I felt the Same Contempt . . . then that I do now,"[4] were familiar notes in his writing.[5] "Neither Youth nor Childhood," he said, "is Folly or Incapacity. Some Children are Fools & so are some Old Men. But There is a vast Majority on the side of Imagination or Spiritual Sensation."[6] When in *A Descriptive Catalogue* (1809), therefore, he reported on those great spirits in art and literature which he considered inspired, one may regard the attitude not a new one in 1809. He said then: "Poetry as it exists now on earth, is the various remains of ancient authors, Music as it exists in old tunes or melodies, Painting and Sculpture as it exists in the remains of Antiquity and in the works of more modern genius, is Inspiration, and cannot be surpassed; it is perfect and eternal. Milton, Shakespeare, Michael Angelo, Rafael, the finest specimens of Ancient Sculpture and Painting and Architecture, Gothic, Grecian, Hindoo and Egyptian, are the extent of the human mind. The human mind cannot go beyond the gift of God, the Holy Ghost."[7] In the company of the inspired, Blake recognized only two poets. From one, Milton, his memory became stored with multifarious elements which were transmuted into new forms of beauty. It would be of great interest to know when and how from the work of the other, Shakespeare, he began to record in his mind characters and ideas which were later to appear in *King Edward the Third*. Since he left no record of his reading, and since the chronological order of the youthful poems cannot be accurately determined, one can know only that he discovered the second inspired poet before 1783, for there are demonstrable traces of Shakespeare's influence in Blake's early poems.

It was not so much a question this time of Blake's search for Shakespeare as of his inability to escape him. Even though Blake was not interested in the critical examination of texts and in the production of new editions, he still could have read the advertisements of the editors' work and the controversial articles in the newspapers, have seen the books in the shops, and, doubtless, have found them on the tables of the homes which he entered. Basire would certainly have had one or more of the new editions which came between Rowe's edition in 1709–10, and I. Reed's production of the edition of Johnson and Steevens in 1778–80.[8] Anyone living during David Garrick's dramatic career could hardly have escaped catching something of the enthusiasm which he generated. The only evidence that Blake ever attended the theatre is in a letter to William Hayley, April 25, 1805, in which he referred to William Henry West Betty thus: "The town is mad: young Roscius, like all prodigies, is the talk of everyone. I have not seen him, and perhaps never may. I have no curiosity to see him, as I well know what is within compass of a boy of fourteen; and as to real acting, it is like historical painting, no boy's work."[9] But this does not preclude the possibilities that he witnessed some of the plays acted by Garrick, Macklin, and others.

During the years when many kinds of interest in Shakespeare were manifest, Blake was spending his days in Westminster Abbey, where on every hand were silent reminders of those royal personages about whom Shakespeare constructed many of his plays. He could hardly have kept his mind from those same royal characters whose remains lay beneath the stones, and Gilchrist[10] indulges in the hope that he may have been present when the tomb of Edward the First was opened by the Society of Antiquaries for whom Basire worked. It was in these days that Blake made drawings of Edward the Third[11] and Queen Philippa from their tombs, the engravings of which, signed by Basire but thought to be by Blake, appeared in Richard Gough's *Sepulchral Monuments of Great Britain.*[12] It may have been this study of effigies, and possibly

some reading in chronicle history about their subjects, that
gave Blake his special knowledge of Edward the Third, who,
for some reason, held a permanent interest for him. Edward
the Third reappears as the subject of one of the Visionary
Heads[13] or Spiritual Portraits which Blake sketched to please
his friend, John Varley, in 1820.[14]

Edward the Third had been the subject of two earlier plays
in English. Another by an anonymous writer was printed too
late to have affected the *Poetical Sketches*.[15] With the first of
the two earlier plays Blake seems not to have been acquainted,
for apart from a few lines (I, 1, 8–11) on the general subject
of freedom, and the identity of the name "Montacute," it
touches Blake's play at no point. It was a play attributed to
William Mountfort,[16] acted at the Theatre-Royal, and printed
in 1691. The second play about King Edward the Third is
called *The Raigne of King Edward the Third*,[17] published in
1596, one of the fourteen plays in the Shakespeare Apocrypha.
It was, however, first included in an edition of Shakespeare
by J. Payne Collier in 1878. It had been ascribed to Shakespeare by E. Capell when, on the title-page of his *Prolusions,*
he listed the play as "thought to be writ by Shakespeare."
Prolusions appeared in 1760, at just the right time to have
been accessible to Blake in the next ten or fifteen years. There
are some hints that Blake may have known it; however, it
must be remembered that since similar ideas and locutions are
also in Shakespeare, Blake's source could as well have been
Shakespeare's plays as this.[18]

There is yet another play, printed in the year of its first
performance at Drury Lane in 1750, which sank into obscurity
until Kemble revived it for the stage in 1783. William Shirley, the author, said on the title-page that it is "An Historical
Tragedy, Attempted after the Manner of Shakespeare."[19] It
is unlikely that Blake knew it. The resemblances seem to have
been the coincidences of a common source, for the plays are
so far apart in tone, in manner, in poetic character, and in action that one is reluctant to think that the likenesses are anything more than conventional details present in any chronicle
play which sets forth patriotically the pride and power of a
nation.

Whatever were the sources of his interest,[20] Blake was strongly enough concerned with Edward the Third to begin an experiment of composing a drama about him. Among several discernible influences Shakespeare's plays share with James Thomson's *Liberty* in making the principal contribution to this dramatic fragment. It is upon *King Edward the Third* alone of the early poems that the Shakespearean influence is strong, and it has four phases: plot, ideas, characterization, and language.

King Edward the Third opens with a scene laid on the coast of France where the army is told that the English will come to take revenge for those "brave Lords who fell beneath the bloody axe at Paris." (p. 31, l. 6.) The scene closes with the king's saying:

> Into three parties we divide by day,
> And separate march, but join again at night:
> (p. 31, ll. 12–13.)

In *The Raigne* this same action is indicated, but there King Edward definitely assigns three divisions, one to Prince Edward, one to the Earl of Derby, and one to himself.[21] The second scene, laid in the English Court, represents Lionel, Duke of Clarence, on the advice of Queen Philippa, calling the lords together to consider the preservation and extension of England's commerce that was preyed upon by the French "small ships of war." Percy and the bishop contend briefly over whether or not the merchants are rich enough to defend themselves. The bishop winning the argument, Percy agrees to use every means "to bring the Gallic rovers under." (p. 35, l. 10.) The third scene is at Cressy on the morning of the battle. This scene is the longest one, and is given entirely to a philosophical discussion among King Edward, the Prince of Wales, Sir Thomas Dagworth, and Sir John Chandos. This scene has many figures of speech, often extended but always well sustained, and truer than those Blake used elsewhere in the *Poetical Sketches*. It has no action and scarcely any preparation for action, except in the sense of the imminence of battle and the brief conflicts of character that arise principally from the fears which cause Sir Thomas Dagworth to petition the king for leave to return to England. The forthcoming battle, unrelated to great human interests or frailties at strife, or to forces controlled by fate, was not a sufficiently dramatic basis of a plot.

Scene 4 is laid in Sir Thomas Dagworth's tent where his servant William philosophizes in the manner of Touchstone, while he burnishes Sir Thomas's armor. In the midst of William's loquacious scene another of his kind, Peter Blunt, enters to provide a bit of news and a touch of characterization. Still no action is furthered. Scene 5, again laid in Sir Thomas Dagworth's tent, consists of a dialogue between Sir Thomas Dagworth and Sir Walter Manny. The latter is deeply affected by the thought of those who will die in battle. Sir Thomas Dagworth replies in philosophical speeches, and, by his eulogy of the glorious nation that will rise from bloodshed, he wins Sir Walter Manny's determination to fight until he dies. Apart from the slight advance made in characterization, there is still no action. Scene 6, and the last, laid in the king's tent, is composed entirely of the minstrel's song, reciting reminiscences of the past, and prophesying the glorious empire that will rise. The fragment ends without the establishment of any real plot, and, in the absence of the remainder of the play, one cannot see that even the characterization, although it progresses somewhat through the scenes, contributes to dramatic action.

To judge of Blake's intentions from the unfinished play is difficult. It seems that the events he planned to use in the play were those of the "fatal day of Cressy." (p. 52, l. 3.) No scenes showing the opposing forces, the French army or king, were given. The theme upon which he constructed his characterizations, which seems to be the purported theme of the play, is that of fear. Blake could well have taken his suggestion from Shakespeare's *Henry the Fifth,* II, iv, 47–64, 84–95.[22]

The first resemblance to Shakespeare's plays seen in *King Edward the Third* is in the introductory lines where King Edward addressed God in the character in which He is portrayed in the Old Testament:

O THOU, to whose fury the nations are
But as dust! maintain thy servant's right.
(p. 29, ll. 1–2.)

This is King Henry's conception of God revealed in his prayer
(*Henry the Fifth,* IV, i, 306–309):

> *King Henry.* O God of battles! steel my soldiers'
> hearts.
> Possess them not with fear. Take from them now
> Their sense of reckoning, if the opposed numbers
> Pluck their hearts from them.

and to whom he referred in I, ii, 289–296:

> But this lies all within the will of God,
> To whom I do appeal; and in whose name
> Tell you the Dauphin I am coming on
> To venge me as I may, and to put forth
> My rightful hand in a well-hallow'd cause.
> So get you hence in peace; and tell the Dauphin
> His jest will savour but of shallow wit,
> When thousands weep more than did laugh at it.—

Blake's picture of the soldiers is strongly suggestive of those
described by Shakespeare:

> Such an army of heroes
> Ne'er shouted to the Heav'ns, nor shook the field.
> . . . the man
> Were base who were not fir'd to deeds
> Above heroic, having such examples.
> (p. 38, ll. 17–22.)

This is the general idea expressed in *King Henry the Fifth,*
III, i, 17–18, 24 ff.:

> On, on, you noblest English,
> Whose blood is fet from fathers of war-proof!
>
> .   .   .   .   .   .
>
> . . . And you, good yeomen,
> Whose limbs were made in England, show us here
> The mettle of your pasture; let us swear

That you are worth your breeding, which I doubt not;
For there is none of you so mean and base,
That hath not noble lustre in your eyes.

The praise of the heroes of war was naturally frequent in Shakespeare's historical plays both because they drew from chronicle history and because of the patriotic ideals of the time. Blake's firsthand knowledge of a soldier's life was too meager to supply details of battle, and hence he would have seen them imaginatively as Shakespeare presented them.

That Shakespeare contributed the theme of fear is possible from the frequency with which the idea appears in his plays. When King Henry the Fifth in disguise spoke with his soldiers, he described himself thus: "His ceremonies laid by, in his nakedness he appears but a man; and though his affections are higher mounted than ours, yet, when they stoop, they stoop with the like wing. Therefore, when he sees reason of fears as we do, his fears, out of doubt, be of the same relish as ours are; yet, in reason, no man should possess him with any appearance of fear, lest he, by showing it, should dishearten his army." (IV, 1, 110–117.) When Blake represented Sir Thomas Dagworth as having walked incognito among the soldiers just as King Henry did, he had much talk of fear, which he, too, allied with reason:

> . . . while Reason, in her
> Frail bark, can see no shore or bound for vast
> Ambition.   (p. 44, ll. 18–20.)[23]

Sir Thomas Dagworth's fear that his king will run away (p. 37, ll. 1–6) is paralleled in *Henry the Fifth* in the king's speech (IV, iii, 112–113):

> There's not a piece of feather in our host—
> Good argument, I hope, we will not fly—

The effect of the king's presence upon Sir Thomas Dagworth is like that described in the *Prologue* of Act IV of *Henry the Fifth:*

> A largess universal like the sun
> His liberal eye doth give to every one,
> Thawing cold fear,   (ll. 44–46.)

When Sir Thomas Dagworth talked of fear, and asked leave to return to England, there seems to be an allusion to the situation described by King Henry (IV, iii, 34–39):

> Rather proclaim it, Westmoreland, through my host,
> That he which hath no stomach to this fight,
> Let him depart. His passport shall be made,
> And crowns for convoy put into his purse.
> We would not die in that man's company
> That fears his fellowship to die with us.

This theme of fear[24] plays in and out of the third scene of *King Edward the Third* until it becomes of greatest importance. It is the basis of the delineation of Sir Thomas Dagworth's character; it is the point of his criticism of the king. It seems to be the cause of the delay in the progress of the war. It is the subject of the petition Sir Thomas Dagworth made to the king, which tests the king's attitude toward battle; it is the subject of the philosophizing in the scene. It directs the only semblance of action and makes the only link between the episodic scenes.

The mention of "thy servant's right" in Blake's opening lines recalls the topic that is the basis in *King Henry the Fifth* of the discussion between the king and his nobles about advancing toward the French throne. The Archbishop of Canterbury said regarding it (I, ii, 130–131):

> O, let their bodies follow, my dear liege,
> With blood and sword and fire to win your right;

King Henry also (ll. 291–293) talked about putting forth his "rightful hand in a well-hallow'd cause." The first scene of *The Raigne* is an exposition of Edward's claims to the French throne, obviously necessary in any play involving this action.

King Henry the Fifth and the Earl of Westmoreland talked about the number of men engaged in battle (IV, iii, 15–50). The Earl of Westmoreland wished that but "one ten thousand" of the idle in England were to fight. King Henry said:

> If we are mark'd to die, we are enow
> To do our country loss; and if to live,
> The fewer men, the greater share of honour.
> (IV, iii, 20–22.)

This idea is very like the one in Sir Walter Manny's words
with which the fifth scene of Blake's play opens:

> *Sir Walter.*   Sir Thomas Dagworth, I have been
> weeping over the men who are to die today.
>
> *Dagworth.*   Why, brave Sir Walter, you or I may
>   fall.   (p. 50, ll. 11–13.)

Sir Thomas Dagworth's later speech in the same scene con-
tinues the subject:

> Thousands of souls must leave this prison-house,
> To be exalted to those heavenly fields,
> Where songs of triumph, palms of victory,
> Where peace, and joy, and love, and calm content,
> Sit singing in the azure clouds, and strew
> Flowers of heaven's growth over the banquet-table:
>   (p. 51, ll. 16–21.)

These lines remind one also of a passage in *The Raigne* where
talk of death and fear closely resemble Blake's thoughts.[25]
They also sound a note that is very near the central meaning
of Blake's thinking about death, a note that he was never to
alter in his later works.

When Blake represented the general's moving unknown
among the soldiers, there is an obvious imitation of King
Henry's action among his soldiers. But the episode in Shakespeare's play drew other response from Blake. When the un-
recognized king talked to his men, one of them, Bates, expressed his belief that the king might wish himself elsewhere,
and added his own wish to be away from France. King Henry
replied (IV, i, 129–134):

> *King Hen.*   I dare say you love him not so
> ill to wish him here alone, howsoever
> you speak this to feel other men's minds.
> Methinks I could not die anywhere so contented
> as in the King's company, his cause being just
> and his quarrel honourable.
>
> *Williams.*   That's more than we know.

Bates. Ay, or more than we should seek after;
for we know enough, if we know we are the King's
subjects. If his cause be wrong, our obedience
to the King wipes the crime of it out of us.

Blake must have registered in his mind the fallacy in the reasoning of these speeches, for the sophistry of Bates's speech
he put into the speech of William to Sir Thomas Dagworth:

Will. Then if ambition is a sin, we are all
guilty in coming with him, and in fighting for him.

Dagw. Now, William, thou dost thrust the
question home; but I must tell you, that guilt
being an act of the mind, none are guilty but
those whose minds are prompted by that same
ambition.   (p. 48, ll. 3–8.)

It would seem that for the general theme of his play, for
many of the ideas, and for the principle outline of character
and event, Blake took Shakespeare's *King Henry the Fifth*
most directly as his model. But his play contains ideas that are
reminiscent of ideas found elsewhere in Shakespeare's work.
One instance is the idea of Sir Thomas Dagworth in the lines:

. . . look upon Edward's face—
No one can say he fears. But when he turns
His back, then I will say it to his face,
He is afraid; he makes us all afraid

.   .   .   .

Audley. . . . Your fear
Is of a different kind then from the King's;
He fears to turn his face, and you to turn
your back.—
I do not think, Sir Thomas, you know what
fear is.   (pp. 36, ll. 7–11; 37, ll. 4–7.)

This may be a modification of Caesar's speech in *Julius Caesar*
(II, ii, 10–12):

Caesar shall forth. The things that threaten'd me
Ne'er look'd but on my back; when they shall see
The face of Caesar, they are vanished.[26]

Involved with the idea of fear is that of flattery. The latter in Decius's speech about Caesar (II, i, 207–208) :

> But when I tell him he hates flatterers
> He says he does, being then most flattered.

is echoed in the dialogue between William and Sir Thomas Dagworth:

> *Dag.* . . . flattery is delicious, even from the
> lips of a babbler.
> *Will.* I never flatter your honour.
> *Dag.* I don't know that.
> *Will.* Why you know, Sir, when we were in
> England, at the tournament at Windsor, and
> the Earl of Warwick was tumbled over, you
> ask'd me if he did not look well when he fell?
> and I said, No, he look'd very foolish; and you
> were very angry with me for not flattering you.
> *Dag.* You mean that I was angry with you for
> not flattering the Earl of Warwick.
> (pp. 49, ll. 26–27 ; 50, ll. 1–10.)[27]

From *Julius Caesar* may have come another detail in *King Edward the Third*. King Edward says:

> The world of men are like the num'rous stars,
> That beam and twinkle in the depth of night,
> Each clad in glory according to his sphere;—
>
> .   .   .   .
>
> . . . and some perhaps
> The most obscure at home, that scarce were seen
> To twinkle in their sphere, may so advance,
> That the astonish'd world, with up-turn'd eyes,
> Regardless of the moon, and those that once were
> bright,
> Stand only for to gaze upon their splendor ![28]

Caesar said (III, i, 60–67) :

> But I am constant as the northern star,
> Of whose true-fix'd and resting quality
> There is no fellow in the firmament.

> The skies are painted with unnumb'red sparks,
> They are all fire and everyone doth shine;
> But there's but one in all doth hold his place.
> So in the world; 'tis furnish'd well with men,
> And men are flesh and blood, and apprehensive;

There are two points of comparison in the following parallel between Hotspur's lines in the *First Part of Henry the Fourth* (I, iii, 194 ff., 302) and the prince's ideas in *King Edward the Third*. First, the point of view of the elder auditors toward the youths shows the same kind of tolerance. Second, both princes have the same manner of confronting danger, a similar zest for action, and a similar boldness. Sir Thomas Dagworth's description of the prince reminds one of Hotspur:

> He is a young lion. O I have seen him fight,
> And give command, and lightning has flashed
> From his eyes across the field; I have seen him
> Shake hands with death, and strike a bargain for
> The enemy;   (p. 36, ll. 17–21.)[29]

The prince in *The Raigne* is also described as a vigorous, eager fellow.[30] Another episode which makes one think Blake may have remembered the play, *The Raigne,* is a very dramatic scene of the knighting of the prince. In *King Edward the Third* the prince is knighted, but Blake made of it only a sort of gesture, and gave the event nothing of the dramatic force of the scene in the old play, thus emphasizing the sense of its borrowed quality.

To return to the parallel between Hotspur and the prince in *King Edward the Third,* the thoughts of the two young men are much alike. Hotspur said (*First Part of Henry the Fourth,* I, iii, 197–198, 301–302):

> *Hot.* . . . O, the blood more stirs
> To rouse a lion than to start a hare!
> *North.* Imagination of some great exploit
> Drives him beyond the bounds of patience.
>
>   .   .   .   .
>
> *Hot.* . . . O, let the hours be short
> Till fields and blows applaud our sport!

Compare now the prince's speech:

> . . . In truth, I am too full;
> It is my sin to love the noise of war.
> . . . my blood, like a spring-tide
> Does rise so high, to overflow all bounds
> Of moderation;
>
> .   .   .   .
>
> Then if we must tug for experience,
> Let us not fear to beat round Nature's wilds,
> And rouze the strongest prey;
>> (pp. 44, ll. 13–14; 45, 16–17.)

This zest for battle was also characteristic of the Black Prince in *The Raigne*.[31] Before the battle of Shrewsbury, King Henry the Fourth said to the prince (V, i, 1–3):

> How bloodily the sun begins to peer
> Above yon busky hill! The day looks pale
> At his distemperature.

Expectant of battle, Sir Walter Manny similarly spoke:

> O Dagworth, France is sick! the very sky
> Tho' sunshine light it, seems to me as pale
> As the pale fainting man on his death-bed,
> Whose face is shewn by light of sickly taper!
>> (p. 51, ll. 10–13.)

Another interesting reminiscence appears in the speech of King Edward to Sir John Chandos:

> O noble Chandos; think thyself a gardener,
> My son a vine, which I commit unto
> Thy care; prune all extravagant shoots, and guide
> Th' ambitious tendrils in the path of wisdom;
> Water him with thy advice, and Heav'n
> Rain fresh'ning dew upon his branches. And,
> O Edward, my dear son! learn to think lowly of
> Thyself, as we may all each prefer other—
> 'Tis the best policy, and 'tis our duty.
>> (p. 43, ll. 20–28.)

Blake's figure of speech unquestionably came from the gar-
dener scene in *Richard II* (III, iv, 29–40, 55–57, 61–64).

Much of the characterization in Blake's play is felt to be
derived from Shakespeare, as, for example, the characterization of King Edward from that of King Henry the Fifth;
but, because it is the impression gained sometimes from the
total presentation of Blake's characters, sometimes from a
single phase of it which links itself with a concept of Shakespeare's characters gained also from a whole impression, it is
impossible, even with tedious explanation, to support with
concrete evidence the likenesses discerned. It is the intangible
correspondence which one feels strongly and believes to be inherent in the drama that makes one willing to accept Richard
Garnett's comment on Blake's play: *"Edward Third . . .*
proves two things: first that Blake was destitute of all dramatic faculty; secondly, that, notwithstanding, few have so
thoroughly assimilated Shakespeare."[32] In spite of the elusive
quality of the evidence, some resemblances between characterizations may be mentioned. William's artlessness suggests
the Shakespearean fools, and his remarks remind one of
Touchstone in particular. Peter Blunt,[33] through his inconse-
quent, breathless narrative, is akin to the comic, witless knave
bearing his name in *Romeo and Juliet*. His answer to Sir
Thomas Dagworth's question as to who the musician was:

> O aye, I forgot to tell that; he has
> got the same name as Sir John Chandos,
> that the prince is always with—the wise
> man, that knows us all as well as your
> honour, only e'nt so good natur'd.
> (p. 49, ll. 13–17.)

seems an allusion to the situation between Sir John Falstaff
and Prince Hal, and to the personality of Falstaff. But Blake
made no further use of Falstaff's characteristics in the portrait of Sir John Chandos. Blake was more impressed by the
dignified, princely characters of the royal persons or by
Touchstone's type of philosopher than by the comic character
of Falstaff's type. His humor was not cultivated in Falstaff's

direction. Fluellen's part, possibly because of the unusual speech, made a more lasting impression than Falstaff did.

When Blake introduced the "little Welshman with a fiery face" whose scrap of speech, "pig enough to light another pattle," is certainly reminiscent of Fluellen in *Henry the Fifth,*[34] he curiously transferred to his Welshman a characteristic "fiery face," which was part of Fluellen's description of Bardolph. (*King Henry the Fifth,* III, iv, 107–110.) Blake's further description of the Welshman, "I told him he look'd like a candle half burn'd out," recalls the chief justice's remark to Falstaff (*Second Part of Henry the Fourth,* I, ii, 177): "What! you are as a candle, the better part burnt out."[35]

The characters in *King Edward the Third,* while more fully portrayed than the action is outlined, are not yet fully realized. Blake selected well-marked types of characters—a prince, a bishop, a man of commerce, and a warrior; but he could not give them personality enough to lift them from the level of the type, or to give them much individuality in their separate classes. Perhaps, if Blake had completed his play, the characterizations of the first part would not seem so slight. It is likely, however, to judge from his lack of ability to achieve well-drawn, clearly limned portraits in his later work, that he had not the kind of dramatic sense that enabled him to give life and personality to his figures. There is a strange absence of personalities, other than purely symbolical ones in his later work and, after Thel and Tiriel, he was unable to bestow upon the persons much individual human character. Symons suggested a plausible reason for this when he said: "There are no men and women in the world of Blake's poetry, only primal instincts and the energies of the imagination."[36] Compared with the later characterizations, these early ones in *King Edward the Third* are more nearly "men and women." The king resembled King Henry the Fifth in his aspirations for the realm and his zestful demands for the loyal allegiance of his subjects, and he is a far more idealized person than the historical Edward the Third, just as Shakespeare's Henry the Fifth was more ideal than the historical one. Sir Thomas Dagworth is the expositor of the play, and in him there is a flash of wit and a philosophical, poetic bent of mind. Sir John

Chandos and Sir Walter Manny, both more emotional than Sir Thomas Dagworth, are patriotic and brave. In all three there need to be traits of character in conflict to make dramatic complications. There are none. They are portraits as static as if painted on separate canvases. Whatever human likenesses there are in Blake's drama, they were the result of the influence of Shakespearean characters. They were soon to be replaced by the grotesque figures of his own creation; thereafter, unlike Bunyan whose personifications were so sharply and truly drawn that one remembers meeting the individuals in the last walk down the street, Blake's allegorical figures moved in an atmosphere that more or less dimmed their individual features and left them as the shapes in an ill-sorted dream.

A more obvious contribution of the Shakespearean plays to *King Edward the Third* is seen in the language. Blake's eye saw more easily through the imagery involved in phrases and figures of speech than his pen was able to delineate characters with driving dramatic force. Hence there are many echoes of word or phrase. They mainly tell the range of his familiarity with the Shakespearean plays.

Sir Thomas Dagworth's description of King Edward's soldiers included one of whom he spoke:

> A raw-bon'd fellow t'other day pass'd by me,
> I told him to put off his hungry looks—
> He answer'd me, "I hunger for another battle."
> (p. 41, ll. 19-20.)

"Raw-boned fellow" recalls Alencon's description of the English soldiers in the *First Part of Henry the Sixth*. It is interesting that there is an allusion to Blake's favorite king in the same passage, which reads (I, ii, 28-36):

> Froissart, a countryman of ours, records,
> England all Olivers and Rolands bred
> During the time Edward the Third did reign.
> More truly now may this be verified.
> For none but Samsons and Goliases
> It sendeth forth to skirmish. One to ten!
> Lean, raw-bon'd rascals! who would e'er suppose
> They had such courage and audacity?

The phrase "hungry looks" in Blake's lines brings Caesar's telling description of Cassius to mind. (*Julius Caesar,* I, ii, 191–193.)

Blake surely remembered some ideas or images from the passages in Shakespeare's plays which record his deep horror of the charnel houses of his day.[37] Sir Walter Manny mentioned the charnel house by name:

> I seem to be in one great charnel-house,
> I seem to scent the rotten carcases!
>
> (p. 52, ll. 5–6.)

and it is pictured in *Fair Elenor:*

> Fancy returns, and now she thinks of bones,
> And grinning skulls, and corruptible death,
>
> (p. 7, ll. 13–14.)

Such thoughts may have been emphasized by the solitary months in Westminster Abbey.

William's reasoning with Sir Thomas Dagworth about whether the soldiers were all guilty in coming with the king is an attempt to present the kind of logic in which Touchstone indulged his wit with Corin over the shepherd's life; and there is, besides, an identity of phrase in the two selections:

> Thou art a natural philosopher, and
> knowest truth by instinct; while reason runs
> aground, as we have run our argument.
>
> (p. 48, ll. 11–13.)

Touchstone remarked to Corin in *As You Like It* (III, ii, 33), "Such a one is a natural philosopher. . . ."

The appeal which Shakespeare made in the prologues to *Henry the Fifth* for the spectators to use their imaginations to supply what the stage did not present would have been in accordance with Blake's own fancy. The beginning of the *Prologue to King Edward the Fourth:*

> O For a voice like thunder, and a tongue
> To drown the throat of war!

reminds one of the opening *Chorus to Henry the Fifth:*

> O for a Muse of fire, that would ascend
> The brightest heaven of invention,

Likewise, the prologues to *Henry the Fifth* suggested to Blake that the future battle of Cressy should be reported as seen in the prince's imagination:

> Methinks I see them arm my gallant soldiers,
> And gird the sword upon each thigh, and fit
> Each shining helm, and string each stubborn bow,
> And dance to the neighing of our steeds.
> Methinks the shout begins, the battle burns;
> Methinks I see them perch on English crests,
> And roar the wild flame of fierce war, upon
> The thronged enemy!   (p. 44, ll. 6–13.)

"Honest-seeming brow" in *Samson* (p. 65, l. 19) rephrases Shakespeare's "seeming brow of justice" in *First Part of Henry the Fourth,* IV, iii, 83. In *Milton,* Blake incorporated Shakespeare's "Gives to airy nothing a local habitation and a name" (*A Midsummer Night's Dream,* V, i, 16–17) as "Giving to airy nothing a name and habitation."[38] In *A Descriptive Catalogue* (1809) Blake said regarding his sixth picture: "This Picture was done many years ago, and was one of the first Mr. B. ever did in Fresco."[39] For a title to this picture, he chose: "A Spirit vaulting from a cloud to turn and wind a fiery Pegasus—Shakespeare."[40] This line is a distorted phasing of a line in *First Part of Henry the Fourth,* IV, i, 108–110. In Blake's *55th Proverb of Hell*[41] is an allusion to the caterpillar which Mr. Damon thinks[42] came from the *Second Part of Henry the Sixth.* The use of the word in *Milton,* "Who creeps into the State Government like a caterpiller to destroy,"[43] is even nearer the application Shakespeare gave it in *Richard II,* II, iii, 166, in "The caterpillars of the commonwealth."

There is one aspect of the dramatic fragment, *King Edward the Third,* and of the prologues to the other projected plays, *King Edward the Fourth* and *King John,* which must not be ignored. This is Blake's attitude toward war. It is not possible to condense the matter into a single assertion, because in these selections there are inconsistencies which seem inexplicable except as one recalls that the work was experimental, and, in the varied expression of ideas and ideals, more reflective than is generally considered of the contributing influences which themselves were contradictory. The Old Testament, Shakespeare's historical plays, Ossian, and even the contemporary patriotic verse,[44] reflective of the conflicts which were gathering force in America and in France, all added something. For example, there is expressed throughout the scenes the picturesqueness of military preparation and of action such as those who never participated in war seem yet able to describe. There is the glorification of the nation—a theme nationalistic in origin, yet seemingly universal, a theme upon which Shakespeare's history plays were naturally constructed. This includes the praise of the hero, the exultation in victory, the poetic and lyrical glory in the prowess and exalted position of the nation. Mingled with these ideas are pointed assertions about the forces that cause war: commercial rivalry, desire for personal fame, and ambition for power. There are telling sentences about the horror and futility of warfare.

But there are other phases of the problem of Blake's attitude toward war which one must believe represent his own personal feeling and convictions. His lifelong hatred of falsehood, of oppression of the weak, and of tyranny surely were not new to the prophetic books. Lyrics like those in the *Songs of Experience* are burdened with the sense of the tyrannical forces oppressing human life. *Auguries of Innocence* plainly states the effect of war and the place greed has in the making of it:

> Nought can deform the Human Race
> Like to the Armour's iron brace.
> When Gold & Gems adorn the Plow
> To peaceful Arts shall Envy Bow.[45]

The temper of Blake's mind in childhood and youth accorded with the ideals of liberty expressed in the play. Hence it would appear that Blake's real thought[46] was to be found not so

much in the ideas derived from the sources cited as in such
lines as the bishop spoke:

> Sweet Prince! the arts of peace are great,
> And no less glorious than those of war,
> Perhaps more glorious in the phlosophic [*sic*] mind.
> When I sit at my home, a private man,
> My thoughts are on my gardens, and my fields,
> How to employ the hand that lacketh bread.
> If Industry is in my diocese,
> Religion will flourish; each man's heart
> Is cultivated, and will bring forth fruit:
> This is my private duty and my pleasure.
>
> (p. 32, ll. 9–18.)

There is still another reason to believe that Blake's own personal attitude was condemnation of war. The *Prologue* intended for *King Edward the Fourth* is so entirely condemna-
tory, so unified in its mood, so intense in its feeling, and so
frank in placing the blame for war upon the rulers and minis-
ters that it seems as if Blake were uttering his innermost convictions. This prologue and the one to *King John,* which certainly related more realistically the wretchedness resulting
from war than was told in *King Edward the Third,* show his
increasing hatred of war. These prologues have more unified
and clear-cut statements condemning war. *A War Song to
Englishmen,* which ends the group of pieces dealing with war,
is a very successful song of its genre; but in temper and purpose, it stands apart from the prologues. If one supposes that
Blake moved from the position where, boylike, he delighted in
the picturesqueness of war and glorified the heroism celebrated in all battle songs, to the place where he condemned
war, then *A War Song to Englishmen* would have been written much earlier than the prologues.[47] A clear understanding
of Blake's real thought is hindered by the fact that so much
of his later poetry related a continuous struggle of forces, a
warfare without ceasing, furious and dire. It was a struggle,
however, among spirits, objectified by the imagery of warfare,
a struggle Blake more fully engaged in than he ever could
have engaged in actual battle. One reason that Blake entered

so fully into Milton's war of the angels in *Paradise Lost* is
that it was essentially a clash of spiritual forces.

The contradiction between Blake's attitudes, at one time
glorifying war, at another condemning it, is to be found in
Shakespeare,[48] and it illustrates again, as *An Imitation of
Spencer* did, that any adherence to sources which were too
consciously imitated or were not fully assimilated became a
formidable obstacle to the clearest expression of himself.
Blake's attempts at drama give one the idea that he tried variously to express certain personal convictions which Shakespeare both inspired and deepened in his mind. His choice of
the dramatic form was only a natural consequence of his admiration for Shakespeare's mastermind, and one must not
allow either the imitative character of the play or its essential
failure to conceal the original features of it. One of these is
the convictions and attitudes personal to Blake himself. When
Sir John Chandos, in *King Edward the Third,* drew his ad-
mirable comparison between age and youth, one sees a description of Blake himself in the youth who

> . . . impatient takes the wing,
> Seizes the fruits of time, attacks experience,
> Roams round vast Nature's forest, where no bounds
> Are set, . . . till tir'd at length, sated and tired
> With the changing sameness, old variety,
> We sit us down, and view our former joys
> With distaste and dislike.   (p. 45, ll. 1–18.)

These lines tell the story of Blake's youth, his impatience with
ordinary restrictions which did not allow him freedom, his
paradoxical willingness to undergo apprenticeship, his experimentation with new forms of art and poetry, his restiveness
under the discipline and exactions of engraving, and his final
independent behavior. Again when the prince replied to Sir
John Chandos, Blake speaks out of his own experience:

> . . . I know,
> That youth has need of age to point fit prey,
> And oft the stander-by shall steal the fruit
> Of th' other's labour.   (p. 45, ll. 25–28.)

The especial significance of this comment is that probably at the time Blake wrote these lines at Basire's he saw his work passed under Basire's name. In spite of this, Blake kept his respect for Basire, and the remainder of the prince's speech tells further how Blake regarded the matter:

> . . . but the pure soul
> Shall mount on native wings, disdaining
> Little sport, and cut a path into the heaven
> of glory,
> Leaving a track of light for men to wonder at.

The terms of apprenticeship may have prevented the bitterness Blake later showed toward those who "stole the fruit of his labour," and he was yet able to view the matter philosophically. This is one of the few touches in the *Poetical Sketches* that reveal the mystic nature of the youthful Blake, an early revelation of the gift with which he was endowed.

Certain allusions to Shakespeare after 1783, in connection with Blake's pictures, point to an early knowledge of Shakespeare and to the permanence of his influence. In *A Descriptive Catalogue* (1809), describing Number XVI, "The Penance of Jane Shore," Blake said the drawing was done "thirty years before," which would put it in 1779. If he took the suggestion from the reference in *Richard the Third*, there is the possibility of his early acquaintance with another play. In the *Rossetti MS.*[49] there is a sketch (p. 96) intended for *The Gates of Paradise*, which has written below it the line from *Hamlet* (I, v, 182), "Rest, rest, Perturbed Spirit." Similarly on page 21 of the *Rossetti MS.*, beneath a sketch of figures associated symbolically with a flower resembling a rose, is a quotation from Sonnet 15: "Everything that grows Holds in perfection but a little. . . ." On design No. 7 of the "Illustrations to Dante," made in Blake's last years, appears: "As Shakespeare said: 'Nature, thou art Goddess.'" This could be from the line in *King Lear* (I, iv, 297)[50] or from *The Winter's Tale* (II, iii, 104).

Blake made drawings and engravings for *As You Like It, Julius Caesar, Hamlet, Henry the Eighth, Richard the Third,*

*First Part of Henry the Fourth, Macbeth, A Midsummer
Night's Dream, Romeo and Juliet,* and *Timon of Athens.*[51] It
cannot be assumed that these were his favorite or most familiar plays because so many other considerations entered into
the illustration of books. It does indicate a number with which
he certainly was familiar; for the rest one must accept the resemblances hitherto cited, if not also many that are too subtle
to be separated, set forth, or described. If Richard Garnett was
right in saying that those most deeply indebted to Shakespeare
are least disposed to reproduce his style,[52] then *King Edward
the Third* is more reliant upon Shakespeare than it is possible
to demonstrate. It was Garnett's opinion that Blake's mind was
so saturated with Shakespeare that it could only express itself
in Shakespearean form: "The drama is childish, but the feeling approaches Shakespeare as nearly as Keats's early poems
approach Spenser. The imitation, being spontaneous and un-
sought, is never senile, but every line reveals a youth whose
soul is with Shakespeare, though his body may be in Golden
Square. Yet the reproduction of Shakespeare's manner is
never so exact as to conceal the fact that the poet is writing in
the eighteenth and not in the sixteenth century."[53] One quality that Garnett must have appreciated in Blake's "reproduction of Shakespeare's manner" is the metrical form. Blake's
genius being lyrical, *King Edward the Third* is most notable
for its lyrical beauty, for the sheer poetic quality of the figures
of speech which abound in it, and the imaginative and emotional suggestiveness of them. The degree or extent to which
Blake failed in his effort to write drama is thus largely explained by the nature of his genius. It is not a failure which
could be due to the kind of imitation which "pilfered from
the first creation."[54] Blake fell short of attainment for the
reason which Gray gave West for the failure of his own imitation of Shakespeare: "Such is the misfortune of imitating
the inimitable."[55]

CHAPTER VI

SOME CONTEMPORARY INFLUENCES

WHEN Gilchrist began his account of Blake's *Poetical Sketches,* in the chapter called "A Boy's Poems," he quoted the phrase that Malkin had applied to the verse of the eighteenth century, "verse of polished phraseology and subdued thought," and then enumerated some of the writers whom that phrase called to mind. Next he questioned: "Where, beyond the confines of his own most individual mind, did the hosier's son find his model for that lovely web of rainbow fancy already quoted? ['How sweet I roam'd'] I know of none in English literature. For the *Song* commencing 'My silks and fine array,' . . . with its shy evanescent tints and aroma as of pressed rose-leaves, parallels may be found among the lyrics of the Elizabethan age: an alien though it be in its own. The influence of contemporary models, unless it be sometimes Collins or Thompson [*sic*], is nowhere in the volume discernible; but involuntary emulation of higher ones partially known to him: of the *Reliques* given to the world by Percy in 1760;[1] of Shakespere, Spenser, and of other Elizabethans."[2] There could be no more excellent example than this to show how easy it is for critics and biographers to accept a pleasing generalization and to incorporate it, unchallenged, as certain truth in a new work. Gilchrist accepted Malkin's information without question; by repeating it, he thus gave it the sanction of his authority as first biographer. Swinburne, prompted by the appearance of Gilchrist's *Life* to write his long essay on Blake, likewise had no doubt concerning what Gilchrist had said, and he repeated it. The idea being thereby established, later writers have merely elaborated upon it. In doing so they have ignored the possibility of the importance to Blake of the writers in his own century.

It is curious how vigorously the critics have denied Blake's debt to his century. It is almost as if they knew that, if they once admitted the strength of the debt, they would break with a sacred tradition. E. de Selincourt in a recent Oxford lecture paid his homage to Gilchrist's dictum by granting that Blake caught "echoes of the Elizabethans that had long grown faint," but he added that Blake's greatest debt to his age—to Ossian —was "wholly deplorable."[3] Oswald Crawfurd in 1874 minimized Blake's debt to his age, with the possible exception of Thomson in the "pastoral verse" and of Chatterton in the "mould in which he fashioned his poetry," but he acknowledged that the *Poetical Sketches* "anticipated all the men of that school which claims for itself to have begun a new era in poetry, an era distinguished by the very marks which are most characteristic of Blake's own Muse."[4] Arthur Symons in 1909 said apologetically that "some rags of his time did cling about him, but only by the edges."[5] C. H. Herford in a lecture on Blake, October 26, 1927, in Manchester, categorically stated that Blake completely ignored the "literary authorities and fashions of his day."[6] In such fashion have the critics spoken. Without question or sufficient investigation, they have repeated the early suppositions of Malkin as if they were facts.

There have been, however, a few dissenters. In 1927, in an introduction to the *Catalogue of the Blake Centenary Exhibition,* presented by the Burlington Fine Arts Club, the writer [Laurence Binyon] gave much importance to the influence of Gothic art and Michelangelo upon Blake, and called Blake a "child of his own age as well as a rebel against it," for "more of it clung to him than he knew."[7] He referred, of course, to Blake's artistic work but, as Blake was in his drawing and painting, so was he in his poetry. Of all the critics who have spoken about the *Poetical Sketches,* T. S. Eliot has shown the most discernment. He said: "His early poems show what the poems of a boy of genius ought to show, immense power of assimilation. Such early poems are not, as usually supposed, crude attempts to do something beyond the boy's capacity; they are, in the case of a boy of real promise, more likely to be quite mature and successful attempts to do something small. So with Blake. . . . But his affection for certain Elizabethans is not so surprising as his affinity with the very best work of his own century. He is very like Collins, he is very eighteenth century."[8] Blake was greatly indebted to the eighteenth century. In some respects this indebtedness is not so significant as his indebtedness to Milton or to the Bible; nor is it so subtle and essentially poetic as was his relation to Spenser or to Shakespeare, but it touched more people and was much more extensive than has ever been explained.

However far away from his own times a poet may stray who ventures in quest of minds most akin to his own, he yet cannot escape his contemporaries. If Blake's critics failed to see this influence, it is partly due to their effort to identify him with the inferior rather than with the excellent work of the century; but the same ability that led him to recognize Milton, Spenser, and Shakespeare enabled him to select the best from his own day. His knowledge of the older masters gave him a standard for selection from the multitude in his own period. Thomson, speaking prophetically, in the ode in *Alfred: A Masque,* usually designated "Rule Britannia," said:

> The Muses, still with freedom found,
> Shall to thy happy coast repair:[9]

The last stanza of Blake's *To the Muses* seems like a reply to Thomson. He expressed his feeling that there were few whom he could regard as highly as he regarded the "bards of old":

> How have you [the Muses] left the antient love
> That bards of old enjoy'd in you!
> The languid strings do scarcely move!
> The sound is forc'd, the notes are few!
> (p. 18, ll. 13–16.)

This is discerning criticism for a youth to make for it shows that he was fully aware of the poets of his own day. It recalls a similar tribute Thomson paid to the older poets:

> Or, turning thence thy view, these graver thoughts
> The muses charm—while, with sure taste refined,
> You draw the inspiring breath of ancient song,[10]

Such an attitude as Blake held in the quotation above is indicative of the mistrust many writers had of the poetic achievement in their own century;[11] it was written before voices that were comparable to Blake's had yet spoken.[12]

One writer of the eighteenth century whose influence upon Blake was marked and important is James Thomson. There are no statements in biographies or letters to give a clue to which works of Thomson Blake knew or how early he read them. Numerous editions of Thomson, and much verse imitative of him, contributed to the magazines and miscellanies, show how widely acquainted the public was with him. The first interesting association between Thomson and Blake is the correspondence between the ideas of the two poets about poetry. To the second edition of *Winter* in June, 1726, Thomson added what was his "apology for poetry." In it he declared that poetry is "the most charming power of imagination, the most exalting force of thought, the most affecting touch of sentiment."[13] Such ideas so phrased would have caught Blake's attention; and to the following paragraph he would have given his full assent: ". . . let poetry once more be restored to her ancient truth and purity; let her be inspired from heaven, and in return her incense ascend thither; let her exchange her low, venal, trifling, subjects for such as are fair, useful, and magnificent; and let her execute these so as at once to please, instruct, surprise, and astonish: and then of necessity the most inveterate ignorance, and prejudice, shall be struck dumb; and poets yet become the delight and wonder of mankind." (p. 240.) Blake never ceased to believe in the divine inspiration of his own work.[14] Who knows but that Thomson's plea for poetry may not have given Blake incentive to write? Who knows that Thomson's description of a true poet did not become an ideal toward which Blake strove, for, point by point, it corresponds with the leading traits of his character. Thomson described the true poet as ". . . one of genuine and unbounded greatness and generosity of mind; who, far above all the pomp and pride of fortune, scorns the little addressful flatterer; pierces through the disguised designing villain; discountenances all the reigning fopperies of a tasteless age: and who, stretching his views into late futurity, has the true interest of virtue, learning, and mankind entirely at heart—a character so nobly desirable that to an honest heart it is almost incredible so few should have the ambition to deserve it." (p. 240.) Thomson urged the choice of "great and serious sub-

jects" for poetry in place of "unaffecting fancies, little glitter-
ing prettinesses." He concluded: "A genius fired with the
charms of truth and nature is tuned to a sublimer pitch, and
scorns to associate with such subjects." (p. 240.) Then he
cited the book of Job as an example of a noble and ancient
book. Such ideas would have been of encouragement to the
youthful Blake and have pointed a way to him as he question-
ingly addressed the Muses about the proper province of poetry:

> Whether on Ida's shady brow,
>   Or in the chambers of the East,
>
>   .   .   .   .
>
> Whether in Heav'n ye wander fair,
>   Or in the greeen [*sic*] corners of the earth,
> Or the blue regions of the air,   (p. 18.)

Interested as Blake was in the traditions of early Britain,[15]
his attention would also have been caught by Thomson's *Alfred: A Masque,* played and published in 1740, but acted after
a period of sixteen years at the Drury Lane Theatre on October 9, 1773.[16] From it he could have taken a suggestion for his
play, *King Edward the Third.* In Act II, scene 3, the hermit
summoned through the *Genius of England* the spirits of Edward the Third, Philippa, and the Black Prince, and of them
said:

> A soverign's great example forms a people.
> The public breast is noble, or is vile,
> As he inspires it. In this EDWARD'S time,
> Warm'd by his courage, by his honor rais'd,
> High flames the *British* spirit, like the sun,
> To shine o'er half the globe: and where it shines,
> The cherish'd world to brighten and enrich.
>
>   .   .   .   .
>
> . . . I see him now
> On *Cressy's* glorious plain! The father's heart,
> With anxious love and wonder at his daring,
> Beats high in mingled transport. Great himself,
> Great above *jealousy,* the guilty mark
> That brands all meaner minds, see, he applauds

The *filial excellence,* and gives him scope
To blaze in his full brightness!—Lo again,
He sends him dreadful to a nobler field:
The danger and the glory all his own![17]

Here is the exact situation Blake sketched in *King Edward the Third,* and the same conception of character of both the king and the prince that Blake portrayed. The masque has no other characters or situations like those in Blake's play, but there are similarities in ideas which are phrased differently. There are, for example, the thoughts that manhood may be noble though clad in "homely russet" if the heart be true (pp. 8–9); that the "hind, whose toil is all his wealth" (p. 13) is superior to the sovereign who cannot save his people; that "what proves a hero great is never to despair" (p. 15); that "we can but die at last" (p. 13); that each must have his portion of sorrow which the brave "bear without repining" (p. 26); that "true courage lags not in its course, weighing action with cold wisdom That borders near on cowardice" (p. 36); and, finally, that "Britannia shall rule the waves; Britons never will be slaves." (pp. 42–43.)

Another of Thomson's plays, the tragedy of *Edward and Elenora,* which was prohibited for political reasons from representation on the stage in 1739, may have been the origin of Blake's early historical engraving, "Edward and Elinor," assigned to 1779, although Russell[18] suggested it may have been begun by Blake at the period of his study at the Royal Academy. It may be one of the drawings Malkin said was made during the "holiday hours of his apprenticeship."[19] Blake announced the historical engraving in his *Prospectus* dated October 10, 1793. The drawing for this is presumably the one that was cut in two to form two pages of *Vala.*[20] It represents Queen Eleanor sitting with King Edward beneath a canopy, while she sucks the poison from his wound from which a physician has extracted an arrow. Attendants and warriors stand about the central group. This episode is the central one of Thomson's play, and, while Blake could have learned it from many historical sources, it is possible he learned it from Thomson's play.

Another one of Blake's pictures of significance to the early poetry, which is thought to have been influenced by Thomson, is the one generally known as "Morning," or "Glad Day," names which were first given it by Gilchrist.[21] This picture inscribed "W. B. inv. 1780," is a line engraving, 9⅞ in. x 7⅜ in. This is reproduced as Plate 4 in Laurence Binyon's *Engraved Designs.* It represents a nude figure of more nearly classical line and proportion than usually seen in Blake's figures, that seems standing, almost poised, on a "mountain's brow."[22] The right foot, slightly raised from the ground, is extended to the side as if the figure were in motion or had not quite ceased from the action of alighting. The arms are outstretched in almost level line. The features are those of a youth, and the hair is in ringlets so disordered as to resemble the flames often conventionalized in the later symbolic pictures. It recalls the line in Macpherson's *Fingal,* "His hair flies from his head like a flame."[23] The light that glows about his head contrasts strongly with the darker base where creatures are in startled movement as if trying to make an immediate escape—a bat-like creature that might be the tail of a serpent, an item that was to reappear in his pictures of later years with strange inevitability. Even here, these creatures are doubtless symbolical. Ellis, with his usual inventiveness, asserted that this drawing was made by Blake "from himself . . . in his triumphant announcement that he had found at home the solution of his artistic problem of form."[24] This is extremely unlikely because the figure is much taller than Blake was and much more slender than he was even as a youth. Russell[25] sees in the face a resemblance to the picture of Blake drawn by his wife, to which opinion Mona Wilson assents.[26] She reproduces the latter in her *Life.* A later impression of the print Blake inscribed with the lines:

> Albion arose from where he labour'd
>   at the Mill with slaves:
> Giving himself, for the Nations, he
>   danc'd the dance of Eternal Death.[27]

The figure seen in this print is strikingly like two others. One is that of "Satan Arousing the Rebel Angels" (1808), repro-

duced as Plate 63 in Wright's *Life.*[28] The figure is poised in
almost identical position, except that the arms are raised above
the head. The face, however, is of very different character
from that of the youth in the early print. The second figure
appears in Plate 76 in *Jerusalem,*[29] in which almost the iden-
tically poised figure stands in adoration before the Saviour on
the Cross. The only difference here is that it is the left foot
that is extended to the side instead of the right. The repetition
of this figure is impressive of the idea that in it Blake incorporated a symbolism dear to his heart,[30] and whether it meant
to him Eternal Youth, or Albion dancing the Eternal Dance,
there was probably little distinction in Blake's conception of
each. As he once later (*c.* 1810) said:

> Re-engraved Time after Time,
> Ever in their youthful prime,
> My designs unchang'd remain.
> Time may rage but rage in vain.
> For above Time's troubled Fountains
> On the Great Atlantic Mountains,
> In my Golden House on high,
> There they Shine Eternally.[31]

A third state of the picture shows that the symbolical creatures have been removed, and slight alterations have been made
in the position of the limbs, while the youthful face, more exultant and more elated, yet has a classical serenity that makes
it correspond more nearly with the classical aspect of the figure. This third state is a color print dated 1794. Russell described it as an impression of the 1780 engraving done in
opaque color commonly used in the *Prophetic Books.*[32] Darrell Figgis, who reproduced it as Plate 69 in the *Paintings of
William Blake,* said it was an impression of the engraving
colored by hand and then stamped from millboard, "a colour-
printed drawing."[33] Binyon disagreed because of the larger
dimensions of the plate, and thought it was more probably a
monotype, painted on copper and then printed.[34] It was reproduced in color lithography as the frontispiece to Keynes's
Bibliography. It is this third state of the picture which is definitely associated with Thomson's poetry.

Russell suggested that the design is likely to have been inspired by the lines in *Romeo and Juliet:*

> Night's candles are burnt out, and jocund day
> Stands tiptoe on the misty mountain tops.[35]

This is a pleasing association between one of Blake's most beautiful pictures and the figurative meaning in Shakespeare's lines; but Thomson's *Summer,* whence came other influences upon Blake, reveals lines which not only give the outline of Blake's picture perfectly but fill in the colors and suggest the meaning. Whether Blake consciously tried to illustrate the lines, or whether unconsciously he utilized them in painting his own conception of the poem, first presented to his mind by Thomson, cannot be known, but the picture in either case fits Thomson's lines:

> But yonder comes the powerful king of day
> Rejoicing in the east. The lessening cloud,
> The kindling azure, and the mountain's brow
> Illumed with fluid gold, his near approach
> Betoken glad. Lo! now, apparent all,
> Aslant the dew-bright earth and coloured air,
> He looks in boundless majesty abroad,
> And sheds the shining day, that burnished plays
> On rocks, and hills, and towers, and wandering streams
> High-gleaming from afar. Prime cheerer, Light!
> Of all material beings first and best!
> Efflux divine! Nature's resplendent robe,
> Without whose vesting beauty all were wrapt
> In unessential gloom; and thou, O Sun!
> Soul of the surrounding worlds! in whom best seen
> Shines out thy Maker! may I sing of thee?   (p. 56.)

That the image of these lines was mirrored in Blake's mind is apparent again in the fact that between 1795 and 1804 he recurred to it, and expressed it plainly in the lines in *Vala:*

> So Urizen spoke; he shook his snows from
>   off his shoulders & arose
> As on a Pyramid of mist, his white robes
>   scattering

> The fleecy white: renew'd, he shook his
>   aged mantles off
> Into the fires. Then, glorious bright,
>   Exulting in his joy,
> He sounding rose into the heavens in naked
>   majesty,
> In radiant Youth;[36]

The majestic, radiant, and joyous personality is the same as in Thomson's poetry and in both Blake's picture and his verses. Thomson's emphasis of color is upon "the fluid-gold" that "burnished" plays over everything. This is the dominance of color in Blake's picture. There is besides "the kindling azure," "the coloured air," the "dew-bright earth" which describe the scene in the picture. Blake so fully reproduced the imagery in Thomson's description that when one meets the lines in *Liberty:*

> . . . Lo! from their ashes rose,
> Gay-beaming radiant youth, the phoenix State,

(p. 387, ll. 1044–1045) one sees a significance Blake may have wished to embody in the picture.[37] Blake was keenly sensitive to the pictorial qualities of Thomson's poetry, but he was also interested in his ideas.

Most people share Samuel Johnson's attitude toward Thomson's *Liberty* when he said, *"Liberty,* when it first appeared, I tried to read, and soon desisted. I have never tried again, and therefore will not hazard either praise or censure."[38] Hannah More, however, knew it well enough to quote it on the title-page of *Slavery, a Poem.*[39] What was it that attracted Blake to it? In the first place, Blake's early intense sense of patriotism made him alert to what was said or written on the subject. He naturally would have observed a contemporary recording of ideas which were in tune with those he admired in Shakespeare. There is, besides, an excellent chance that he was brought definitely in touch with a circle of people who were reading and discussing *Liberty.* In 1768, Thomas Bentley became a partner of Josiah Wedgwood and took charge of the London firm in St. Martin's Lane where the Etruria wares were sold. It was on the recommendation of Bentley that John

Flaxman was engaged by Wedgwood the latter part of 1774,[40] in which year the London shop was moved to new quarters in Portland Place, Greek Street, Soho, within the neighborhood of the home of Basire and of Blake's parents. Bentley was a great admirer of Thomson's poems, and sought to interest others apparently, since he "infected Wedgwood with his [Thomson's] love of nature, and especially his poem 'Liberty.'"[41] Thus again one sees the possibility of an earlier acquaintance between Blake and Flaxman than has been previously known. But, if Blake had not learned of *Liberty* through these associations, he would have been drawn to it if he had heard that it was a "Poem . . . thrown into the form of a Poetical Vision."

There is a passage in *Liberty* which, in the substance of what the action covers, in inferences about characters, ideals, and ideas, although not in language, may have furnished argument for *Edward the Third:*

> 'But when an Edward, and a Henry breathed
> Through the charmed whole one all-exerting soul;
> Drawn sympathetic from his dark retreat,
> When wide-attracted merit round them glowed;
> When counsels just, extensive, generous, firm,
> Amid the maze of state, determined kept
> Some ruling point in view; when, on the stock
> Of public good and glory grafted, spread
> Their palms, their laurels—or, if thence they
>   strayed,
> Swift to return, and patient of restraint;
> When regal state, pre-eminence of place,
> They scorned to deem pre-eminence of ease,
> To be luxurious drones, that only rob
> The busy hive; as in distinction, power,
> Indulgence, honour, and advantage first—
> When they too claimed in virtue, danger, toil
> Superior rank, with equal hand prepared
> To guard the subject and to quell the foe:
> When such with me their vital influence shed,
> No muttered grievance, hopeless sigh was heard;
> No foul distrust through wary senates ran,
> Confined their bounty, and their ardour quenched;

On aid, unquestioned, liberal aid was given;
Safe in their conduct, by their valour fired,
Fond where they led victorious armies rushed;
And Cressy, Poitiers, Agincourt proclaim
What kings supported by almighty love
And people fired with liberty can do.'

(p. 381, l. 840–p. 382, l. 867.)

Here are the dominating Edward; the idea of just counsel;
the effectiveness of politics; the sense of public good; the
glory; the scorn of luxury and ease; the emphasis upon honor
and valor; the sacred person of the king; the inspiration given
by liberty—all ideas of Blake's play.[42]

If one considers that *King Edward the Third* is concerned
definitely with a forthcoming battle and the preparations for
it, and if one considers the period it is supposed to represent,
there is a curious emphasis put upon commerce. Clarence
speaking to the assembled lords said:

Yet, with your kind assistance, Lords, I hope
England shall dwell in peace; that while my father
Toils in his wars, and turns his eyes on this
His native shore, and sees commerce fly round
With his white wings, and sees his golden London,
And her silver Thames, throng'd with shining spires
And corded ships; her merchants buzzing round
Like summer bees, and all the golden cities
In his land, overflowing with honey,
Glory may not be dimm'd with clouds of care.
Say, Lords, should not our thoughts be first to
    commerce?

The bishop answered:

Sweet Prince! the arts of peace are great,
And no less glorious than those of war, . . .

.   .   .   .

My thoughts take in the gen'ral good of the whole,
And England is the land favour'd by Commerce;
For Commerce, tho' the child of Agriculture,
Fosters his parent, who else must sweat and toil,
And gain but scanty fare. Then, my dear Lord,

> Be England's trade my care; and we, as tradesmen,
> Looking to the gain of this our native land.
> (p. 31, l. 20–p. 32, l. 7; p. 32, ll. 9–16.)

Compare the ideas thus expressed with Thomson's lines about Commerce[43] (pp. 366, ll. 316–321; 369, ll. 422–426, 432–438):

> . . . 'and Commerce thus,
> Of toil impatient, flags the drooping sail.
> Bursting, besides, his ancient bounds, he took
> A larger circle; found another seat,
> Opening a thousand ports, and charmed with toil
> Whom nothing can dismay far other sons.
>
> . . . .
>
> . . . 'and peddling commerce plied
> Between near joining lands. For Britons, chief,
> It was reserved, with star-directed prow,
> To dare the middle deep, and drive assured
> To distant nations through the pathless main.
>
> . . . .
>
> . . . 'Theirs the triumph be,
> By deep invention's keen pervading eye,
> The heart of courage, and the hand of toil,
> Each conquered ocean staining with their blood,
> Instead of treasure robbed by ruffian war,
> Round social earth to circle fair exchange
> And bind the nations in a golden chain.'

The idea in the last lines repeats the lines from Thomson's *Summer:*

> . . . hence burnished war
> Gleams on the day; the nobler works of peace
> Hence bless mankind; and generous commerce binds
> The round of nations in a golden chain.
> (p. 58, ll. 136–139.)

The imagery in Blake's lines is even closer to the following passage from *Liberty:*

> 'The times I see whose glory to supply,
> For toiling ages, commerce round the world
> Has winged unnumbered sails and from each land

Materials heaped that, well employed, with Rome
Might vie our grandeur, and with Greece our art!'
(p. 408, ll. 569–573.)

.   .   .   .

'Trade, joined to these, on every sea displayed
A daring canvas, poured with every tide
A golden flood.'   (p. 383, ll. 569–573.)

The same note is struck in "Rule Britannia":

To thee belongs the rural reign;
Thy cities shall with commerce shine;
All thine shall be the subject main,
And every shore its circles thine.[44]

It is interesting to hear a later echo of this in a fragment of
verse from Blake's notebook:

Spirit, who lov'st Brittannia's [*sic*] Isle
Round which the Fiends of Commerce smile . . .[45]

Blake's picture of Liberty as a person comes directly from
Thomson's representation. In *King Edward the Third,* Blake
wrote:

"Liberty shall stand upon the cliffs of Albion,
"Casting her blue eyes over the green ocean:"
(p. 55, ll. 11–12.)

Thomson's description was:

Its guardian she, the Goddess, whose staid eye
Beams the dark azure of the doubtful dawn.
(p. 370, ll. 464–465.)

The remainder of Blake's stanza, closing *King Edward the
Third,* reads:

"Or, tow'ring, stand upon the roaring waves,
"Stretching her mighty spear o'er distant lands;
"While, with her eagle wings, she covereth
"Fair Albion's shore, and all her families."
(p. 55, ll. 13–16.)

Thomson introduces the closing section of *Liberty* with a similar idea:

> Here ceased the Goddess; and her ardent wings,
> Dipped in the colours of the heavenly bow,
> Stood waving radiance round, for sudden flight
> Prepared, when thus impatient burst my prayer:
>
> .   .   .   .
>
> . . . Straight with her hand,
> Celestial red, she touched my darkened eyes.
> As at the touch of day the shades dissolve,
> So quick, methought, the misty circle cleared
> That dims the dawn of being here below;
> The future shone disclosed, and, in long view,
> Bright rising eras instant rushed to light.
>> (p. 408, ll. 549–552, 558–564.)

Here are the same emanation of color, the same attribute of
wings, the same aloofness. Blake expressed the same general
idea of the governing, protecting part that the goddess played,
which is found similarly expressed by Thomson in other lines:

> 'High shining on the promontory's brow,
> Awaiting me, she stood with hope inflamed,
> By my mixed spirit burning in her sons,
> To firm, to polish, and exalt the state.'
>> (p. 371, ll. 475–478.)

Again Thomson wrote:

> An island-goddess now; and her high care
> The queen of isles, the mistress of the main.
>> (p. 313, ll. 33–34.)

The "mistress of the main," the heaven-sent, Blake visualized,
and to her he gave more human value in his description of her:

> . . . if so, we are not sovereigns
> Of the sea; our right, that Heaven gave
> To England, when at the birth of nature
> She was seated in the deep, the Ocean ceas'd
> His mighty roar; and fawning, play'd around
> Her snowy feet, and own'd his awful Queen.
>> (p. 34, ll. 17–22.)

Thomson has a long passage which praises the life of independence (p. 395, ll. 120–158), an extract from which will show how closely Blake followed the idea:

> 'Hail! independence, hail! heaven's next best gift
> To that of life and an immortal soul!
> The life of life! that to the banquet high
> A sober meal gives taste; to the bowed roof
> Fair-dreamed repose, and to the cottage charms.
>
> . . . .
>
> . . . 'Nor can those
> Whom fortune heaps, without these virtues, reach
> That truce with pain, that animated ease,
> That self-enjoyment, springing from within,
> That independence, active and retired,
> Which make the soundest bliss of man below:
> But, lost beneath the rubbish of their means,
> And drained by wants to nature all unknown,
> A wandering, tasteless, gaily wretched train,
> Though rich, are beggars, and though noble, slaves.'
>   (p. 396, ll. 124–128, 147–156.)

Sir John Chandos said to the prince in *King Edward the Third*:

> Courage, my Lord, proceeds from self-dependence;
> Teach man to think he's a free agent,
> Give but a slave his liberty, he'll shake
> Off sloth, and build himself a hut, and hedge
> A spot of ground; this he'll defend; 'tis his
> By right of nature: thus set in action,
> He will still move onward to plan conveniences,
> 'Till glory fires his breast to enlarge his castle,
> While the poor slave drudges all day, in hope
> To rest at night.   (p. 43, ll. 4–13.)

Closely allied to this topic is the idea Thomson expressed elsewhere in *Liberty*:

> '. . . Then stood untouched the solid base,
> Of Liberty, the liberty of the mind;'
>   (p. 331, ll. 246–247.)

Blake's response to this is seen in:

> . . . let Liberty
> Blaze in each countenance, and fire the battle.
> The enemy fight in chains, invisible chains, but
> heavy;
> Their minds are fetter'd; then how can they be
> free, . . .   (p. 30, ll. 1–4.)

Blake's phrase, "Their minds are fetter'd," recalls Thomson's use of the idea in "soft enchanting fetters of the mind," and "thought unfettered ranges" of *Liberty*.[46] Closely allied to this idea is another which Thomson expressed as:

> 'Thus human life, unhinged, to ruin reeled,
> And giddy reason tottered on her throne.'
>   (p. 360, l. 99.)

which Blake turned to account as "Reason's fine-wrought throne. . . ." (p. 46, l. 19.)

Sir Thomas Dagworth, in his indirect approach to the king about his fears, enumerated a number of creatures: dog, wolf, lion, stag, crane, and snake. It seems a strange piece of writing for Blake, incongruous, and unlike any passage elsewhere in the *Poetical Sketches*. It seems as if it were a recollection of Thomson's lines in *Liberty:*

> 'These her delights—and by no baneful herb,
> No darting tiger, no grim lion's glare,
> No fierce-descending wolf, no serpent rolled
> In spires immense progressive o'er the land
> Disturbed.'   (p. 393, ll. 43–47.)[47]

Thomson's *Liberty,* although probably less widely read than his *Seasons,* was of importance to Blake, and *King Edward the Third* is indebted particularly to it for many ideas, images, and phrases. Blake's interest in *Liberty* is but a foreshadowing of his increasing passion for liberty that later was to express itself in many directions: hatred of man-made moral codes which enchained the human spirit; hatred of materialism and commercialism which imprisoned the human being, body and soul; hatred of systems of rationalization which closed in upon

spiritual existence. Even as early as the *Poetical Sketches,* reflections from Thomson's *Liberty* were indicative of his restiveness under these repressions.

It is plain from many echoes in his shorter poems that Blake
also knew the *Seasons.* Both Thomson and Blake conceived of
Spring as a personage to whom each addressed himself. But
there is a difference. Spring became a human personality to
Blake; to Thomson she remained an abstraction which never
escaped the bounds of his theorizing. If both men had the gift
of poetic vision, it was Blake who also had the gift of communication of his vision to others. For example, one can cite
the beginning of the two poems on Spring. Thomson wrote:

> Come, gentle Spring, ethereal mildness, come;
> And from the bosom of yon dropping cloud,
> While music wakes around, veiled in a shower
> Of shadowing roses, on our plains descend.
> (p. 3, ll. 1–4.)

Blake's Spring also dwelt above the earth, and to her Blake
spoke:

> O THOU, with dewy locks, who lookest down
> Thro' the clear windows of the morning; . . .
> . . . all our longing eyes are turned
> Up to thy bright pavillions:
> (p. 1, ll. 1–2, 3–7.)

Blake had the ability to choose from many details, accurately
observed by Thomson, the essentially poetic item which he reproduced, not on broad canvas as a panorama which was
Thomson's style, but in miniature. The selective eye of the
artist saw the significance in accustomed things. An example
of Blake's fusing of Thomson's multiple detail into an organic
unit, the essence of which is almost delicately symbolical compared with the more expository manner of Thomson, is seen
in Blake's song, "Love and harmony combine," which begins:

> LOVE and harmony combine,
> And round our souls intwine,
> While thy branches mix with mine,
> And our roots together join.

> Joy upon our branches sit,
> Chirping loud, and singing sweet;
> (p. 12, ll. 1–6.)

For this, something came from Thomson's *Nuptial Song:*

> A genial spirit warms the breeze;
> Unseen, among the blooming trees,
> The feathered lovers tune their throat,
> The desert growls a softened note,
> Glad o'er the meads the cattle bound,
> And love and harmony go round.
> (p. 431, ll. 9–14.)

Something also of similar idea and manner came from *Spring:*

> When first the soul of love is sent abroad
> Warm through the vital air, and on the heart
> Harmonious seizes, . . .
> . . . all alive at once their joy o'erflows
> In music unconfined . . .
> . . . Every copse . . .
> Deep-tangled, tree irregular, and bush . . .
> Are prodigal of harmony.
> (p. 25, ll. 582–598.)[48]

Closely associated with this idea of the harmonious music of the birds is the passage in Thomson's *Spring:*

> Full swell the woods; their very music wakes,
> Mixed in wild concert, with the warbling brooks
> Increased,   (p. 10, ll. 198–200.)

In one phrase Blake condensed all that Thomson's several lines have said:

> . . . turn
> Thine angel eyes upon our western isle,
> Which in full choir hails thy approach, O Spring!
> (p. 1, ll. 2–4.)

Thomson was fond of representing the sounds of nature. Again he described the birds:

> . . . The jay, the rook, the daw,
> And each harsh pipe, discordant heard alone,
> Aid the full concert; while the stock-dove breathes
> A melancholy murmur through the whole.
>
> (p. 26, ll. 610–613.)

From the "full concert" Blake selected only one sound, which he reported so that it carried much more suggestion:

> Thy sweet boughs perfume the air,
> And the turtle buildeth there.
> There she sits and feeds her young,
> Sweet I hear her mournful song;
> And thy lovely leaves among,
> There is love: I hear her tongue.
>
> (p. 12, ll. 11–16.)[49]

Thus, also, Blake summed up what Thomson says in this passage:

> 'Tis love creates their melody, and all
> This waste of music is the voice of love,
> That even to birds and beasts the tender arts
> Of pleasing teaches. (p. 26, ll. 614–618.)

Thomson undertook to describe the absence of sounds. In *Spring* he wrote:

> . . . Gradual sinks the breeze
> Into a perfect calm; that not a breath
> Is heard to quiver through the closing woods,
> Or rustling turn the many-twinkling leaves
> Of aspen tall. The uncurling floods, diffused
> In glassy breadth, seem through delusive lapse
> Forgetful of their course. 'Tis silence all,
> And pleasing expectation. (p. 9, ll. 155–162.)

In one of the most daring figures of speech Blake—or anyone else—ever wrote, he expressed the silence that Thomson had striven to express through so many verses. Blake's comparison, although technically faulty, achieved the effect desired by its startling paradox in *To the Evening Star:*

> . . . Let thy west wind sleep on
> The lake; speak silence with thy glimmering eyes,
> And wash the dusk with silver.   (p. 5, ll. 8–10.)

"Wash the dusk with silver" is an artist's presentation of the lines of Thomson. Blake's words fused the senses into a single act of perception in which color and sound are realized as aspects of the same thing.

Ample suggestive detail for the following quotation from Blake's *To Summer* came from Thomson's *Spring* and *Summer:*

> Beneath our thickest shades we oft have heard
> Thy voice, when noon upon his fervid car
> Rode o'er the deep of heaven; beside our springs
> Sit down, and in our mossy vallies, on
> Some bank beside a river clear, throw thy
> Silk draperies off, and rush into the stream:
> Our vallies love the Summer in his pride.
> > (p. 2, ll. 7–13.)

In *Spring,* Thomson wrote:

> . . . but when the sun
> Shakes from his noon-day throne the scattering
>   clouds,
> Even shooting listless languor through the deeps,
> Then seek the bank where flowering elders crowd,
>
> .   .   .   .
>
> Or lie reclined beneath yon spreading ash
> Hung o'er the steep,   (pp. 19–20, ll. 443–450.)

A similar scene is in *Summer:*

> Hence let me haste into the mid-wood shade,
> Where scarce a sunbeam wanders through the
>   gloom,
> And on the dark-green grass, beside the brink
> Of haunted stream that by the roots of oak
> Rolls o'er the rocky channel, lie at large
> And sing the glories of the circling year.
> > (p. 53, ll. 9–14.)

This idea of "singing the glories" of the season is present in Blake's *Autumn,* where Autumn sings the "lusty song of fruit and flowers." The characteristic of Summer's pride is true of Thomson's Summer; the "fervid car" of Blake's *Summer* is in Thomson's picture, the sun's "beaming car." Thomson's *Autumn* opens with lines descriptive of the "jovial" figure who, "well-pleased," tunes the "Doric reed." The suggestion of revelry is clear in Blake's *Autumn:*

> . . . there thou may'st rest,
> And tune thy jolly voice to my fresh pipe;
> And all the daughters of the year shall dance!
> Sing now the lusty song of fruit and flowers.
>
> (p. 3, ll. 3–6.)[50]

The difference between their manner of devising a personification is shown in Thomson's and Blake's *Summer*. Both dealt with essentially the same factors. Blake described Summer's "ruddy limbs and flourishing hair." Thomson wrote:

> Nor to the surface of enlivened earth,
> Graceful with hills and dales, and leafy woods,
> Her liberal tresses, is thy force confined;
>
> (p. 58, ll. 130–133.)

Thomson added "tresses" as an appositive to explain literally the meaning of his personification. This expository method of enforcing his picture, contained within the personification, gains objectivity by making both factual. Blake, through the lack of explanation, put upon the the reader the necessity of seeing the personification which he himself visualized and fully realized. Its directness and vividness convey the required implication.

Blake's *To Winter* differs in its indebtedness to Thomson's poem about the same season from the poems of the other seasons. It shows a higher degree of assimilation of the elements involved and greater independence in the treatment of them. The result is new aspects of beauty, wrought by the play of the imagination upon the old elements that he had drawn together. The periodicals and miscellanies were filled with poems imitative of one or all of Thomson's seasons, ranging

from the absurd personification of Winter as a feminine character[51] to Winter as an old pilgrim.[52] They were one and all
filled with stock expressions,[53] trite and ineffective. Blake enhanced the meaning and value of what he utilized from Thomson by the charm and originality of his expression. The idea
of Winter as a ruler, for example, is not new. Thomson stated
the idea quite as a matter of fact:

> . . . Dread Winter spreads his latest glooms,
> And reigns tremendous o'er the conquered year.
> . . . Horror wide extends
> His desolate domain.
> (p. 223, ll. 1024–1025, 1027–1028.)

Blake put the same idea metaphorically in a single sentence:

> . . . I dare not lift mine eyes;
> For he hath rear'd his sceptre o'er the world.
> (p. 4, ll. 7–8.)

Again, instead of Thomson's almost prosaic manner in:

> And see where surly Winter passes off
> Far to the north, and calls his ruffian blasts:
> (p. 4, ll. 11–12.)

Blake condensed the details at the same time that he enlarged
the personification:

> The north is thine; there hast thou built thy dark
> Deep-founded habitation.   (p. 4, ll. 2–3.)

Likewise, where Thomson wrote:

> And Winter oft at eve resumes the breeze,
> Chills the pale morn, and bids his driving sleets
> Deform the day delightless;   (p. 4, ll. 19–21.)

Blake rendered the whole idea:

> . . . and in his hand
> Unclothes the earth, and freezes up frail life.
> (p. 4, ll. 11–12.)

Similarly, where Thomson said:

> The North-east spends his rage, and, now shut up
> Within his iron caves,   (p. 9, ll. 143-144.)

Blake added to the lines just quoted:

> Shake not thy roofs,
> Nor bend thy pillars with thine iron car.
>   (p. 4, ll. 3-4.)

Blake conceived of Winter in terms of a person, not as an abstraction, "the direful monster, whose skin clings to his strong bones," striding over the rocks. He not only makes one see the figure—the person—, but he maintained such a consistently true point of view toward his personality that he enlists one's feelings, until Blake's own exclamation about the victim of Winter's power, "Poor little wretch!" seems the most natural response. There is no better example of Blake's anthropomorphic view of nature. Winter to him was a fully realized personality.

Blake followed Thomson's plan of utilizing a scene at sea. Thomson's description of the storm[54] fills many pages, the entire scene of which Blake condensed, unified, and crystallized, added a suggestion of plot, increased the sense of destruction and terror, and enforced the characterization—all in a few lines:

> He hears me not, but o'er the yawning deep
> Rides heavy; his storms are unchain'd; . . .
>
>   .   .   .   .   .   .
>
> He takes his seat upon the cliffs, the mariner
> Cries in vain. Poor little wretch! that deal'st
> With storms;   (p. 4, ll. 4-5, 13-15.)

It is but representative of the manner in which Blake handled what he remembered from Thomson. The pictorial element he always kept, but he condensed material until there was no waste either in details seen or in details felt. In fact, one feels more by not being required to see too much. His treatment compared with Thomson's reminds one of a phrase he used in

Jerusalem, "He seiz'd the bars of condens'd thoughts to forge them."[55] Undramatic as Blake was in his *King Edward the Third,* he was yet able to give a certain dramatic touch, restrained and simple, to his personifications that heightened their sensibility and gave them life.

There remains one curious circumstance about Thomson's influence upon Blake. Although it is clear that Blake knew both *Liberty* and *The Seasons,* there is no indication whatever that he knew *The Castle of Indolence.* As Spenser's allegory had not appealed to Blake, so it seems that Thomson's imitation of Spenser's allegory likewise did not appeal. It is to be observed, too, that Blake reflected nothing of the philosophy of nature Thomson set forth in his poetry. There is nothing, for example, in Blake's early poems to show that the seasons "as they change . . . are but the varied God." "The rolling year is full of Theé," said Thomson. Except for this idea, the first twenty lines of Thomson's *A Hymn to the Seasons* outline Blake's four seasons. But there is none of Thomson's moralizing. It was the artist's eye that selected the pictorial detail—the images that were not photographic, but such as were visioned by an insight into their significance. Although Thomson was diffuse, he was never false; being romantic, he revealed a fresh world of beauty, intimate and sometimes mysterious; but Thomson's consciousness of the manifestation of the divine in nature was not mystic in the sense of the perception which Blake was later to attain. Although Blake did not express himself in as mystical terms as he later used, the great difference between Thomson's view of nature and Blake's lay in the farther realms to which Blake's imagination was, even in his youth, able to penetrate. This is borne out by his remark in 1816 about Wordsworth's title: "Influence of Natural Objects In calling forth and strengthening the Imagination in Boyhood and early Youth."[56] Blake said: "Natural objects always did & now do weaken, deaden & obliterate Imagination in me. W. must know that what he writes valuable is not found in Nature. Read Michael Angelo's Sonnet, Vol. 2, p. 179:"[57] Blake's later "double vision" which enabled him to see the twofold essence of nature that he described in:

> For double the vision my Eyes do see,
> And a double vision is always with me.
> With my inward Eye 'tis an old Man gray;
> With my outward, a Thistle across my way.[58]

is thus early made manifest in the way in which he either altered details about nature which he took from Thomson, or ignored others that held no interest for him.

Thomson's influence was considerable both in importance and in extent.[59] It was by no means a "feeble reflection" as suggested by Crawfurd, nor a "rag of his time" as remarked by Symons, nor complete "ignorance of the literary authorities and fashions of his day" as Herford stated. There are some evidences that Blake read the work of Mark Akenside, William Collins, and Thomas Gray, but the extent and character of their influence were much less than that of Thomson. The very title of Akenside's poem, *The Pleasures of Imagination,* would have drawn Blake to it, holding as he did ideas that finally led him to assert, "The world of Imagination is the world of Eternity." Akenside's interpretation of poetry as the one of the arts that uses language as an instrument of imitation to express objects of the imagination would have interested Blake. In the *General Argument* to the 1772 edition, the thought of a poet as a man of genius destined by nature to excel, whose imagination was endowed with powers which other men cannot share, would have brought Blake's assent. Early in the poem Akenside expressed his theory of inspiration, concluding that

> . . . from heaven descends
> The flame of genius to the human breast,
> And love and beauty, and poetic joy
> And Inspiration.[60]

Akenside described the "laughing Autumn"[61] and the "gloomy north, with iron swarms, Tempestuous pouring from her frozen caves"[62] that is reshaped into the habitation of Blake's Winter. It is the arrangement of words and the cadence in the verse rather than the language or the ideas wherein Blake's resemblance lies. For example, Akenside wrote:

> . . . Hither turn
> Thy graceful footsteps; . . . let thy eyes
> Effuse the mildness of their azure dawn;
> And may the fanning breezes waft aside
> Thy radiant locks, dissolving as it bends
> With airy softness from the marble neck
> The cheek fair-blooming.[63]

There is, also, a similar choice of details in a comparable passage in Blake's *To Spring:*

> . . . turn
> Thine angel eyes upon our western isle
> Which in full choir hails thy approach . . .
> . . . let us taste
> Thy morn and evening breath.
>   (p. 1, ll. 2–4, 10–11.)

Many of the resemblances in Akenside are of such conventional character that they reappear in Collins and in Thomson. They are of little importance except as they indicate how Blake conformed to some of the manners or fashions of his time.

The revival of interest in Collins's poetry after his death, when Fawkes and Woty and Dodsley included his poems in their collections, and when in 1765 Langhorne edited the collected edition that was reprinted in 1771 and 1781, was surely strong enough to have affected Blake. Meyerstein is of the opinion that the youthful Chatterton, Blake's exact contemporary, was influenced by Collins.[64] Some idea of the currency of Collins's poetry may be seen in the fact that in *Lloyd's Evening Post* for May 10, 1783, Collins's "How sleep the brave" was printed with the title, *On Lord Robert Manners,* with no attribution to Collins as the author.[65]

Because it is not a simple matter to separate what is imitative in the poetry of Collins from what is original, it is impossible to be sure that the likenesses one sees in Blake came from Collins or from Collins's sources. In a general way, Blake resembles Collins in the vividness, the simplicity, and the truth of his personification. The same heightened but re-

strained sensibility is common to both. But Blake's personifications have a personal existence and identity with which Collins never quite endowed his abstractions. It is to be noted
that the personifications in *The Couch of Death* and in *Contemplation* are more nearly in the tradition of Collins than of
Macpherson, whose influence in them is strong and demonstrable. One notes the use of the same details, conventional to
be sure, of dew, blossoms, and coursers of the day in Blake's
poems on the seasons.

Although there are in Blake's "My silks and fine array"
phrases that recall Collins's poem, "Young Damon of the
Vale is dead," Blake could not have known the poem since it
was first published in the *Public Advertiser,* March 7, 1788. It
is, therefore, an instance of how both poets were indebted to a
common source, Shakespeare. Collins wrote:

> His shroud, which Death's cold damps destroy,
> Of snow-white threads was made, . . .
>
> .   .   .   .
>
> Ah, no! his bell of peace is rung,
> His lips are cold as clay.
>
> .   .   .   .   .   .
>
> Ah me! how many a true-love show'r
> Of kind remembrance fell![66]

Blake wrote:

> Bring me an axe and spade,
>   Bring me a winding sheet;
> When I my grave have made,
>   Let winds and tempests beat:
> Then down I'll lie, as cold as clay.
> True love doth pass away!
>   (p. 11, ll. 13–18.)

In *Hamlet,* IV, v, 35–39, Ophelia sang:

> "White his shroud as the mountain snow,
>   Larded with sweet flowers;
> Which bewept to the grave did not go
>   With true-love showers."

"Bring me yew to deck my grave," in the same poem of Blake, recalls Collins's *Dirge in Cymbeline:*

> . . . With hoary moss, and gather'd flowers,
> To deck the ground where thou are laid.
>
> When howling winds, and beating rain,
> In tempests shake the sylvan cell;[67]

The storm represented in this passage was kept by Blake in the quotation cited above. Of "decking" somebody with something there had been no end since classic times; nor was the phrase, "dewy fingers," uncommon from as long ago. But who knows that it was not Collins's lines,

> When Spring, with dewy fingers cold,
> Returns to deck their hallow'd mold,[68]

that gave Blake the line in *To Spring,* "O deck her forth with thy fair fingers"? (p. 2, l. 1.)

Gray seems to have done much conscious borrowing, for he added footnotes to tell his sources. One need not, therefore, be in doubt as with Collins. Blake's resemblance to Gray lies in two parallels. In the *Hymn to Adversity* Gray wrote:

> Bound in thy adamantine chain
> The Proud are taught to taste of pain,
> And purple Tyrants vainly groan
> With pangs unfelt before, unpitied and alone.[69]

In Blake's *Prologue to King John* is the phrase, "Tyranny hath stretched his purple arm." In a later poem, *The Grey Monk,* Blake recurred to the same idea:

> "Thy hand of Vengeance found the Bed
> "To which the Purple Tyrant fled;"[70]

The setting in Gray's *Ode to Spring:*

> Where'er the oak's thick branches stretch
> A broader browner shade;
> Where'er the rude and moss-grown beech
> O'er-canopies the glade,

> Beside some water's rushy brink
> With me the Muse shall sit, and think . . .[71]

reminds one of the scene in Blake's *To Summer:*

> Beneath our thickest shades . . .
> . . . beside our springs
> Sit down, and in our mossy vallies, on
> Some bank beside a river clear,
> > (p. 2, ll. 6–10.)

That these three poets, Akenside, Collins, and Gray, interested Blake at all shows that they had qualities of the imagination that appealed to him, for they illustrate the trend in poetry that was frankly stated by Joseph Warton in the *Advertisement* to his *Odes on Various Subjects:* "The Public has been so much accustom'd of late to didactic Poetry alone, and Essays on moral Subjects, that any work where the imagination is much indulged, will perhaps not be relished or regarded. The author therefore of these pieces is in some pain least [*sic*] certain austere critics should think them too fanciful and descriptive. But as he is convinced that the fashion of moralizing in verse has been carried too far, and as he looks upon Invention and Imagination to be the chief faculties of a Poet, so he will be happy if the following Odes may be look'd upon as an attempt to bring back Poetry into its right channel."[72]

Occasional reference has been made to the fact that Blake at one time owned a copy of the first edition of Percy's *Reliques of Ancient Poetry.* His copy, formerly a part of the library of George Herbert Palmer but now in the Wellesley College Library, bears on the flyleaf the inscription, not in Blake's handwriting:

> Mary Ann Linnell
> The gift of M[r] W. Blake.

A typewritten note pasted inside the front cover reads: "First edition—A copy given by the poet Blake to Mary Ann (Budden), second wife of the painter, John Linnell, with whom Blake became intimate in 1818, and for whom he engraved his Illustrations to the book of Job." Volume I shows that the first seventy-four pages have been well used, but the section from page 161 to the end, given to the ballads associated with Shakespeare, has had very hard usage. The other two volumes show no particular use, making it seem probable that they have been added to the set since Blake's ownership. In Volume I there are numerous emendations in the text of *The Aged Lover Renounceth Love,* done in Blake's handwriting. Blake's use of the *Reliques* is seen in these external details, but his knowledge of the collection is further manifest in the reflections of it in his poetry, demonstrating the error Damon made in saying that the "influence of Percy is limited entirely to the use of the old and virile ballad form."[73]

The most interesting influence of the *Reliques* is found in Blake's *Mad Song.* It shows the influence of no one single poem, but is a compound of many. There are six "mad songs" in Percy's second volume, all written from the point of view of the first person, as is Blake's *Mad Song.* The second one, *The Distracted Puritan,* is of religious content, and except for the rhythm of a few lines seems to have been unused by Blake. The broad humor of the first one, *Old Tom of Bedlam,* affected Blake's poem in no way. The general theme of all but *The Distracted Puritan* parallels the theme of Blake's *Mad Song.* All emphasize the frantic, tortuous nature of madness; all seek pity for their woe. The last four songs attribute madness to love, or to being in love. There is nothing in Blake's poem that speaks of love; rather there is a suggestion that the madness is over his poetry. The first stanza of *The Lunatic Lover* puts emphasis upon the nighttime, in witches being abroad, and moonlight. *Old Tom of Bedlam* has the lines:

> Through the world I wander night and day . . .
>
> . . . .
>
> For time will stay for no man:
>> (II, 344, ll. 9, 15.)

Blake wrote:

> After night I do croud,
> And with night will go;
>> (p. 15, ll. 19–20.)

One of the strange fancies of *The Lunatic Lover* is:

> Methinks in a spangled cloud
>   I see her enthroned on high,
> Then to her I crie aloud,
>   And labour to reach the sky.
>   (II, 351, ll. 37–40.)

> .   .   .   .

> To the elysian shades I post
>   In hopes to be freed from care,
> Where many a bleeding ghost
>   Is hovering in the air.
>   (II, 352, ll. 61–64.)

From *The Distracted Lover* come similar ideas:

> Furies tear me,
> Quickly bear me
> To the dismal shades below!
>   Where yelling and howling.
>   And grumbling, and growling,
> Strike the ear with horrid woe.
>   (II, 356, ll. 25–30.)[74]

This imagery, with part of the phrasing, Blake turned into:

> . . . My notes are driven:
> They strike the ear of night,

> .   .   .   .   .   .

> Like a fiend in a cloud
> With howling woe,
>   (p. 15, ll. 12–13, 17–18.)

The phrase, "like a fiend in a cloud," Blake used twice later, both times in versions of *Infant Sorrow:*

> My mother groan'd! my father wept.
> Into the dangerous world I leapt;
> Helpless, naked, piping loud:
> Like a fiend hid in a cloud.[75]

The *Lunatic Lover* also has

> I lye on the barren soil,
>> And bitterly complain:
> Till slumber hath quieted me,
>> In sorrow I sigh and weep;
>>> (II, 352, ll. 43–46.)

The Lady Distracted with Love has, "My pulse beats a dead march for lost repose" (II, 354, l. 22), and *The Distracted Lover* has

> I GO to the Elysian shade,
>> Where sorrow ne'er shall wound me;
> Where nothing shall my rest invade,
>>> (II, 385, ll. 1–3.)

Blake's use of these ideas is in his opening lines, as a sort of invocation:

> Come hither, Sleep,
> And my griefs unfold: (p. 15, ll. 3–4.)

Blake rephrased the lines from *Old Tom of Bedlam:*

> In vaine with cryes
> I rent the skyes
> For pity is not common. (II, 344, ll. 16–18.)

as

> Lo! to the vault
> Of paved heaven
> With sorrow fraught
> My notes are driven: (p. 15, ll. 9–12.)

The storm described in *The Lady Distracted with Love* is utilized in Blake's *Mad Song.* The first has

> Cold, cold despair, disguis'd like snow and rain,
> Falls on my breast; bleak winds in tempests blow;
>> (II, 354, ll. 19–20.)

Blake wrote:

> They [my notes] make mad the roaring winds,
> And with tempests play. (p. 15, ll. 15–16.)

When Blake wrote:

> For light doth seize my brain
> With frantic pain. (p. 15, ll. 23–24.)

he but restated more figuratively Tom of Bedlam's complaint:

> Mad Tom is come into the world againe
> To see if he can cure his distempered braine.
>   (II, 344, ll. 3–4.)

Blake could hardly have read the mad songs in the *Reliques* without recalling the words of King Lear as the storm raged around him. King Lear said:

> . . . the tempest in my mind
> Doth from my senses take all feeling else
> Save what beats there. (III, iv, 12–14.)

Edgar, disguised as the shivering "Tom o' Bedlam," complained of the "foul fiend" who misled him, and repeated "Tom's a-cold." (III, iv, 50–59.) Hence Blake's opening lines:

> The wild winds weep
> And the night is a-cold; (p. 15, ll. 1–2.)

seem more reminiscent of Shakespeare than of the *Reliques*.

In rhythm, Blake definitely played a variation upon the fourth stanza of *Old Tom of Bedlam:*

> When me he spyed,
> Away he hyed,
> For time will stay for no man:
> In vain with cryes
> I rent the skyes,
> For pity is not common. (II, 344, ll. 13–18.)

Blake's handling of these details within *Mad Song* illustrates again what he meant by seeing with a "double vision"; he dis-

cerned in the spirits and fiends lurking in surrounding objects
a life and a meaning which lifted his personifications above
their conventional and abstract nature. The number and order
of lines as well as the rhyme scheme differ, but the meter,
which is more important for the effect, is very like Blake's.
Saintsbury has eulogized Blake's *Mad Song* in his history of
prosody as showing "a new birth of prosody." He based his
judgment upon the pure verse-effect, undivorced from thought
and yet independent of it, upon the "ineffable music" which
was prosodic rather than musical, upon the "true blend of
freedom and order." Saintsbury considered it a "marvel forever" that Blake, with delicacy and unerringness, effected freedom and variety in the interchange of metrical units.[76] De
Selincourt, in contradiction to his feeling against Ossian's
power over the *Poetical Sketches,* praised *Mad Song* for the
haunting music with which the "turbid passion of the maniac"
is so sympathetically heard in the wildness of night that the
demented one, hugging his anguish, turns from "the sweet
comforts of day."[77] The enthusiastic response which Blake's
Mad Song aroused from both Saintsbury and De Selincourt
indicates how well Blake reinvested the old with new cogency;
but both critics seem unaware of how much of the old songs
became a part of the new. In ideas, in imagery, in phrasing,
in rhythm, Blake's debt to no one was more direct than that of
his *Mad Song* to Percy's *Reliques.*[78]

Gilchrist says that Blake sang old ballads in youth.[79] They
doubtless were from other sources besides the *Reliques,* and
to them Blake owed his own attempt at balladry, if not certain aspects of some of his lyrics. In the *Reliques* is the poem,
The Friars of Orders Gray, a medley of fragments of old poetry out of which Percy made a composite poem. Knowing the
manner of its composition may have led Blake to imitate it.
The general theme of "true love"[80] is that of "My silks and
fine array"[81] where the test of true love is the same, and where
the manner and tone of Blake's lament are very similar to
those of the ballads. Blake's *Gwin, King of Norway,* in the
metrical pattern of a ballad as illustrated in *The Child of Elle*
or in *Edom o' Gordon,* has a number of details that show the
influence of *Hardyknute* in the *Reliques.* In the first place

there are similar settings of the castle high on a hill with the
Norse enemy spread out in great numbers below. Where
Hardyknute had a leading character described as

> Proud Norse with giant body tall,
>   Braid Shoulder and arms strong,
>   (II, 98, ll. 225–226.)

Blake described his character, "Godred the giant rous'd himself." (p. 19, l. 13.) There is a similar summons to battle. In
Hardyknute it is described thus:

> He hes tane a horn as grene as glass,
>   And gien fine sounds sae shrill,
> That treis in grene wod schuke thereat,
>   Sae loud rang ilka hill. (II, 91, ll. 61–64.)

Blake summarized these ideas in *Gwin, King of Norway:*

> Godred the giant rous'd himself
>   From sleeping in his cave;
> He shook the hills, and in the clouds
>   The troubl'd banners wave. (p. 19, ll. 13–16.)

Similarly the consequent action was condensed by Blake:

> And now the raging armies rush'd,
>   Like warring mighty seas; (p. 22, ll. 1–2.)

from the passage in *Hardyknute:*

> "Zonder my valiant sons and ferss
>   Our raging revers wait
> On the unconquerit Scottish swaird
>   To try with us their fate."
>   (II, 95, ll. 157–160.)

The outcome of the battle was told in *Hardyknute:*

> But bludy bludy was the field,
>   Or that lang day was done.
>   (II, 96, ll. 183–184.)

The same emphasis is kept and made even greater by Blake:

> The god of war is drunk with blood,
>   The earth doth faint and fail;
> The stench of blood makes sick the heav'ns;
>   Ghosts glut the throat of hell!
>   (p. 23, ll. 1–2.)

When the summons was sent forth to rouse the forces to action in the Scottish ballad, there is similarity to the summons to battle in *Gwin, King of Norway*. The response in each case is prompt. Many of these details linking Blake's ballad to *Hardyknute* are combined with details derivative of Chatterton and Ossian.

Blake's other ballad, *Fair Elenor,* is of an entirely different type. It, too, owes much to Percy's *Reliques*. Elenor, spelled variously, is the name of the queen or lady in *Sir Aldingar, Hardyknute, Queen Eleanor's Confession, Fair Rosamund, Lord Thomas,* and *Fair Ellinor*. Blake altered the situation, found in *Sir Aldingar,* of the attempt to dishonor the lady by having the severed head of Elenor's husband warn her of such a purpose of the "cursed duke." *Fair Elenor* has a perfectly conventional ballad ending. Christabelle, in *Sir Cauline,* expired over the body of her dead lover as Elenor did over the head of her husband. Christabelle

> . . . layde her pale cold cheek to his,
> And thus she made her moane. (I, 53, ll. 294–295.)

while Elenor "sank upon the steps on the cold stone her pale cheeks." (p. 7, ll. 5–6.) So end *Fair Margaret* and *Sweet William's Ghost, Sir John Grehme,* and *Barbara Allen*. Blake's title has a model in *Fair Margaret* or *Fair Rosamund*.

Other details of *Fair Elenor* link Blake to the Gothic tales. The machinery of them—the haunted, echoing vaults, the underground passages, the spectres, the chill and the gloom—was borrowed by many writers of prose and verse. It was a prevailing fashion,[82] nowhere so much at its best as in Walpole's *The Castle of Otranto* to which certain details of *Fair Elenor* relate directly. The passages involved from *The Castle of Otranto* are stated consecutively so that one can see, in their

accumulative effect, more clearly the details drawn upon for
Fair Elenor.

When Manfred made his declaration to Isabelle:[83]

> She shrieked, and started from him. . . .* That Lady, whose
> resolution had given way to terror the moment she had quitted
> *Manfred,* continued her flight to the bottom of the principal stair-
> case. There she stopped, not knowing, whither to direct her steps,
> nor how to escape. . . . As these thoughts passed rapidly through
> her mind, she recollected a subterraneous passage, which led from
> the vaults of the castle. . . .† An awful silence reigned through-
> out these subterraneous regions, except, now and then, some blasts
> of wind that shook the doors. . . . Every murmur struck her with
> new terror; . . . She trod as softly as impatience would give her
> leave,—yet frequently stopped, and listened to see if she was fol-
> lowed. In one of these moments she thought she heard a sigh. She
> shuddered, and recoiled a few paces. In a moment she thought she
> heard the step of some person. Her blood curdled; . . . Yet the
> sound seemed not to come from behind; . . . and the steps she
> heard were too distinct to proceed from the way she had come.
> . . .‡ She was ready to sink under her apprehensions . . . she
> felt for the door; and having found it, entered trembling into the
> vault, from whence she had heard the sigh and steps. . . .§ She
> advanced eagerly toward the chasm, when she discerned a human
> form, standing close against the wall. She shrieked, believing it
> the ghost of her betrothed Conrad . . . ‖ Frederick's blood froze
> in his veins. . . .¶

Elenor's progress through the castle in the first three stanzas
of *Fair Elenor* parallels the details of action above. In the fifth
stanza there is the sound of footsteps "of one that fled." The
apprehensions, the shrieking, the being "froze to stone with
fear," the "fleeing from fear" are all reproduced in *Fair
Elenor*. Conrad is the name Blake gave the lover whose ghost
returned to the lady in *Woe, Cried the Muse,* a fragment of
prose, not included in the *Poetical Sketches,* but generally
thought to have been written before 1777.[84] It is little more
than a practice sketch for the prose that was included in the
Poetical Sketches.

That Blake was not interested in the "Gothic" details except as narrative accessories seems clear from the change in

the emphasis and in the effect of the story. He centered attention on Elenor, not so much by her flight, animated by fears, as by the mistake the murderer made in not recognizing her when he thrust her own husband's head into her arms for delivery to herself. The ballad's interest thenceforth is in the emotional response to her full awareness of the burden she carried. Had Blake been merely copying, he could not have gone further than other poems on kindred subjects had gone —the mere externals of "Gothic" setting. As it was, he gave the imaginative realization of Elenor's tragedy; and the lyrical rendering of her poignant lament,[85] kept within bounds that "Gothic" emotions knew not, lifts it above its derivations into a plane of originality. *Fair Elenor* illustrates the curious refinement that a thorough knowledge of old ballads made of the cruder substance prevalent as "Gothic" poetry and fiction.

Except for the work of Chatterton and Macpherson, such are the principal evidences of how Blake's *Poetical Sketches* was affected by the writers of the eighteenth century whose imaginative energy was great enough to have fired Blake's own imagination. The musical notes, the bright images, the potent ideas which came to him from the best in his century quickened the quality of genuine poetry. One may indeed say with Mr. Eliot: "He was very eighteenth century."

CHAPTER VII

"IMAGINATION KINDLED AT ANTIQUE FIRES"

O NE of the most significant contacts which Blake made with the poetic work of his own time has been over-looked by those who have written about him since Gilchrist published his *Life* in 1863. This oversight is not a matter of accepting early authority without verification, for Gilchrist, who is the only early writer to comment on the sub-ject, did not err in his statement, except that it did not go far enough when he said: "In a few of the poems, the influence of Blake's contemporary, Chatterton,—of the *Poems of Row-ley, i.e.,* is visible."[1] Symons, recognizing that the influence of Chatterton was present, explained that it was an influence "which could hardly have found its way to Blake before the year 1777."[2] Damon went farther in saying that the *Adver-tisement* to the *Poetical Sketches* made a misstatement because "if these poems were written before 1777, Blake could not have seen Chatterton's *Miscellanies* (June, 1778) ; yet Chat-terton's *Godred Crovan, A Poem,* must, with Percy's *Reliques,* have been responsible for *Gwin, King of Norway. Gwin* was hastily written, and it is not at all in the style of the rest of the book. It seems likely that this was a late piece included with Blake's earlier poems ; . . ."[3] Keynes accepted Damon's position, as did Mona Wilson.[4] De Selincourt, with more fi-nality, asserted in his lecture of 1933 : "Of his contemporaries Chatterton alone had gained metrical effects comparable with his, and Blake, when he wrote his *Poetical Sketches,* had read no Chatterton."[5]

It is true that Chatterton's *Miscellanies* did not appear un-til 1778, and that his first volume of poetry, the so-called *Rowley Poems,* did not appear until February 8, 1777.[6] Within a year there were three editions of the latter. With the third edition (1778) an appendix was issued in which the editor,

Tyrwhitt, endeavored to prove that the poems were not Rowley's but Chatterton's. It is true, besides, that Blake owned a copy of this edition in which his autograph is written in ink on the title-page.[7] Blake's first acquaintance with Chatterton was not with this third edition, or even with the *Miscellanies* of 1778. The work of Chatterton which exerted influence upon Blake's *Poetical Sketches* appeared nine years before the first collected edition. The *Town and Country Magazine* printed the following, all sent from Bristol, and all signed, "D.B.":

1. *Letter on Saxon Tinctures.* I, 100. February, 1769.
2. *Ethelgar. A Saxon Poem.* I, 144–146. March, 1769.
3. *Kenrick. Translated from the Saxon.* I, 174–175. April, 1769.
4. *Cerdick. Translated from the Saxon.* I, 233–235. May, 1769.
5. *Saxon Achievements.* I, 245. May, 1769.
6. *Elinoura and Juga.* I, 273. May, 1769. This was modernized in the June number by "S. W. A. Aged 16"—probably Chatterton himself.
7. *Godred Crovan. A Poem. Composed by Dopnal Syrric Scheld of Godred Crovan, King of the Isle of Man.* I, 425–428. August, 1769.
8. *The Hirlas. Composed by Bleythyn, Prince of North Wales.* I, 574–575. October, 1769.
9. *Antiquity of Christmas Games.* I, 623–625. December, 1769.
10. *The Hirlas. Translated from the Ancient British of Owen Cyfeliog, Prince of Powys.* I, 683. Supplement, 1769.
11. *Elegy to the Memory of Mr. Thomas Phillips of Fairford.* I, 711. Supplement, 1769.
12. *Gorthmund. Translated from the Saxon.* II, 486–489. September, 1770.

"D.B." was a pseudonym[8] of Chatterton which he used frequently. In November, 1769, the editor of the *Town and Country Magazine* announced in *Acknowledgments to our Correspondents,* "D.B. *of Bristol's Favours will be gladly re-*

ceived."[9] This reflects somewhat the readers' approval of the new magazine which made its appearance in January, 1769, after elaborate preliminary announcements in other periodicals.

These contributions were not the only works of Chatterton available to Blake before 1778. In the *London Magazine* for May, 1770 (XXXIX, 268–269, 320–322), there appeared two of the *African Eclogues: Narva and Mored* and *The Death of Nicou.* These were both signed "C." The third *African Eclogue, Heccar and Gaira,* was printed in February, 1770 (I, 86–87) in the *Court and City Magazine,* where also in July, 1770, appeared *An African Song* (I, 326–327). In the *Lady's Magazine* for January, 1771 (II, 271), was printed *Cuthold, Translated from the Saxon,* signed "Asaphides," another of Chatterton's pseudonyms. The *Westminster Magazine* printed in January, 1775, the *Song to Ælla,* which was reprinted in Evans's *Old Ballads* in 1777 (I, 32–33). *Ælla, The Tragycal Enterlude,* first appeared in the edition of 1777; but the famous song from it, "O Sing unto my roundelay," was first printed January, 1775, in the *Westminster Gazette,* and was reprinted in April, 1777, in the *Gentleman's and London Magazine* (XLVII, 299), a fact not previously recorded. It was modernized in 1783, and set to music for three voices by Stephen Paxon. In June, 1772, *The Bristowe Tragedie, or The Execution of Sir C. Bawdin* was published[10] in apparently two states, for the copy in the British Museum has two title-pages, one stating that it would be sold by M. Goldsmith at No. 20 Paternoster Row, and the other that it would be sold by T. Newbery in St. Paul's Churchyard. Mr. Meyerstein has a copy with only the Goldsmith imprint.[11] Five hundred copies of the Newbery imprint seem to have been published at half a crown each.[12] Finally, a series of twelve letters signed "A Hunter of Oddities" appeared[13] in the *Town and Country Magazine* during its first year. These, with other prose pieces during 1769–70, signed by various names, have not been enumerated because from them there is no sign of influence upon Blake's *Poetical Sketches.*

Apart from these printed sources, which after all comprise a goodly number of examples of Chatterton's writings which Blake could easily have known, Blake had other chances to become interested in Chatterton. The activity of the Juvenile Club in Bristol had helped to draw attention to the contributions which came from Bristol to the London magazines. How alert Blake was to poetic endeavors elsewhere is signified by an allusion in *Jerusalem:*

> Bath, healing City! whose wisdom, in midst of Poetic Fervour, mild spoke thro' the Western Porch :[14]

If the ambitious efforts of Lady Miller and her followers at Bath were known to him, Blake certainly would not have missed anything to be learned of Chatterton whose untimely death produced such a tangled web of public attack and defense, of evasion and forthright acceptance, of criticism and laudation that it caught, among many others, Walpole, Gray, Johnson, George Cumberland (one of Blake's later friends), Herbert Croft, and Thomas Warton. Anyone alert to news could not have missed this influence.[15] Blake probably made an allusion to Chatterton in *Jerusalem* when he said, "Bristol & Bath, listen to my words, & ye Seventeen, give ear!"[16]

Furthermore, at Basire's home much discussion would have gone on among the group of antiquarians who figured in the controversy. The president of the Society of Antiquaries was Jeremiah Milles, who later (1792) brought out an edition of the *Rowley Poems.* Another prominent antiquarian was the Reverend Michael Lort, whose impartial investigations furnished some of the most authentic information available. Still another whom Blake could have heard talk at Basire's was Jacob Bryant. It is to be noted that Blake referred to him by name in the *Descriptive Catalogue* in his discussion of the picture, "The Ancient Britons."[17] Bryant, in 1781, published his *Observations upon the Poems of Thomas Rowley.*[18] Blake gave further proof that he listened to much controversy on the subject of Rowley and Chatterton; in *An Island in the Moon,* written within a few years of the *Poetical Sketches* and obviously intended to satirize people whom he heard discuss all manner of subjects, Blake, with something of the abruptness of transition and inconsequence of argument which Lewis Carroll was to immortalize many years later, reported what impressed him about all the learned talk to which he listened:

Here Aradobo look'd Astonish'd & ask'd if he understood Engraving.

Obtuse Angle Answer'd, indeed he did.

"Well," said the other, "he was as great as Chatterton."

Tilly Lally turn'd round to Obtuse Angle & ask'd who it was that was as great as Chatterton.

.   .   .   .

"Pray," said Aradobo, "is Chatterton a Mathematician?"

"No," said Obtuse Angle. "How can you be so foolish as to "think he was?"

"Oh, I did not think he was—I only ask'd," said Aradobo.

"How could you think he was not, & ask if he was?" said Obtuse Angle.

"O no, Sir. I did not think he was, before you told me, but "afterwards I thought he was not."

.   .   .   .

Then Aradobo began, "In the first place, I think, I think in "the first place that Chatterton was clever at Fissie Follogy, "Pistinology, Aridology, Arography, Transmography, Phizog- "raphy, Hogamy, Hatomy, & hall that, but, in the first place, he "eat very little, wickly—that is, he slept very little, which he "brought into a consumsion; & what was that that he took? Fis- "sic or somethink,—& so died!"[19]

A second important influence is that of the work of James Macpherson, perhaps better known as Ossian. From the day in 1760, when the slender volume of seventy pages, named *Fragments of Ancient Poetry, Collected in the Highlands of Scotland, and translated from the Gaelic or Erse Language,* appeared, until long after the Highland Society printed (1807) the long-delayed original Gaelic texts, controversy had raged over the genuineness of *Fragments* in 1760, of *Fingal* in 1762, and of *Temora* in 1763. The influence of these works spread far and wide. There were imitations, parodies, paraphrases, and metrical renderings by many who had an ear for Ossianic cadences. Some even found new treasures in the Highlands, as Thomas Bridges who announced in the *Advertisement* to his poem, *The Battle of the Genii,* "from the Erse" that ". . . the great MILTON took his Hint of the Battle of the Angels, from the original Erse, in which it was written, and stiled the

Battle of the Genii; . . ."[20] Still another made Ossian an Israelite in whom dwelt no guile.[21] What Walpole called the "flimsy giantry of Ossian"[22] made its way everywhere.

The exact dependence of Blake upon Ossian is difficult to determine because Chatterton was an intermediary. The work of Chatterton that was printed in the *Town and Country Magazine,* generally called his Saxon pieces, was directly imitative of Ossian. The internal evidence found in the examination of this dual relationship seems to show that the greater influence of Ossian upon Blake came through Chatterton, although there was some direct use made of Ossianic matter.

In general, one may say that from Ossian Chatterton's Saxon pieces drew the substance and plan of the narratives: their fighting chiefs, the fearful slaughter, the ominous and omnipresent cloud effects, and the tempests. From Ossian, also, Chatterton's narratives took figures of speech, especially those based upon objects in nature such as rocks, trees, and meteors, and the exaggeration and monotonous repetition of a detail, which singly would have had considerable force and often much charm. Thence, also, came the songs in praise of the hero, and the exhortations. Finally there was much indebtedness in vocabulary. To understand Blake's connection, one must consider in addition to such basic matter as the contents just enumerated the treatment of such details as, in particular, the manner and tone and effect of their use.

An analysis of Ossian is complicated by the repetitions so that it is difficult to find from any one passage what an accumulated mass of them will convey. This can be seen first in the fact that the scenes of battle and tempest are inevitably portrayed together: "As autumn's dark storms pour from two echoing hills, towards each other approach the heroes.—As two dark streams from high rocks meet, and mix and roar on the plain; loud, rough and dark in battle meet Lochlin and Innis-fail. Chief mixed his strokes with chief, and man with man; steel, clanging, sounded on steel, helmets are cleft on high. Blood bursts and smoaks around.—Strings twang on the polished yews. Darts rush along the sky. Spears fall like the circles of light that gild the stormy face of night. As the troubled noise of the ocean when roll the waves on high; as the last peal of the thunder of heaven, such is the noise of battle. Though Cormac's hundred bards were there to give the war to song; feeble were the voices of a hundred bards to send the deaths to future times. For many were the falls of the heroes; and wide poured the blood of the valiant." (I, 18–19.) "As roll a thousand waves to the rocks, so Swaran's host came on; as meets a rock a thousand waves, so Innis-fail met Swaran. Death raises all his voices around, and mixes with the sound of shields.—Each hero is a pillar of darkness, and the sword a beam of fire in his hand. The field echoes from wing to wing, as a hundred hammers that rise by turns on the red son of the furnace." (I, 21–22.) "Such were our words, when Gaul's loud voice came growing on the wind. He waved on high the sword of his father, and rushed to death and wounds. As waves white-bubbling over the deep come swelling, roaring on; as rocks of ooze meet roaring waves: so foes attacked and fought. Man met with man, and steel with steel. Shields sound; men fall. As a hundred hammers on the son of the furnace, so rose, so rung their swords. . . . I rejoiced in my secret soul, when his sword flamed over the slain. They fled amain through Lena's heath: and we pursued and slew. As stones that bound from rock to rock; as axes in echoing woods; as thunder rolls from hill to hill in dismal broken peals; so blow succeeded to blow, and death to death, from the hand of Oscar and mine." (I, 79–80.) It was the noise of battle that Macpherson emphasized—noise of shields clanging, of rolling waves breaking on rocky shores, of thunder, of axes felling trees, of shrieks of dying warriors[23]—but a battle was never represented without also the presentation of the disturbed elements of nature. Macpherson must have visualized an army as just another item in a struggle of the elements; repeatedly he so described the onrush of battle: "Then dismal, roaring, fierce, and deep the gloom of battle rolled along; as mist that is poured on the valley, when storms invade the silent sunshine of heaven. The chief moves before in arms, like an angry ghost before a cloud; when meteors inclose him with fire; and the dark winds are in his hand." (I, 39.) Active and aggressive forces of war are repeatedly compared to the movement of sea or streams in Macpherson's work. At one time he wrote: "The foe came forth in arms. The strife is mixed at Rath-col, like the roar of streams." (II, 218.) At another time, he wrote: "Where broken hosts are rolled away, like seas before the wind." (II, 101.) Still another time he wrote: "He drew his sword, a flame, from his side; and bade the battle move.—The tribes, like ridgy waves, dark pour their strength around." (II, 69.)

Compare now what Chatterton and Blake did with such details as these several extracts have exhibited. In *Kenrick*, Chatterton described the pursuit of Mervin by Egward: "Like the rage of a tempest was the noise of the battle: like the roaring of the torrent, gushing from the brow of the lofty mountain." (*Town and Country Magazine*, I, 175.) Blake related in *Gwin, King of Norway:*

> And now the raging armies rush'd
> Like warring mighty seas; (p. 22, ll. 1–2.)

Chatterton reported in *Godred Crovan:* ". . . like the noise of torrents rolling down the high mountains, is the noise of the flight." (*T. and Co. Mag.,* I, 426.) In Blake's *Gwin, King of Norway* this appeared as:

> The trampling horse, and clanging arms
> Like rushing mighty floods! (p. 20, ll. 3–4.)

Chatterton drew many Ossianic details together in briefer form. In *Godred Crovan* he wrote: "The son of Henna drew forth his band to the plan [*sic*]; like a tempest they fell upon the foe; they were astonished, they fled." (*T. and Co. Mag.,* I, 427.) In *King Edward the Third*, Blake wrote:

> Our fathers move in firm array to battle,
> The savage monsters rush like roaring fire;
> Like as a forest roars with crackling flames,
> When the red lightning, borne by furious storms,
> Lights on some woody shore; the parched heavens
> Rain fire into the molten raging sea!
> (p. 54, ll. 7–12.)

Into this was introduced the idea of the effects of fire and heat, which were in Chatterton's lines in *Godred Crovan:* ". . . like the fires of the earth he burnt up the ranks of the foe."

(*T. and Co. Mag.*, I, 428) and in *Kenrick:* "like red lightnings of heaven he burnt up the ranks of the enemy." (*T. and Co. Mag.*, I, 175.) When Blake wrote in *King Edward the Third:*

> The smoaking trees are strewn upon the shore,
> Spoil'd of their verdure! O how oft have they
> Defy'd the storm that howled o'er their heads!
>   (p. 54, ll. 13–15.)

he gave an interesting example of the metamorphosis of subject matter. Macpherson used details with abandon. Without loss of any significant aspect, Chatterton selected those which he needed for a dramatic but pictorial narrative; and, while he fell into the error of repetition for the sake of attaining the style of Ossian, he still economized in substance. Blake, with the eye of an artist, perceived qualities which he could fuse with his own symbols into a new vision. This same compression is seen again in a comparison between Chatterton's passage in *Godred Crovan* and one in Blake's *Gwin, King of Norway:* ". . . the warriors are like the stars of the winter night. The noise of a multitude is heard from the hills: Godred set his troops in order for war, they are seen on the brow of the hill. . . . Godred Crovan bent his anlace on the shield: the warriors upon the mountain heard the sound of silver shield, swift as the hunted stag they fly to war, they hear the noise of battle, the shout of onset swells in the wind, the loud din of the war increases, as the thunder rolling from afar; they fly down the mountains, where the fragments of the sharp rock are scattered around. . . ." (*T. and Co. Mag.*, I, 426, 428.) Blake used a similar detail when he represented the taking of the shield by the leader (a different action, but the same intent), the speedy rallying of the soldiers, the sound of battle, the suggestion of thunder, and the descent from a hill. These Blake recorded:

> Down Bleron's hills they dreadful rush,
>   Their cry ascends the clouds;
> The trampling horses, and clanging arms
>   Like rushing mighty floods!
>   (p. 20, ll. 1–4.)

The significance of the action which Blake phrased as "reared his shield" is seen in another part of *Godred Crovan:* "The wolf of Norway beat his anlace on his silver shield; the sons of war assembled around him. Swain of the cleft-hill shook the spear on his left; and Harald the Black, the lion of Iceland on his right, dyed in gore. . . . Swain prepares for war; he sounds the brazen helmet, his followers lift high the deadly spear . . . he seized the flaming banner, and sounds the silver shield." (*T. and Co. Mag.,* I, 425.) In *Gwin, King of Norway,* Blake wrote·

> Then suddenly each seiz'd his spear,
> And clashing steel does ring.
> (p. 20, ll. 23–24.)

Chatterton, with a similar scene in mind in *The Hirlas,* wrote: "The warriors of the hill stood round their chief," (*T. and Co. Mag.,* I, 583) which Blake retained in *Gwin, King of Norway:*

> Like reared stones around the grave
> They stand around the King;
> (p. 20, ll. 21–22.)

This is a combination of two ideas in Ossian. In *Cathloda,* Macpherson wrote: "The chiefs stood silent around, as the stones of Loda, on their hill." (II, 258.)

In the longer passages from Chatterton and Blake quoted above, there are a few other details to be stressed. The use made of "hills" is very curious. In neither Ossian nor Chatterton's Saxon pieces does one ever see actual hills. Chatterton added many descriptive touches of nature which showed that he saw and felt more about nature than Macpherson;[24] yet his "hills" never became more real than those in Ossian. A "hill" is merely a vague generalized place, and whether it was meant to serve any purpose, as an eminence, a fortress, or a power, is at no place clear, definite, or convincing. This generalized conception Blake retained, and, unlike what he usually did, he seemed not to have made of it anything more than the Ossianic generality—indistinct and unreal. Two details, however, link his usage more nearly to Chatterton's than to Macpherson's. In *Gwin, King of Norway,* Blake wrote:

> The battle faints, and bloody men
>   Fight upon hills of slain. (p. 22, ll. 19–20.)

The phrase, "hills of slain," was not Ossian's; Chatterton used it often. In *Godred Crovan* Chatterton wrote: ". . . like a tempest they rage, like a rock he repels their assault; hills of slain arise around him, . . . victory sat on his helm, death on his anlace. Wilver . . . shakes the crooked sword as he rages upon the hills of the slain. . . ." (*T. and Co. Mag.,* I, 425, 428.) Blake again in *The Couch of Death* wrote "the bosom of the lofty hill drank in the silent dew," (p. 62, ll. 23–24) which is Chatterton's "lofty hill" in *Cerdick,* "The rose-crowned dawn dances on the top of the lofty hill" (*T. and Co. Mag.,* I, 233), and in *Ethelgar:* ". . . and the black clouds sit on the brow of the lofty hill; . . . thou shalt stand firm in the days of temptation, as the lofty hill of Kinwulph; . . . Edwina stood on the brow of the lofty hill, like an oak in the spring. . . ." (*T. and Co. Mag.,* I, 144, 145.)

It is a strange fact that, for all the fighting and slaying that were depicted in the Ossianic works, there was not the emphasis put upon blood that was put by Chatterton and Blake. Slaughter was as generalized a matter in Ossian as was a hill. Once in *Comala* Macpherson wrote, "O Carun, roll thy streams of blood, for the chief of the people fell." (I, 129.) This Blake rendered in *Gwin, King of Norway:*

> A sea of blood; nor can the eye
>   See to the trembling shore!
>   (p. 22, ll. 7–8.)

Another time, in *Croma,* Macpherson phrased it, "Days! wherein I fought; and conquered in the field of blood." (I, 348.) This Blake phrased in *Gwin, King of Norway:*

> The husbandman does leave his plow,
>   To wade thro' fields of gore;
>   (p. 21, ll. 1–2.)

Chatterton also wrote "sea of blood" and "lake of blood" in *Godred Crovan* and in *The Death of Nicou*.[25] In *Godred Crovan* there was another detail that was kept by Blake: "Tatwalin sat by his side, he sung sweet as the birds of spring, he fought like the hungry lion . . . like two wolves they rage in the war, their shields are red with blood." (*T. and Co. Mag.,* I, 425, 428.) In *King Edward the Third,* Blake used the same details:

> Your ancestors came . . .
> (Like lions . . .)
> Heated with war, fill'd with blood of Greeks,
> With helmets hewn, and shields covered with gore . . .
>
>   .   .   .   .
>
> . . . wild men
> Naked and roaring like lions,
>   (pp. 53, ll. 10–14; 54, l. 4.)

To Chatterton's particular phrasing of the same elements of battle, Blake was indebted. Where Chatterton wrote in *Godred Crovan:* ". . . Hear, ye sons of blood, whilst the horn of mirth is refreshing your souls, . . . Morvor and Essyr raged like sons of blood, thousands fell around them. . . . Sons of blood! said the immortal Wecca . . ." (*T. and Co. Mag.,* I, 425, 426, 427), Blake wrote in *Gwin, King of Norway,* "The num'rous sons of blood." (p. 19, l. 18.) This same association of ideas and the unusual phrasing in *Cerdick* point to Chatterton as the source of Blake's lines in *Gwin, King of Norway:*

> The god of war is drunk with blood,
>   The earth doth faint and fail;
> The stench of blood makes sick the heav'ns;
>   Ghosts glut the throat of hell!
>   (p. 23, ll. 1–4.)

The lines from *Cerdick* are: ". . . the enemies are swept away; the Gods are glutted with blood, and peace arises from the solitary groves." (*T. and Co. Mag.,* I, 234.) The phrase in Chatterton's *The Hirlas,* "his spear flies to thy breast, and

his followers drink thy blood" (*T. and Co. Mag.,* I, 683),
Blake altered somewhat to

> Earth smokes with blood, and groans and
>   shakes,
> To drink her children's gore, (p. 22, ll. 5–6.)

Ossian frequently used another detail of warfare which is illustrated by this passage from *Fingal:* "The sword of Fingal
descended, and cleft his shield in twain." (I, 96.) Chatterton,
with his ability to add realism to what he took from Ossian,
wrote in *Godred Crovan:* "Harald the Black stood on the
bridge, he swelled the river with gore; he divides the head of
Edmund. . . ." (*T. and Co. Mag.,* I, 425.) Blake, with more
vividness still, used the same action and the same choice of
words in his *Gwin, King of Norway:*

> Down from the brow unto the breast
> Gordred his head divides! (p. 23, ll. 15–16.)[26]

Blake's *Gwin, King of Norway,* while it is forceful and
vivid in these details of warfare, has a reality as opposed to
artificial composition that gives a greater singleness of impression than anything he ever found in Ossian gave. To effect
this result, which surpassed his sources, Blake turned to account those qualities of the old ballads which gave more feeling and simplicity and directness than Macpherson ever knew.
The old ballads never shrank from things gruesome or bald
when they were a part of the scene. Such aspects exist in Ossian, but they are dimmed to indistinctness by Macpherson's
manner.

Perhaps no detail is more characteristic of Macpherson's
work than his use of "ghosts," of which examples are innumerable. One time "a thousand ghosts shriek at once on the
hollow wind" (I, 62); another "the ghosts of night shriek
afar." (I, 75.) They "fly on clouds and ride on the winds" or
"rest in caves and talk of mortal men." (I, 35.) Chatterton
mentioned few ghosts and then in quite a different manner.
His chiefs were as strong as the tower of Pendragon, as "furious as the souls of unburied warriors." (*T. and Co. Mag.,* I,

425.) Blake's usage in *Gwin, King of Norway* is closer to Ossian:

> When thousand deaths for vengeance cry
> And ghosts accusing groan! (p. 23, l. 9.)

Fingal pictures the scene for the ghosts as a "dark and stormy cloud, edged round with the red lightning of heaven." (I, 77.) This image appears in Blake's scene:

> Like the tall ghost of Barraton[27]
> Who sports in stormy sky,
>
> .　　.　　.　　.　　.　　.　　.
>
> Thro' the red fev'rous night.
> (pp. 21, ll. 9–10; 22, l. 16.)

Macpherson used "meteors" almost as commonly as "ghosts" and with much the same effect. Chatterton's use of the figure is so slight that Blake was probably affected by Ossian in his description:

> The King is seen raging afar,
> With all his men of might;
> Like blazing comets, scattering death[28]

One detail common to all three is the phrase, "lean on their spears," which probably came to Ossian from biblical[29] usage. Ossian described the pale-faced warrior: "he leaned on his spear and rolled his red eyes around." (I, 81.) "Cerdick leans upon his spear and sings the praises of the Gods." (*T. and Co. Mag.*, I, 234.) Blake wrote:

> Our fathers, sweating, lean on their spears
> and view
> The mighty dead.　　(p. 54, ll. 16–17.)[30]

So far most of the details have been shared in common by Macpherson, Chatterton, and Blake. A great many details Blake drew from one of his contemporaries, but not from both.

In *King Edward the Third* occurs an interesting phrase, "fame's wide trophied hall." Homer, Chaucer, and Spenser would seem possible sources for such a figure of speech, but in no one was anything found to justify concluding that Blake discovered the idea there. But from the recurrence as well as the dominance of the hall of the chieftain in Ossian, and from the association of ideas in certain passages, it is thought that Ossian probably gave Blake the figure of speech. For example from *Sul-malla* comes this passage: "Amidst the song we sat down, in Connor's echoing hall. . . . Not unmarked, said the maid, by Sul-malla, is the shield of Morven's king. It hangs high, in Conmor's hall, in memory of the past; when Fingal came to Cluba, in the days of other years." (II, 224, 225.) In *Temora,* where much was said of Ossian's hall, the fifth book begins: "Thou dweller between the shields that hang on high in Ossian's halls, descend from thy place, O harp, and let me hear thy voice."

In mood and setting, although not in phrasing, the last paragraph of *The Couch of Death* is reminiscent of the closing of *Temora:* "Evening came down on Moi-lena, Grey rolled the streams of the land. . . . Pleasant, from the way of the desert, the voice of music came. It seemed, at first, the noise of a stream, far-distant on its rocks. Slow it rolled along the hill like the ruffled wing of a breeze, when it takes the tufted beard of the rocks, in the still season of night." *The Couch of Death,* however, owes more to Chatterton than to Ossian. Macpherson rarely attempted anything tender or fanciful; rather he strove for sublimity and grandeur. Chatterton's imitations of Macpherson's work have many passages of almost idyllic simplicity and tone. These moods of Chatterton's Saxon pieces, and especially *Ethelgar,* imposed their effects upon Blake's *Couch of Death* as some comparisons will reveal. Blake wrote: "THE veiled Evening walked solitary down the western hills, and Silence reposed in the valley; the birds of day were heard in their nests, rustling in brakes and thickets; and the owl and bat flew round the darkening trees; all is silent when Nature takes her repose." (p. 60, ll. 1–6.) In *Godred Crovan* appeared the same ideas similarly expressed: "Tatwallin arose, and sung, 'When the flowers arose in the verdant meadows, when the birds of spring were heard in the grove of Thor, the son of Victa prepared his knights for war; . . .'" (*T. and Co. Mag.,* I, 427), as in *Cerdick,* too, appeared the following:

"The rose-crowned dawn dances on the top of the lofty hill. Arise, O Cerdick, from thy mossy bed, for the noise of chariots is heard in the valleys." (*T. and Co. Mag.,* I, 233.) This particular use of "hear" appears twice in *The Hirlas,* and once in *Ethelgar.* (*T. and Co. Mag.,* I, 573, 683.) Blake's use of "rustling" also appears in *Ethelgar:* ". . . his soul, like the lark, every morning ascended the skies, and sported in the clouds: when stealing down the steep mountain, wrapt in a shower of spangling dew, ev'ning came creeping to the plain, closing the flowers of the day, shaking her pearly showers upon the rustling trees; then was her voice heard in the grove, as the voice of the nightingale upon the hawthorne spray." This passage, so in accord in mood and feeling with *The Couch of Death,* especially emphasizes the passage in Blake's prose: "As the voice of an omen heard in the silent valley when the few inhabitants cling together." (p. 61, ll. 24–26.)

From the following passage in *Ethelgar* Blake may have taken the striking phrase, "the morning's brow," in *To Mrs. Ann Flaxman*[31] as well as a similar image to the one in *To Morning:* "The morn awoke the sun: who, stepping from the mountain's brow, shook his ruddy locks upon the shining dew; AElgar arose from sleep; he seized his sword and spear, and issued to the chace." (*T. and Co. Mag.,* I, 145.) The passage in *The Couch of Death,* beginning "O my son, my son, I know but little of the path thou goest! But lo, there is a God, who made the world; stretch out thy hand to Him" (p. 61, ll. 7–10) is in thought rather than phrasing a recollection, blended with biblical allusion, of the following in *Ethelgar:* "Know, O man! said a member of the blessed, to submit to the will of God; he is terrible as the face of the earth, when the waters sunk to their habitations; gentle as the sacred covering of the oak; secret as the bottom of the great deep; just as the rays of the morning. Learn that thou art a man, nor repine at the stroke of the Almighty, for God is as just as he is great." (*T. and Co. Mag.,* I, 146.)

In the passage from *Cerdick* quoted above, there was mention made of "chariots." This minor detail, slight in itself, illustrates the difference between Blake's relation to Ossian and his relation to Chatterton. In Ossian there is frequent reference to cars of the warriors, but the word "chariot" is not used except once when Macpherson referred to "two dark clouds that are the chariots of ghosts." (I, 66.) In *Fingal* one reads such passages as "The car, the car of battle comes, like the flame of death; the rapid car of Cuchullin, the noble son of Semo." (I, 16.) This car is fully described, as is each horse, Sulin-Sifadda and Dusronnel. Its sole purpose is to set off the hero, for it does not enter the battle nor appear again in the narrative. Similarly the heroes who often are described with the stock epithets, "car-borne"—the "car-borne Colmar," the "car-borne Lathmon," the "car-borne Clathan"[32]—are never seen in chariots. This is a stereotyped device of Macpherson's description and is used merely decoratively. Chatterton and Blake, on the other hand, not only used the word "chariot" but had chariots and horses actually participate in battle and become a part of the carnage resulting from it. In the following passage in *Gwin, King of Norway,* and the next from *Cerdick* this use is illustrated, as is also a similarity in the detail of the scene, the "pestilence" of one being comparable to the "hail" of the other. Blake wrote:

> Gwin leads his host as black as night,
>   When pestilence does fly.
>
> With horses and with chariots—
>   And all his spearmen bold,
> March to the sound of mournful song,
>   Like clouds around him roll'd.
>   (p. 21, ll. 11–16.)

Cerdick reads: ". . . the noise of the chariots is heard in the valleys . . . thick as the hail in the howling storm, drive down the mountains side the son of the tempest; the chariot, and the horse, roll in confusion to the blood-stained vale." (*T. and Co. Mag.,* I, 233.) The latter recalls Blake's lines in *King Edward the Third:*

> When confusion rages, when the field is in flame,
> When the cries of blood tear horror from heav'n,
> And yelling death runs up and down the ranks,
>   (p. 29, ll. 6–8.)

This, in turn, has other reminiscences from *Godred Crovan:*
". . . there fought *Godred Crovan,* death sat on his sword,
the yelling breath of the dying foe shook his banner . . ."
(*T. and Co. Mag.,* I, 428) and from the line that described the
death of Morval: ". . . the weapon perforated, he yelled like
a wolf of the mountain, he died." (*Ibid.*) Chatterton attributed the same action to Winter in *Kenrick* that Blake did to
his Winter. The first wrote: "When winter yelled through the
leafless grove: when the black winds rode over the roaring
winds . . ." (*T. and Co. Mag.,* I, 174) and the second:

> He hears me not, but o'er the yawning deep
> He rides heavy; . . .
>
> . . . and the monster
> Is driv'n yelling to his caves beneath
> Mount Hecla.   (p. 4, ll. 5–6, 15–16.)

Macpherson had innumerable ghosts, meteors, and eagles[33]
—all things seen in the air—but of an authentic vision of reality from which a true poet's imagination takes wing, there is
little. With Chatterton it is entirely different. He frequently
used animals as a basis of some comparison which was exactly
visioned. Some of Blake's lines suggest equally apposite images, although usually heightened somewhat beyond Chatterton's comparisons. In *Godred Crovan,* Chatterton wrote: "Os-
pray, like a lion, ravages the band of Elgar." (*T. and Co. Mag.,*
I, 426.) In *The Hirlas* he wrote of warriors—"they fought
with the rage of lions." (*T. and Co. Mag.,* I, 683.)[34] Expressing the same figurative meaning, Blake wrote:

> Beneath them roll'd like tempests black,
> The num'rous sons of blood;
> Like lions whelps, roaring abroad,
> Seeking their nightly food.
>   (p. 19, ll. 17–20.)

The action in these lines resembles that attributed to the wolf
in *Kenrick* when Chatterton described the fury of Ceolwulf:
"he followed Kenrick, like a wolf roaming for prey." (*T. and
Co. Mag.,* I, 175.)[35] After describing Ealward in *Godred Cro-*

van, Chatterton wrote: "See he sleeps with the chiefs upon the skin of the wolf," which may have had echo in Blake's memory when he wrote in *King Edward the Third:*

> I know the wolf
> Is dangerous to fight, not good for food
> Nor is the hide a comely vestment.
>   (p. 45, ll. 22–24.)

In *Heccar and Gaira,* Chatterton appropriately chose the tiger, "pawing in his rage [that] bids the black archers of the wild engage," who, prowling came, "Dreadful his voice, his eyes a glowing flame."[36] The picture in these lines may have contributed to the fund of imagery out of which Blake's *Tiger* later came. Certainly the latter poem utilized two phrases from Chatterton's poems, both of which were unquestionably accessible to Blake by the time he wrote *The Tiger.* In an *Epistle to the Reverend Mr. Catcott* are these lines, in connection with Chatterton's discussion of inspiration:

> As nothing by my mother-tongue I speak;
> Else would I ask, by what immortal power
> All nature was dissolved as in an hour.[37]

The second is in *The Elegy to the Memory of Mr. Thomas Phillips of Fairford:*

> Say what bold number, what immortal line
> The image of thy genius can reflect?[38]

Macpherson's influence upon Blake has generally been considered "wholly deplorable," to use De Selincourt's phrase. This judgment has largely been due to the obscurity of the merits of Ossian by a sort of prejudice against what was proved spurious, enforced by revolt against the surfeit of repetition in matter, imagery, and phrasing. Ossian has an abundance of faults, but its widespread influence proved that in its own character it had power. To explain that power would mean an analysis of Ossian's indebtedness to Homeric epic, to biblical imagery, to Miltonic sublimity. In style of sentence, in descriptive phrase, in cadence of his prose, Macpherson's work gave Blake much upon which he continued to build. Macpherson, eventually at least, checked the lyrical note in Blake; but it gave impetus to Blake's experimentation with rhythm and with concepts of grandeur. Ossian was, above all, a romantic experience to the youthful Blake, and, as such, satisfied a certain boyish love of adventure. It was not wholly a bad influence, else the *Songs of Innocence and Experience* would never have been an interlude between the *Poetical Sketches* and his prophetic books wherein he returned to the Ossianic manner.

Chatterton's part was something otherwise. His poetic and nearly lyrical imitations of Ossian served to sustain the lyrical and the poetic in Blake. Blake's rhythm and cadence are nearer those of Chatterton than those of Ossian; his sentence structure is nearer Chatterton's. The form of his similes and their brevity as well as the substance of the comparisons in them are more like Chatterton's than Ossian's. There are a number of associations between Chatterton's and Blake's that are independent of Ossian.[39] Chatterton's *Bristowe Tragedy* contributed some interesting things to Blake. In the first place, its verse pattern is exactly that of *Gwin, King of Norway*, true ballad form. Secondly, in a few details there is significant association of ideas.

At no place in Ossian is there mention of children. Women characters are frequent, to supply the voice of lamentation for the heroes. But in Blake's poem, one reads:

> . . . our wives
> And children cry for bread:
>
> .   .   .   .
>
> Their wives and children weeping loud,
> Follow in wild array, . . .
>
> .   .   .   .
>
> The cries of women and of babes
> Over the field doth fly.
> (pp. 19, ll. 9–10; 20, ll. 5–6; 22,
> ll. 11–12.)

In *The Bristowe Tragedy*, Chatterton specifically stated in regard to Charles Bawdin:

> Hee has a spouse and children twaine,
>   "Alle rewyn'd are for aie;
> "Yff thatt you are resolv'd to lett
>   CHARLES BAWDIN die to-daie."[40]

Earlier he recorded:

> Butt whenne hee came, hys children twaine
>   And eke hys lovynge wyfe,
> Wythe brinie tears dydd wett the floore,
>   For goode SIR CHARLESES lyfe.[41]

From Chatterton also came the emphasis upon vultures and gore in the wake of battle. *The Bristowe Tragedy* reads:

> "Sae lett hym die!" DUKE RICHARD sayde,
>   "And maye echone oure foes
> "Bende downe theyre neckes to bloudie axe,
>   And feede the carryon crowes."
>
>   .   .   .   .
>
> "Youre sonnes and husbandes shalle bee slayne,
> "And brookes wythe bloude shall flowe."[42]

Parallel to this, *Gwin, King of Norway* has:

> The rest did fill the vale of death,
>   For them the eagles strive.
> The river Dorman roll'd their blood
>   Into the northern sea;
>   (p. 23, ll. 19–22.)

Into the narrative of crude horrors that has moved through three pages, Blake suddenly interpolated the ejaculatory comment:

> O what have Kings to answer for,
>   Before that awful throne! (p. 23, ll. 5–6.)

There is nothing else in this key in Blake's poem; yet it is the theme of *The Bristowe Tragedy*. Neither is there any antecedent in *Gwin, King of Norway* for the reference to "that awful throne." This is clearly a transference into Blake's poem of the situation in *The Bristowe Tragedy* where Sir

Charles Bawdin made his specific accusation of King Edward, and of the emphasis Sir Charles put upon being prepared to die.[43] In the accusation Sir Charles said:

> Thou thinkest I shall dye to-daie;
> I have beene dede 'til nowe,[44]

which Blake echoed years later in an inscription he put into an Autograph Album of William Upcott:

> WILLIAM BLAKE, one who is very much
> delighted with being in good Company.
> Born 28 Novr 1757 in London & has died
> several times since.[45]

There are miscellaneous associations between Chatterton and Blake which indicate the range of Chatterton's influence upon Blake. Chatterton wrote a number of satires, and while nothing is known as to what chance Blake had of being familiar with those that were not published in the periodicals, some resemblances lead one to suspect that by some means before 1787 he came to know them. One of the satires, *The Prophecy,* contains the lines:

> When vile corruption's brazen face
> At council-board shall take her place.[46]

The opening line of a song which Cynic sang in Blake's satire, *An Island in the Moon,* was "When old corruption first begun."[47] Another of Chatterton's satires, *Kew Gardens,* contains many allusions to Samuel Johnson, all more or less reviling him. He is alluded to unpleasantly in Blake's satire also. At the point in which the allusion to Dr. Johnson is made, Suction said:

> I say, this evening we'll all get drunk—
> I say—dash!—an anthem, an anthem.[48]

This recalls Chatterton's lines in another satire, *Journal Sixth:*

> May all and every mother's son
> Be drunk before the dinner's done.[49]

Blake and Chatterton made many allusions to Newton, Blake never kindly, Chatterton rarely so. Closely allied to this reference is the attitude of both youths toward religion. When Chatterton was but eleven, he wrote his first religious satire, *Apostate Will;* the same year his poem, *The Churchwarden and the Apparition,* appeared in *Felix Farley's Journal.* A portion of a poem he wrote *To a Lady in Bristol,*

> In natural religion free
> I to no other bow the knee,
> Nature's the god I own:[50]

may have furnished a title for one of Blake's later works, *There is No Natural Religion.* This antagonistic attitude so freely announced shows the adolescence of both writers. In *Journal Sixth* Chatterton devoted many lines to a caricature of Whitefield, among which there is an echo in *An Island in the Moon,* where the antiquarian talks about cats.[51]

It was with Chatterton as it came to be with Blake that when he expressed bitterness or hatreds involving personal acquaintances, he wrote not poetry but inelegant prose or verse. It is a kind of human perversity that Blake should have been impressed by the scurrilous writing of Chatterton when he was also sensitive to the poetry of which Chatterton was capable. But perversity is often youth's way. Blake never wrote any verse, as Chatterton wrote his abusive satires, with the hope of patronage. Even when Blake wrote his one satire, he disguised the names; and his couplets that said stinging things about his friends he concealed all his life in personal notebooks. One must remember in this connection that however interested he was in the products of the whole group of writers who issued their work in the guise of someone else— Macpherson, Walpole, Percy, and Chatterton—, Blake was himself never deceptive. Although the *Poetical Sketches* appeared under the partially disguising initials, "W.B.," it was not an attempt to pretend he was another person. His signatures and his *Descriptive Catalogue* showed that he wished to be identified with what he did. If he later had a turn for concealment, it took the form of an elaborate symbolism. Blake had, therefore, no lament to compare with Chatterton's in *Chatterton's Will.*[52]

With Chatterton Blake had much more in common than with Macpherson, and it is apparent that Chatterton's influence was greater than Macpherson's. Besides these evidences of Chatterton's influence during the years that Blake composed the *Poetical Sketches,* one should note the statement Blake himself made in reply to Wordsworth's remarks in his *Essay, Supplementary to the Preface.* Wordsworth said that his childhood experience in a mountainous country had made him see the spurious imagery and falsehood pervading Ossian, for whereas in nature everything was distinct, in Ossian it was "insulated, dislocated, deadened." "Yet, much as these pretended treasures have been admired," he said, "they have been wholly uninfluential upon the literature of the Country. No succeeding Writer appears to have caught from them a ray of inspiration; no Author in the least distinguished, has ventured formally to imitate them—except the Boy, Chatterton, on their first appearance."[53]

Wordsworth did not know when he wrote this criticism how distinguished one person who did in a manner imitate Ossian would become; but Blake's own comment on the above passage denies that Macpherson and Chatterton were "uninfluential." He said: "I believe both Macpherson & Chatterton that what they say is ancient is so. I own myself an admirer of Ossian equally with any poet whatsoever, Rowley & Chatterton also."[54] Blake's indebtedness to these two most imaginative contemporaries, sometimes subtle and sometimes bald, is nevertheless so significant of how deeply Blake felt their power that it is strange for Meyerstein to lament that Chatterton could not, like Blake, "be content to escape his century altogether."[55] Only the blinding effect of adherence to the early assumption that from the Elizabethans alone could have come any influence upon the *Poetical Sketches* prevents the critics from acknowledging that Blake did not escape the eighteenth century. With penetrating insight, he knew his century better than most men; with forceful statement he asserted his loyalty to it.

CHAPTER VIII

"POETICAL ORIGINALITY, WHICH MERITED SOME RESPITE FROM OBLIVION"—*Advertisement*

BLAKE'S poetic mind variously recreated the material he derived from his inner experiences with the master-minds in his reading so that he was never indebted in any slavish fashion to his sources. However many elements he seems to have borrowed, the final essence acquired a life of its own. What effected the synthesis of the varied and the multiple into one? What was the real achievement of the *Poetical Sketches?* How do the universality and originality of their author therein express themselves? For, as Leonard Welsted set forth in his *Dissertation concerning the Perfection of the English Language, the State of Poetry, etc.* (1724), ". . . that which truly and lastingly pleases in writing is always the result of a man's own force, and of that first cast of soul which gives him a promptitude to excell. . . ."[1]

That Blake did excel in his first volume of verse, which in lyrical qualities exceeded anything the eighteenth century had yet produced, is a fact easily lost sight of in the mass of evidence stressing his indebtedness to others. But the significance of this indebtedness must be seen in the perspective of the intrinsic worth of the whole achievement, which in turn is dependent upon the individuality of the creator. Blake, from childhood, with a taste that instinctively selected the masters both in poetry and in art, stored his mind bountifully. His selection, mainly without guidance other than his own energy of imagination and his unerring sensitiveness to beauty, becomes all the more remarkable. His imitativeness was an essential process of learning, much as a child learns to do anything else —by experimenting with the model or practice furnished by his elders. From them all he took something. It is not always possible to define in critical terms what that something was, for, as Meyerstein said about Chatterton, "Descent in English poetry, it cannot be repeated too often, is spiritual."[2] Blake's first rendering of all the substance which became his poetical inheritance has not full meaning, therefore, except as it is viewed in terms of the kindred spirits of the past and of those of his own day. Only then is it clear how much more than temporal Blake's work was; how timeless, in fact, it is. If his imitativeness had been merely the continuation of traditions of which he was only artificially or superficially aware, his work would have been stagnant and without continuity in the great current of true poetry that arose in the springs of Helicon and flowed on into succeeding centuries. The forces which Blake imitated inspired but did not control him. They were the substance out of which his creative imagination moulded new forms, whose individuality, as T. S. Eliot phrased it, was even seen in those parts "in which the dead poets, his ancestors, assert their immortality most vigorously."[3]

The *Poetical Sketches* is one of the most enduring works of the eighteenth century. In certain respects it belonged fully to its own time; in many others it presented new and individual characteristics. That Blake naturally followed certain fashions of his day has been seen in his catching the new Ossianic manner which so quickly became trite in the hands of servile copyists; seen again in his attempt at a conventional imitation of Spenser's stanzaic form; in the representation of a homely, realistic scene; in a turn to satire; and in the choice of such hackneyed subjects as *To Spring, To Morning,* or *To the Evening Star.*[4]

Some of Blake's language was the current, stereotyped, poetic usage. The phrases, "deck," "dewy locks," "mossy vallies," "Phoebus fir'd my vocal rage," "boughs perfume the air," "pensive woe," "whisp'ring faint murmurs in the scanty breeze," "deathy dust,"—these link Blake unmistakably to the eighteenth century. Likewise his compound epithets, "honest-seeming brow," "softly-breathing song," "all-worship'd tomb," "deep-founded habitations" are in the style of the current poetic "vocabulary" familiar on any page of the many eighteenth-century miscellanies.[5] Unlearned in the sense in which many of the poets of the eighteenth century were learned, Blake, lacking in classical and formal education, yet showed by the diction in his early poems how advantageously he had read the masters. Nevertheless, he avoided archaisms except the few used to give the suggestion of Spenser in his *Imitation.* What then are the characteristics of Blake's poetic diction which gave it distinction? Contrasted with the standardized and generalized phrases, the stereotyped epithets, and the conventional abstractions of much contemporary verse,[6] Blake's diction was singularly simple and unaffected. There was nothing pretentious or pedantic about it. He could not have sung in such a medium. On the contrary, his vocabulary was tinged with emotion. With the warmth of his imagination, he gave language a luminous quality, a felicity, and a richness of association that belonged to poetic inspiration rather than to studied phrase. It betokened the irradiation of his youthfulness.

These are qualities which also partly explain Blake's figures of speech, which seem not the invention of reason but a discovery with his "double vision" of new resemblances between familiar objects. Lucy Allen Paton has said about Blake's figures of speech: "They serve him in their proper province, as tools for the clear delineation of the pictures with which his fancy is teeming. He never forces them irrelevantly; with the tact of a writer in harmony with his theme, he omits them entirely where the simple narrative pictures the scene or object with sufficient vividness. . . . This use of a figure to suggest an entire scene is frequent in Blake's poems, and serves to connect him strikingly with the romantic movement."[7] Blake often reinvested the imagery he found in his sources in a new imaginative guise which indicated his powers both of observation and of suggestion. He compelled his readers' eyes to follow his; he animated his figures of speech with reality and inner meaning. It is as Osbert Burdett aptly expressed it: "This pictorial quality is characteristic of all the *Poetical Sketches.* It is not merely that the metaphor becomes a symbol, but that the symbol is an image vivid enough to possess an independent life of its own."[8]

Blake's rendering of the imagery from Spenser in his own epithalamium, *To Morning,* is an excellent example of what Burdett calls "an independent life of its own." Even when

Blake's figures of speech are based upon an abstraction, he transfigured it into a poetical emblem with associations of aesthetic truth. The songs, "My silks and fine array," "Love and harmony combine," and "Memory, hither come," illustrate these characteristics. The figures of speech in *Edward the Third* constitute one of the most important phases of Shakespeare's influence upon Blake. They are the strength of the play. They are numerous and well sustained; they are fresh and in keeping with the ideas and emotions being set forth.

Occasionally Blake's figures of speech are faulty. For example, in *The Couch of Death* he said, "the breath of night slept among the leaves of the forest." This, while logically indefensible, is an effective communication of something which had only an ideal existence. At another place, in the same selection, he doubled the figure until it missed his usual lucidity, when he wrote, "like lilies, dropping tears in each other's bosom, they stood by the bed like roses bending over a lake." This overlapping of figures is common in both Chatterton and Ossian. In *To Autumn,* an ill-chosen verb destroyed the force of the comparison of joy to a winged creature:

> ". . . and joy, with pinions light, roves round
> The gardens, or sits singing in the trees."
> (p. 3, ll. 14–16.)

Blake used more metaphors than similes or personifications, a minor fact but significant of the nature of his vision.

Mention has been made of the pictorial qualities of the *Poetical Sketches.* The very title of the book confesses as much. It is an artist's title. Never again after the *Poetical Sketches* did Blake rely upon words alone. Thereafter he worked in two mediums, expressing his ideas and feelings with words and with line and color that illumined the words. One can hardly determine which was first created in the poet-artist's mind. In a letter to William Hayley, October 7, 1803, Blake made an allusion that suggests the intrusion of the poetic upon the artistic work. He referred to the "good-natured Devil" that "was seeking amusement in making Verses to which he constantly leads me very much to my hurt."[9] There were no illustrations made with pen or brush in the *Poetical Sketches,* but one believes from the way Blake's imagination played upon his thoughts that the words were accompanied in his mind by visual imagery. For instance, there is a passage in *King Edward the Third* that suggests the presence in Blake's mind of a picture not unlike one by Raphael:

> . . . the voice of Conscience then
> Sweeter than music in a summer's eve,
> Shall warble round the snowy head, and keep
> Sweet symphony to feather'd angels, sitting
> As guardians round your chair;
>
> (p. 46, ll. 13–17.)

As a matter of fact, the *Poetical Sketches* shows a greater number of pictorial qualities incorporated within the language and figures of speech than the later *Songs* do. There are more phrases designed to convey images. It may be that this is one reason that Blake's latest work seems confused and chaotic, in that as he grew older he spent his richest poetic impulse on the design rather than upon the poetry because then for him the picture more satisfactorily conveyed his symbol and, therefore, his meaning. One does not miss the illustrations for the *Poetical Sketches,* but the *Songs* are not complete without the accompanying designs, since the *Songs* communicate themselves only as the words and pictures are seen together. Max Plowman has said, significantly: "Six years divide Blake's earliest book of poems, *Poetical Sketches,* from the *Songs of Innocence.* Those six years mark the biggest change he ever experienced. In them he passed from the representational to the symbolic poet: from the exquisite traditionalist to the genuine creator: from the youth who re-echoed the loveliest strains in English lyrical poetry to the man who set forth from the Garden of Innocence to trace the course of human life from Eden to the New Jerusalem."[10]

Another original quality of the *Poetical Sketches* is apparent in the response Blake made to nature. As a child he had free access to the fields and countrysides in which he spent many hours. He began one of his poems, "How sweet I roam'd from field to field." One has only to read the passages throughout his later works where he returned to the charm of his early lyrics in the glimpses of scenes or objects in nature, brief but with utter fidelity of observation, to realize that he was in maturity expressing the things that impressed him most deeply as a child. The exultant expressions, for example, with which Blake reported his joy over returning to the country when, in 1800, he went to Felpham, suggest how vital had been his pleasure in nature: "the sweet air & the voices of winds, trees, & birds, & the odours of the happy ground, makes it a dwelling for immortals."[11] It is nature seen at some time, not wholly imagined; seen sometimes, to be sure, as Wordsworth was later to see it, and as Traherne had formerly seen it, with the "inward eye." The pastoral poetry which persisted in lifeless and trite forms even to Blake's day affected him not at all, as did none of the so-called "garden poetry" of those interested in formal landscapes. He escaped, therefore, from the conventionalized praise of innocence and simplicity into the actual presentation of those qualities as they were visible objects of real life. If these natural objects came to be invested with more and more symbolism, it still does not alter the fact that Blake saw vividly and truthfully all the aspects of nature. Wicksteed said in his *Expository Preface:* "Like other painters Blake could see his pictures before he painted them—could see them line for line as he would draw them. . . . And for this reason, with all his visions Blake never deserts the earth. We miss all the virtue of his mighty sanity if we miss this fact. Vision did not transport him into another world. It enlightened him to see this one in all its glory."[12] In her assertion that there is in the early poems not a single touch of "that passionate intimacy with nature which many later passages reveal,"[13] Emily Hamblen seems not to have taken into account the perceptions of nature that went to make the imagery of the lyrics on the seasons, or the penetration into the facts of nature that lay back of the figures of speech in *King Edward the Third,* or the naturalness of "How sweet I roam'd from field to field," or the awareness in *The Couch of Death* of the many elements of nature: the birds (especially the owl and the bat), the "brakes and thickets," "the reed-bordered lake," "the bubbling waters of the brook," the "deer wounded by the brooks," the "cloud tossed by the winds," "the drops of rain glistening" in

the sun, the moon and "stars faintly glimmering in the summer sky." There was no sentimentality in Blake's response to
nature. As an artist, his aim was not merely to copy what he
saw and heard, but to treat it imaginatively in order to convey
to others what was beautiful to him. In this manner of response, Blake identified himself with the romantics, a step beyond the romanticism of Thomson; a step behind that of
Keats.

Blake was a romanticist by nature. The curiosity of his mind,
the adventurous character of his imagination sent him into far
places and unfamiliar fields. His resistance to all restraints
marks him as a romantic. This is seen best in another aspect
of the *Poetical Sketches* in which his originality is also apparent. This is his reaction against the forms of verse then in
vogue. The lyric melody of Blake's early songs causes one to
assume that the form in which they came was entirely a spontaneous thing. No amount of conscious attention to prosody
could have produced any true song if the lyrical note—the free
voice of the poet—had been lacking or even had not been spontaneous. But there are reasons to conclude that Blake definitely
experimented with new forms of verse. In the first place, in
the preface to the first part of *Jerusalem,* Blake's testimony of
how he proceeded with that poem may indicate how he likewise worked at other times. It shows, at least, his point of view
toward composition. He said that at first he considered that a
monotonous cadence was an indispensable part of verse. Then
he said: "But I soon found that in the mouth of a true Orator
such monotony was not only awkward, but as much a bondage
as rhyme itself. I therefore have produced a variety in every
line, both of cadences & number of syllables. Every word and
every letter is studied and put into its fit place; the terrific
numbers are reserved for the terrific parts, the mild & gentle
for the mild & gentle parts, and the prosaic for inferior parts;
all are necessary to each other. Poetry Fetter'd Fetters the
Human Race."[14] To escape fetters was Blake's urgent need
from the first, and the new poetic forms, both in the number
and the beauty of them, in the *Poetical Sketches* show that he
experimented with metrical patterns in an effort to find the one

that fitted the melody in his mind. The fragmentary condition of many of the sketches also speaks of experimentation.

The two most distinctive things about Blake's prosody[15] were the variations he made in any basic measure he used, especially as he substituted one type of foot for another; and the new use to which he put blank verse. The syllabic blank verse familiar through the current imitations of Milton was not flexible enough for him. Hence, when he wrote *King Edward the Third,* he played variations with the cadences of it which gave entirely new effects. It is doubtful that he would have found blank verse so suitable a pattern for his play if he had not studied Shakespeare's prosody. While Marlowe and Shakespeare wrote blank verse charged with lyrical emotion, it had never had the particular use in pure lyrics that Blake's poems on the seasons had. Blake played another variation with it in *Fair Elenor* where he arranged it in quatrains, and still another where he grouped the blank verse of the minstrel's song in *King Edward the Third* into six-line stanzas. The pentameter line was the dominant one, but Blake successfully used a trimeter in "My silks and fine array," and "Memory, hither come," and a tetrameter in *To the Muses. Mad Song* has dimeter measure, with mixtures of iambic, anapestic, and trochaic feet. Here the change from one metrical form to another shows a definite influence of the "mad songs" in Percy's *Reliques,* as has already been discussed. Blake's only use of the heroic couplet was *Blind-man's Buff,* where in scene, tone, and form the poem was in the style of the eighteenth century. *Gwin, King of Norway* is the conventional ballad.

Moving a step beyond blank verse under the influence of Ossian, Blake accomplished a new kind of metrical prose in *The Couch of Death* and *Contemplation* in which he remarkably suited the cadence to speech rhythm. Striving for greater freedom with the rhythm of Milton's *Samson Agonistes,* Blake combined the nonmetrical rhythm of the prose pieces with a basic cadence of speech in *Samson.* He achieved something that was neither blank verse nor free verse, and had never been done before. Yet Rossetti in his early edition (1874) forced *Samson* into regular blank verse. In doing so he lost the particular cadence which was Blake's contribution to the poem. All in all, Blake's experiments with metrical forms illustrate a sound principle of prosody—that it is the departures from a particular pattern that are the secret of poetic rhythm.

With rhyme Blake's ear was less sure. Damon's attitude is that Blake's false rhymes in the *Songs* achieve a certain pleasant effect. T. Sturge Moore spoke to this point, especially in regard to the *Songs:* "My second remark concerns the exquisite ear for what pedants call bad rhymes which Blake shows in the songs. To rhyme 'shade' with 'bed' or 'inns' with 'since' may produce an exquisite effect, or fail to do so, just as mere pat rhymes may be used happily or make the ear ache."[16] Pleasure can hardly be said to result from the false rhymes in the *Poetical Sketches,* as seen, for example, in the early stanzas of "Fresh from the dewy hill."

The *Poetical Sketches* was unlike eighteenth-century verse in other ways. After reading verse contemporaneous with the *Poetical Sketches,* one is impressed by the individuality of Blake because there was so much that he did not imitate, and with which he did not experiment. Blake wrote no epistles in verse; no odes to Camilla, Chloe, or Clarissa; no elegies; no fulsome flattery to countesses or lords; no verses occasioned by the receipt of a hare; no lines to Miss —— on having the toothache. He wrote no ode on the return of any royal personage; no extemporary rhapsody on a trifle, nor any ode to mankind or equally inclusive generality. He wrote no riddle, no fable, no "essay" in rhyme. He wrote no "progress" of anything. He paraphrased no psalm and composed no hymn. He attempted no sonnet. One notes, furthermore, the absence of a quality not only characteristic of the verse of the time but almost inevitable from one of his age. He did not moralize. He was not platitudinous. The philosophy inherent in the figures of speech in *King Edward the Third* is not in the category of dull truisms. His early poems missed the morbid obsession with melancholy and death. In *Fair Elenor* where these ideas appear, they were given the directness and impersonality of the old ballads. Besides, the poems in the *Poetical Sketches* are happy poems—a prelude to the fuller expression of happiness in the *Songs of Innocence.* Charles Gardner, in speaking about Blake's happy childhood, said: "His happiness was creative, and he burst into song when he was eleven in strains that savoured of Ben Jonson, but were wholly fresh and captivating because they were inspired by the first fresh vision of his childhood. There is surely nothing in any language written by a boy of eleven to touch the song: *How sweet I roam'd from field to field.* It is a sudden spring of sparkling water that can never lose its purity."[17] Gardner has expressed here a quality in which Blake anticipated the romanticists—"the first fresh vision of childhood." It is a quality that cannot receive too much emphasis. It is the secret of the irresistible charm of the lyrics of his youth.

Another attribute closely allied to "the vision of his childhood" and also significant of the romantic in Blake was expressed by Symons when he attempted to define the poetry of Blake. He said: "In this verse there is, if it is to be found in any verse, the 'lyrical cry'; and yet, what voice is it that cries in this disembodied ecstasy? The voice of desire is not in it, nor the voice of passion, nor the cry of the heart, nor the cry of the sinner to God, nor the lover of nature to nature. It neither seeks nor aspires nor laments, nor questions. It is like the voice of wisdom in a child, who has not yet forgotten the world out of which the soul came. It is as spontaneous as the note of a bird; it is an affirmation of life; in its song, which seems mere music, it is the mind that sings; it is lyric thought."[18] If this seems like the overstatement of an enthusiast, it still has the essential fact of the lyrical quality which put Blake first in a line of lyric poets of the romantic movement. It has been observed that Blake had little narrative ability and less dramatic, but in the lyrical he excelled. He expressed in poetry without any accompanying theorizing what later romanticists formulated into theories of poetry and then attempted to illustrate by poetry. One of the earliest to recognize Blake's relation to the romantic movement was James Thomson ("B.V.") whose review of Gilchrist's *Life* (1884) contains the following statement: ". . . although he was scarcely listened to at all, while his colleagues held in attention the whole kingdom, the fact may at length be recognized that by him, even more clearly than by them, was anticipated and announced both the event now already past and the event still in process of evolution."[19] Blake's later expressions of his theories about poetry and especially about the imagination also identified him with the romanticists. For instance, in *A Descriptive Catalogue* (1809) is stated an idea to which he doubtless had held for a long time: "Weaving the winding sheet of Edward's race by means of sounds of spiritual music and its accompanying expressions of articulate speech is a bold, and daring, and most masterly conception, . . . Poetry consists in these conceptions; and shall Painting be confined to the sordid drudgery of fac-simile representations of merely mortal and perishing substances, and not be as poetry and music are, elevated into its own proper sphere of invention and visionary conception? No, it shall not be so! Painting, as well as poetry and music, exists and exults in immortal thoughts."[20]

One question remains to be raised about the *Poetical Sketches*. It is important to inquire what happened that the qualities which gave individuality to the *Poetical Sketches* disappeared from Blake's work after the *Songs*. Blake gave one clue to the answer in the passage in *Jerusalem*, quoted at the close of Chapter I, a part of which reads:

> "Wherefore hast thou shut me into the winter
> of human life,
> "And clos'd up the sweet regions of youth and
> virgin innocence
> "Where we live forgetting error, not pondering
> evil,"

When Blake's childhood passed, maturity brought him perplexing problems. Harold Bruce has well described how these impressed Blake: "Blake saw another's woe; he saw poverty, hypocrisy, oppression, militarism, ignorance, prostitution, fear, cruelty,—London's barriers to lightheartedness. At the sight the 'merry notes' of the *Poetical Sketches* died on his lips."[21] In the *Poetical Sketches* and in the *Songs* Blake was not yet reactionary enough to lose the spontaneity of his intuitions or the singleness of his vision. He had not yet begun to support his deeper spiritual affirmations with his own rationalization which was not Reason at all but something still dependent upon

his intuitive and imaginative processes. Since he never lost his
intuitions, they became chaotically allied to a profusion of image and symbolism which had the harmony of the purpose and
sincerity in them, and the essential genius that was Blake's.
Besides, Blake conceived a great mission for himself. He said:

> . . . I rest not from my task!
> To open the Eternal Worlds, to open the immortal
> Eyes
> Of Man inwards into the Worlds of Thought, into
> Eternity
> Ever expanding in the Bosom of God, the Human
> Imagination.[22]

At first he was content to sing; his songs being unheeded, he
was impelled to argue for his beliefs, and no man argues lyri-
cally. Yet his powers of imagination increased, and, given mo-
mentum by the driving fervor of his beliefs and unrestrained
by any discipline, they became fantastic and "gigantic." Blake's
own awareness of the change in himself is seen in a letter he
wrote to William Hayley October 23, 1804, when he said:
"Suddenly, on the day after visiting the Truchsessian Gallery
of pictures, I was again enlightened with the light I enjoyed
in my youth, and which has for exactly twenty years been
closed from me as by a door and by window-shutters . . . for
I am really drunk with intellectual vision whenever I take pencil or graver in hand, even as I used to be in my youth, and as
I have not been for twenty dark, but very profitable, years."[23]
Then, too, as Blake attained more perfectly the character of a
religious mystic, his truest communication was of necessity
the symbol, the only way by which an inexpressible spiritual
experience can be brought to a material embodiment. For these
reasons the work of Blake, after the *Songs,* was of an entirely
different character from the *Poetical Sketches.* There and in
the *Songs* are to be found the lyrics that are magically correct
although entirely strange to his day. It was this very strange-
ness of the *Poetical Sketches* which partly explains the contemporary neglect it suffered. Swinburne, speaking of Blake's
"rare gift of poetical judgment" and "exquisite natural sense
and art," said: ". . . there is no case on record of a man's

being quite so far in advance of his time, in everything that belongs to the imaginative side of art, as Blake was from the first in advance of his."[24] The narrow circulation of the volume, through the failure of Blake to publish it, or even through the destruction of copies, restricted greatly the chances of its being known. Besides this, Blake associated more closely with the circle of artists than with the circle of poets, and even this association was long deferred because of the methods he followed of producing and of publishing his pictures and books. Consequently there was little effect of the *Poetical Sketches* upon his own generation. After 1860 it was a different story.

There has been no wish or attempt to incorporate in this study the opinions of all the people who have written about Blake since Gilchrist, Swinburne, Rossetti, and Shepherd established his position as a poet of high merit; or even since the scholarly editing of Sampson and Keynes gave sound texts with which to study him. Much of this secondary writing has made little contribution to a knowledge of Blake. Much of it is imaginative, or written to support some fantastic theory of his imagined abnormality or of his genius. Perhaps the greater part of the more recent writing has been concerned with an exposition of the meaning of the symbolical works by many persons, holding entirely diverse opinions, each one equally certain that he knows exactly what the meaning is. The position of Blake is in no wise dependent upon any of the expositors. It was made by Blake in the *Poetical Sketches* and *Songs* and by him through them will it be retained.

The rank Blake's *Poetical Sketches* has attained, however, can be seen by comparing two statements widely apart in time. The first is that of Shepherd in his *Preface* to the first reprint of the *Poetical Sketches* in 1868: ". . . if he had written nothing else, he could claim a place second to none among English song-writers. As it is, he can claim also to be the first restorer of our English poetry to the simplicity of its prime—to have chased away with his sweet music the feeble sing-song of Darwin and the flat inanities of Hayley a whole 'sunny decade' and 'gay quinquenniad' before the appearance of Wordsworth, who was at Hawkshead School 'cutting eights' on Esthwaite-

lake when these poems were printed—who was not even born
when some of them were written."[25]

The second is by a Latin professor and poet—whose own
poetry is like the song of a hermit-thrush—who for the moment turned critic, the late A. E. Housman. In the Leslie
Stephen Lecture delivered in Cambridge May 9, 1933, he said,
illustrating his remarks by quoting "Memory, hither come":
"For me the most poetical of all poets is Blake. I find his lyrical note as beautiful as Shakespeare's and more beautiful than
anyone else's; and I call him more poetical than Shakespeare,
even though Shakespeare has so much more poetry, because
poetry in him preponderates more than in Shakespeare over
everything else, and instead of being confounded in a great
river can be drunk pure from a slender channel of its own.
Shakespeare is rich in thought, and his meaning has power of
itself to move us, even if the poetry were not there: Blake's
meaning is often unimportant or virtually non-existent, so that
we can listen with all our hearing to his celestial tune."[26]

If whoever penned the *Advertisement* to the *Poetical
Sketches* could have known the ultimate judgment of the val-
ues of the poems, he might have written of his generous action
with more pride and less apology than are within his words
when he wrote: "Conscious of the irregularities and defects to
be found in almost every page, his friends have still believed
that they possessed a poetical originality, which merited some
respite from oblivion. These their opinions remain, however,
to be now reproved or confirmed by a less partial public." The
"less partial public" has now made the confirmation. Being of
his age, and yet above it, and akin to the true poets of the past,
the youthful Blake has in the *Poetical Sketches* written lyrics
whose "poetical originality" made them a force in the romantic
renaissance of poetry and gave them a place in the Golden
Treasury of Time.

NOTES

CHAPTER I

Since full bibliographical data are given in the references, no separate bibliography is appended. With minor omissions, the form is a reproduction of the title-page. References which have once appeared will make their initial appearance in each chapter thereafter in a shortened form.

1. Benjamin Heath Malkin, *A Father's Memoirs of His Child*. London: . . . Longman, Hurst, Rees, and Orme . . . 1806. pp. xviii–xli.

2. *Ibid.*, pp. x–xi.

3. *Ibid.*, pp. xvi–xvii.

4. *Ibid.*, pp. xvii–xviii.

5. *Ibid.*, p. 157.

6. *Ibid.*

7. Blake also made a portrait for the elder Malkin. Cf. *The Dictionary of National Biography*. XXXV, 424. Confirmed by an entry in *A Catalogue of a Collection of Engraved Portraits* . . . Edward Evans [1836–53]. I, 220. In the British Museum.

8. Malkin, *op. cit.*, pp. 33–34.

9. William Blake, *Poetry and Prose*. Complete in one volume. New York: Random House Inc.; London: The Nonesuch Press. MCMXXVII. p. 529, l. 15. (Edited by Geoffrey Keynes.) Hereafter all references to Blake's writings, except the *Poetical Sketches,* will be made to this edition. Permission to quote this text has been kindly granted by the publisher.

10. Geoffrey Keynes, *A Bibliography of William Blake*. New York: The Grolier Club of New York. 1921. p. 101.

11. Edward Fitzgerald, *Letters and Literary Remains*. London and New York: Macmillan and Co. 1889. I, 21. (Edited by William Aldis Wright.)

12. Keynes, *op. cit.*, p. 347.

13. *The Monthly Review; or Literary Journal, Enlarged*, LI, 216. (October, 1806.)

  The Monthly Magazine; or British Register, XXII, 633. (January, 1807.)

14. John Thomas Smith, *A Book for a Rainy Day; or Recollections of the Events of the Last Sixty Years*. London: Richard Bentley. 1845. p. 96.

15. Allan Cunningham, *The Lives of the Most Eminent British Painters, Sculptors, and Architects*. London: John Murray . . . MDCCCXXX. II, 142–179.

16. The Rev. David Hogg, *Life of Allan Cunningham* . . . Dumfries: John Anderson and Son . . . 1875. p. 289.

17. Alexander Gilchrist, *Life of William Blake*. London and Cambridge: Macmillan and Co. 1863. I, 10.

18. Algernon Charles Swinburne, *William Blake. A Critical Essay*. London: John Camden Hatten . . . 1868. p. 82. (Second edition.)

19. Archibald G. B. Russell, *The Letters of William Blake together with a Life by Frederick Tatham.* New York: Charles Scribner's Sons. 1906. p. xlv. Permission to quote this text has been kindly granted by the publisher.

20. Keynes, *op. cit.,* p. 136.

21. Laurence Binyon, *The Followers of William Blake: Edward Calvert, Samuel Palmer, George Richmond, & their Circle.* London: Halton & Truscott Smith, Ltd.; New York: Minton Balch & Company. 1925. pp. 11–12. Permission to quote this text has been kindly granted by the publisher.

22. Arthur Symons, *William Blake.* London: Archibald Constable and Company Ltd. 1907. p. 21. Permission to quote this text has been kindly granted by the publisher.

23. Alfred T. Story, *William Blake, His Life, Character, and Genius.* London: Swan Sonnenschein & Co.; New York: Macmillan & Co. 1893. p. 1.

24. William Blake, *Works, Poetic, Symbolic and Critical.* London: Bernard Quaritch . . . 1893. I, 2–3. (Edited by Edwin John Ellis and William Butler Yeats.)

25. Allan Cunningham, *The Lives of the Most Eminent Painters and Sculptors.* New York: . . . J. & J. Harper . . . 1831. II, 124. (Family Library.) References hereafter will be to this edition.

26. Russell, *op. cit.,* p. 1.

27. *The London Directory for the Year 1780.* London: Printed for T. Lowndes. p. 17.

28. *Ibid.,* (1784.), p. 16.

29. *The New Complete Guide to all Persons who have any Trade or Concern with the City of London.* London: T. Longman. 1783. p. 20. (Sixteenth edition.)

30. *Post-Office Annual Directory for the Year 1801.* London. p. 23.

31. Cunningham, *op. cit.,* p. 124.

32. Malkin, *op. cit.,* p. xix.

33. Blake, *Poetry and Prose,* p. 973.

34. Malkin, *op. cit.,* p. xix.

35. Mona Wilson, *The Life of William Blake.* London: The Nonesuch Press . . . MCMXXVII. p. 265. Permission to quote this text has been kindly granted by the publisher. Cf. Thomas Wright, *The Life of William Blake.* Olney, Bucks: Thomas Wright. 1929. II, 77.

36. William T. Whitley, *Art in England, 1800–1820.* Cambridge: At the University Press. 1928. pp. 1–2. Permission to quote this text has been kindly granted by the publisher.

37. William T. Whitley, *Artists and Their Friends in England, 1770–1799.* London and Boston: The Medici Society [MCMXXVIII]. I, 237. Permission to quote this text has been kindly granted by the publisher.

38. Blake, *Poetry and Prose,* p. 1066.

39. Russell, *op. cit.,* p. 2.

40. Cunningham surely errs in naming Reynolds, as Blake's later attitude shows. Cf. Blake, *Poetry and Prose,* p. 970.

41. Cunningham, *op. cit.,* p. 124.

42. Russell, *op. cit.,* p. 4.

43. *Ibid.*
44. Blake, *Poetry and Prose,* p. 854.
45. *Ibid.,* p. 66.
46. *Ibid.*
47. Russell, *op. cit.,* p. 2.
48. Blake, *Poetry and Prose,* p. 64. Cf. pp. 61, 62, 75, 77, 78.
49. H. N. Morris, *Flaxman, Blake, Coleridge, and Other Men of Genius Influenced by Swedenborg* . . . London: New Church Press, Limited . . . 1915. pp. 78–79. Permission to quote this text has been kindly granted by the publisher.
50. *The Quest,* XI, 75–76. (1920.) Permission to quote this text has been kindly granted by the publisher.
51. *Minutes of the First Seven Sessions of the General Conference of the New Church,* . . . London: James Speirs . . . 1885. p. xx.
52. Keynes, *op. cit.,* p. 78.
53. Ernest Hartley Coleridge (editor), *Letters of Samuel Taylor Coleridge.* Boston and New York: Houghton Mifflin and Company . . . 1895. II, 685–686.
54. Robert Hindmarsh, *Rise and Progress of the New Jerusalem Church, in England, America, and Other Parts.* . . . London: Hodson & Son, . . . 1861. p. 14. (Edited by the Rev. Edward Madeley.)
55. Carl Th. Odhner, *Robert Hindmarsh, a Biography.* Philadelphia: Academy Book Room, . . . 1895. pp. 74–75. Cf. Hindmarsh, *op. cit.,* pp. 101–104.
56. No one has properly studied the share that Swedenborg's writings have had in the visionary experiences or the thinking of Blake after 1783. Although he seemed to repudiate Swedenborg (Blake, *Poetry and Prose,* pp. 201, 933–948), nevertheless, the influence remained. By way of example of influential items which have not previously been mentioned, there are forty-two propositions in the *Circular Letter* of December 7, 1788 (Hindmarsh, *op. cit.,* pp. 80–83), and the doctrine of concubinage (Odhner, *op. cit.,* p. 29), the practical application of which split the New Church in 1789 (just the year after Blake joined it), and which doubtless was the basis for the rumored decision of Blake to bring a concubine into his house. (Cf. Swinburne, *op. cit.,* p. 14.)
57. Mr. Wright's letter to the author, October 1, 1934, confirmed by Mr. Muir's letter to the author, October 12, 1934. Cf. Wright, *op. cit.,* I, 2.
58. T. Taylor Hamilton, *A History of the Church Known as the Moravian Church.* Bethlehem, Pa.: Times Publishing Co. 1900. p. 84.
59. Daniel Benham, *Memoirs of James Hutton; Comprising the Annals of his Life and Connection with the United Brethren.* London: Hamilton, Adams Co. . . . MDCCCLVI. p. 79. There is a striking resemblance between Blake's *The Lamb* and James Hutton's hymn, "O Lamb of God so mild." p. 99.
60. The Rev. Abraham Reincke, *A Register of Members of the Moravian Church, and of the Persons Attached to Said Church in This Country and Abroad, between 1727 and 1754.* (Transcribed from a MS. in the Archives of the Moravian Church at Bethlehem, Pa. by W. C. Reichel) Bethlehem [Pa.]: H. T. Clauder, Printer. 1873. p. 12.
61. John Thomas Smith, *Nollekens and His Times* . . . London:

John Lane, the Bodley Head; New York: John Lane Company. MCMXX. II, 394. (Edited by Wilfred Whitten.) Permission to quote this text has been kindly granted by the publisher. Cf. Herbert Jenkins, *William Blake. Studies of His Life and Personality.* London: Herbert Jenkins Ltd. . . . MCMXXV. pp. 81–97. (Edited by C. E. Lawrence.)

62. Symons, *op. cit.*, p. 22.

63. *Ibid.*, p. 23.

64. Russell, *op. cit.*, p. 2.

65. Symons, *op. cit.*, p. 28.

66. This shows that Gilchrist was more correct than Cunningham about the date of James Blake's business. Cunningham erroneously gives 1828 as the date of Blake's death. (p. 153.)

67. Russell, *op. cit.*, p. 3.

68. *Ibid.*, p. 2.

69. Blake, *Poetry and Prose*, p. 1069. (November 22, 1802.) Cf. *Letter to Butts*, p. 1062.

70. *Daily Advertiser*, June 25, 1757, quoted in Whitley, *Artists and Their Friends in England, 1770–1799.* II, 249.

71. Malkin, *op. cit.*, pp. xviii–xix.

72. Blake, *Poetry and Prose*, p. 1008.

73. Malkin, *op. cit.*, p. xix.

74. Geoffrey Keynes, "William Blake and the Portland Vase." *The Times Literary Supplement* (London). XXIX, 554. (July 3, 1930.) Cf. C. H. Collins Baker, *Catalogue of William Blake's Drawings and Paintings in the Huntington Library.* San Marino, California. 1938. p. 38.

75. Cf. the principles enunciated in Blake, *Poetry and Prose*, pp. 778–806, 808–824, 970–1015.

76. *Ibid.*, p. 1045.

77. *Ibid.*, p. 975.

78. *London Magazine*, VI, 385. (July, 1737.)

Cf. *Lloyd's Evening Post*, XXIV, 78 (January 20, 1769); XXIV, 270 (March 18, 1769); *The Gazetter and New Daily Advertiser.* (March 14, 1778.)

79. Eliza Meteyard, *The Life of Josiah Wedgwood from his Private Correspondence and Family Papers* . . . London: Hurst and Blackett . . . 1866. II, 292.

Cf. Julia Wedgwood, *The Personal Life of Josiah Wedgwood, the Potter.* London: Macmillan and Co., Limited . . . 1915. p. 157. (Edited by C. H. Herford.)

Cf. Dr. George C. Williamson, *The Imperial Russian Dinner Service. A Story of a Famous Work by Josiah Wedgwood.* London: George Bell and Sons. 1909. p. 19.

80. Archibald G. B. Russell, *The Engravings of William Blake.* London: Grant Richards Ltd. MDCCCCXII. p. 53.

81. *Ibid.*, p. 56.

82. Williamson, *op. cit.*, Plate 665 facing p. 44.

83. *The Town and Country Magazine*, I, 100 (February, 1769), gives an account of Joseph of Arimathea. Blake knew this magazine as will be shown in Chapter VII.

84. Gilchrist, *op. cit.*, I, 13. Cf. *The Morning Post, and Daily Advertiser.* No. 3264. (July 28, 1783.)

85. *The London Chronicle,* LIV, 215. (August 30, 1783.)
86. Russell, *Letters,* pp. 4–5.
87. Malkin, *op. cit.,* p. xix.
88. Blake, *Poetry and Prose,* p. 824.
89. *Ibid.,* p. 808.
90. [R. B. Adam and R. B. Adam, Jr.], *A Letter of William Blake.* [n.p.] [Privately printed]. Christmas, 1929. [p. 3.] Letter to William Hayley, dated October 7, 1803. Permission to quote this text has been kindly granted by the publisher.
91. *Dictionary of National Biography,* III, 358–359. Cf. Gilchrist, *op. cit.,* p. 14.
92. Blake, *Poetry and Prose,* pp. 811, 812, 823.
93. Malkin, *op. cit.,* p. xix.
94. Laurence Binyon, *The Engraved Designs of William Blake.* London: Ernest Benn Limited . . . ; New York: Charles Scribner's Sons. MCMXXVI. p. 62.
95. *Lloyd's Evening Post,* XXVII, 454. (November 9, 1770.)
96. Gilchrist, *op. cit.,* I, 14–15.
97. Blake, *Poetry and Prose,* p. 1040.
98. *Ibid.,* p. 1061.
99. *Ibid.,* p. 1097.
100. *Ibid.,* p. 1092.
101. Gilchrist, *op. cit.,* I, 19–20; Russell, *Engravings,* p. 23; Binyon, *Engraved Designs,* p. 36; W. R. Letheby, *T. L. S.* (London), XXVI, 592. (September 1, 1927.)
102. Blake, *Poetry and Prose,* pp. 793, 847–848.
103. Thomas Maurice, *Westminster Abbey; An Elegaic Poem.* London: J. Dodsley . . . 1784. p. 1.
104. Malkin, *op. cit.,* p. xx.
105. *Ibid.,* pp. xx–xxi.
106. Maurice, *op. cit.,* p. 4.
107. Malkin, *op. cit.,* p. xxi.
108. Blake, *Poetry and Prose,* pp. 41, 302, 390, 399, 477, 489, 528, 626, 630.
109. Joseph H. Wicksteed, *Blake's Innocence and Experience,* . . . London and Toronto: J. M. Dent & Sons Ltd.; New York: E. P. Dutton & Co. MCMXXVIII. p. 103. Permission to quote this text has been kindly granted by the publisher.
110. Blake, *Poetry and Prose,* p. 783.
111. *Ibid.,* pp. 820–821.
112. A. H. Palmer, *The Life and Letters of Samuel Palmer, Painter and Etcher.* London: Seeley & Co. Ltd. . . . 1892. p. 8.
113. Gilchrist, *op. cit.,* I, 303.
114. One story relating to Blake's days in Westminster Abbey is apparently not authentic. Tatham said that Blake, annoyed by the interference from Westminster boys, knocked one of them from the scaffolding where he worked. Upon Blake's complaint, the Dean is said to have ordered the door closed to them, and they have since been excluded. (Russell, *Letters,* pp. 6–7.) The Rev. A. Sargent, Chaplain to his Grace the Archbishop of Canterbury, wrote the author, February 19, 1933, regarding this episode, that there is no record of such action by the Dean and the only known reference is that by Tatham.

115. Russell, *Letters*, p. 7.
116. Blake, *Poetry and Prose*, p. 768.
117. Malkin, *op. cit.*, pp. xxi–xxii.
118. Russell, *Engravings*, p. 53.
119. Gilchrist, *op. cit.*, I, 30.
120. Keynes, *Bibliography*, p. 32.
121. Gilchrist, *op. cit.*, II, 263. Cf. Frances A. Gerard, *Angelica Kauffman, a Biography.* New York: Macmillan and Co. 1893. p. 162.— Angelica Kauffman exhibited in 1776 at the Royal Academy "Eleanor sucking the Poison from the wound of Edward I."
122. Blake, *Poetry and Prose*, p. 806.
123. Malkin, *op. cit.*, p. xxii.
124. Gilchrist, *op. cit.*, I, 28. Cf. Russell, *Engravings*, p. 25.
125. Smith, *Nollekens and His Times*, II, 167.
126. The author is indebted to Mr. W. R. M. Lamb, Secretary of the Royal Academy, for this information, February 24, 1931.
127. Mrs. Bray, *Life of Thomas Stothard, R. A. with Personal Reminiscences.* London: John Murray . . . 1851. p. 20. Cf. Keynes, *Bibliography*, p. 326.
128. Bray, *op. cit.*, p. 21 n.
129. Russell, *Engravings*, pp. 135–146.
130. Blake, *Poetry and Prose*, p. 800.
131. *Ibid.*, p. 802.
132. *Ibid.*, p. 1064.
133. Symons, *op. cit.*, p. 362. Symons reprints the text of the first edition of Nollekens; but in the only text available to the author, the information has been incorporated in the text.
134. Russell, *Letters*, pp. 16–17.
135. Symons, *op. cit.*, p. 45. Cf. Wm. Bray . . ., *The History and Antiquities of the County of Surry.* . . . London: J. White. 1814. III, 341.
136. Gilchrist, *op. cit.*, I, 360.
137. Blake, *Poetry and Prose*, p. 1048.
138. A copy of *Nollekens and His Times*, once owned by Elizabeth Hogarth, contains annotations by J. H. (presumably Joseph Hogarth). One annotation to a section on William Blake reads: "Fred Tatham was Blake's executor and possessed several of his drawings, many of which I purchased from him. Mrs. Blake was hardly the passive creture [*sic*] here described—at all events Tatham did not find her so for she was opposed to everything he did for her benefit . . ." Cf. [Wilfred Partington] "A William Blake Discovery and Its Lesson." *The Bookman* (American), LXXIV, 669. (March, 1932.)
139. Blake, *Poetry and Prose*, p. 585.
140. *Ibid.*, p. 1011.

CHAPTER II

1. Gilchrist, *Life of William Blake*, I, 49.
2. Clarence Gohdes and Paull Franklin Baum (editors), *Letters of William Michael Rossetti concerning Whitman, Blake, and Shelley to Anne Gilchrist and Her Son Herbert Gilchrist* . . . Durham, North

214   *Windows of the Morning.*

Carolina: Duke University Press. 1934. pp. 131–132. Permission to quote this text has been kindly granted by the publisher.

3. William Blake, *Poetical Sketches.* London. 1783. p. 40, ll. 5–23. All references throughout this study will be made to this, the original edition.

4. Blake, *Poetry and Prose,* p. 7, ll. 18–19.

5. Richard Herne Shepherd (editor), *Poetical Sketches* by William Blake . . . London: Basil Montagu Pickering . . . 1806. p. 13, ll. 18–20.

6. Samuel Johnson, *The Rambler.* No. 177, p. 1059, l. 10. (November 26, 1751) London: . . . MDCCLI.

7. Cf. Spenser's *The Faerie Queene,* II, ii, 7.8; III, v, 13.6; III, vi, 46.9; IV, ix, 5.1; V, viii, 50.7; V, xi, 59.7; VI, i, 22.7; *Epithalamion,* l. 70; *Amoretti,* xxi.7; Milton's *Paradise Lost,* X, 219; I, 775; V, 357; Shakespeare's *Merry Wives of Windsor,* III, 5.100. Cf. *The Gentleman's Magazine, and Historical Chronicle,* XXXII, 73. (February, 1762); Mark Akenside, *The Pleasures of Imagination* (London, 1744), Bk. III, 210; Oliver Goldsmith, *She Stoops to Conquer* . . . (London, 1773), V, 12 ff.; Judges 16.7. (Authorized version.)

8. Robert Southey, *The Doctor* . . . London: Longman, Brown, Green, and Longmans. 1847. VI, 127.

9. Henry Crabb Robinson, *Diary, Reminiscences and Correspondence.* London: Macmillan and Co. 1869. I, 338. (Second edition. Edited by Thomas Sadler.)

10. Edward Dowden (editor), *The Correspondence of Robert Southey with Caroline Bowles* . . . Dublin: Hodges, Figgis, & Co. . . . ; London: Green, & Co. . . . 1881. p. 194. (Dublin University Press Series.)

11. Shepherd, *op. cit.,* p. ix.

12. William Blake, *Poetical Works* . . . London: George Bell and Sons . . . 1874. p. 47. (Edited by William Michael Rossetti. The Aldine edition.) Cf. the similarity of phrasing in the *Poetical Sketches,* p. 60. ll. 3–4.

13. *The Academy,* VI, 599–606. (December 5, 1874. No. 135, New Series.)

14. George Saintsbury, *A History of English Prosody from the Twelfth Century to the Present Day.* London: Macmillan and Co., Limited . . . 1910. III, 11–12. Permission to quote this text has been kindly granted by the publisher.

15. The *T. L. S.* (London), p. 548. (October 9, 1919.)

16. *Ibid.,* p. 591. (October 23, 1919.)

17. Verified by a letter to the author, September 29, 1934.

18. Verified by a letter to the author from Roland O. Baughman, Assistant Curator of Rare Books, June 16, 1934.

19. The author is indebted to Mr. J. Wilks, Librarian, for the privilege of examination of this copy, July, 1937.

20. *Book Prices Current* (1910), XIV, 372. No. 5230.

21. Letter to the author from the owner, September 29, 1934.

22. William Blake, *The Poetical Works.* Oxford: At the Clarendon Press. 1905. p. 4. (Edited by John Sampson.)

23. A conspicuous example of condescension is that of Henry Crabb Robinson who, at the time he wrote, had not made Blake's acquaint-

ance. He wrote in January, 1811, in *Vaterländisches Museum,* Band II, Heft I, S. 107–131 (Cf. *The Modern Language Review,* XXII, 137–154. April, 1927) : "Schon im Jahre 1783 ward ein kleines Bändschen unter dem Titel: Poetische Versuche, gedruckt . . . Auf dem Titel ist kein Drucker genannt, und in der Vorrede heiszt es, dasz die Gedichte zwischen dem 13 ten un 20 sten Jahre verfertigt wurden. Sie sind von seher unglichem Werthe. Der Versbau ist meistentheils so lose und sorglos, dasz er eine völlige Unwissenheit der Kunst verräth, wobei zugleich die meisten Stücke von empörender Rohheit und sehr zuruckstoszend sind. Dagegen findet sich auf der andern Seite in einigen dramatischen Bruckstücken wieder eine Wildheit und Grösze der Phantasie, die ein ächt dichterisches Gefühl beglaubigen." Permission to quote this text has been kindly granted by the publisher.

24. The printer of the *Poetical Sketches* is unidentified. A likely printer is Robert Hindmarsh who came to London from Bristol to learn the trade as an apprentice to Josiah Collier, Quaker (Cf. Hindmarsh, *Rise and Progress* . . . p. 8), in a printing house connected with Mr. James Phillips, also a Quaker, at whose shop in 1778, Swedenborg's *Heaven and Hell,* in translation, was printed. While he was yet a young man, Robert Hindmarsh established a shop of his own. By 1782, he had obtained copies of Swedenborg's *Heaven and Hell* and *The Intercourse between the Soul and the Body,* and, by 1783, he had Swedenborg's complete works in Latin. That year those interested first gathered under the leadership of Robert Hindmarsh's father to learn of Swedenborg. Among them was John Flaxman, who, seeking just then someone to print Blake's little book of verse, would, doubtless, have thought of Robert Hindmarsh and been glad to give work to a young printer who, beginning in his own establishment, might have had broken fonts of type, as the printer of the *Poetical Sketches* did have.

25. *The Town and Country Magazine; or Universal Repository of Knowledge, Instruction and Entertainment,* IV, 171. (April, 1772.)

26. *Ibid.,* I, 104–106. (February, 1769.) Cf. I, 328 (June, 1769); I, 440 (August, 1769); II, 216 (April, 1770); II, 608 (November, 1770); XIV, 215. (April, 1782.)

27. *The Monthly Magazine, or British Register,* XXII, 43. (August, 1806.)

28. *The Monthly Ledger, or Literary Repository,* I, 378. (January, 1774.)

29. *The Lady's Magazine; or Entertaining Companion for the Fair Sex* . . . II, 328. (February, 1771.) Cf. the description of the Juvenile Club in *The Town and Country Magazine,* III, 309. (June, 1771.)

30. Cf. [John Gilbert Cooper], *Poems on Several Occasions.* London: J. Dodsley. MDCCLXIV. *Preface* (Written when he "was very young"); Matthew West, *Poems on Several Occasions* (466 subscribers. Written before his seventeenth year); Mary Jones, *Miscellanies in Prose and Verse.* Oxford: J. Dodsley . . . MDCCL. p. v (Written at "a very early age." 1500 subscribers.) The apologetic tone and phrasing of the *Advertisement* suggest the *Advertisement* to the *Poetical Sketches.*

31. Smith, *Nollekens and His Times,* II, 367–368.

32. Russell, *Letters,* p. 8.

33. William Blake, *Poems.* London: George Routledge & Sons,

Limited; New York: E. P. Dutton & Co. [1905]. p. xxiii. (Edited by W. B. Yeats. The Muses Library.)

34. Allardyce Nicoll, *William Blake & His Poetry*. London: George G. Harrap & Co. Ltd. . . . 1922. p. 31. Professor Nicoll was unable to state to the author upon whose authority he named Fuseli as one who aided in printing the *Poetical Sketches*.

35. Smith, *Nollekens and His Times*, II, 369.

36. Smith, *A Book for a Rainy Day*, p. 97.

37. Gilchrist, *op. cit.*, I, 43–44; 45–46.

38. *Ibid.*, I, 44.

39. *The Builder*, XXI, 60. No. 1042. (January 24, 1863.)

40. William T. Whitley, *Art in England, 1821–1837*. Cambridge: At the University Press. 1930. p. 119. Permission to quote this text has been kindly granted by the publisher.

41. *The Builder*, XXI, 60. No. 1042. (January 24, 1863.)

42. There is one interesting speculation which arises from the possibility that Blake knew Charles Burney, the scholar. There seems little doubt that Blake was acquainted with Thomas Traherne's poetry although this has always been considered impossible because it was thought Traherne's work did not reach print until 1903 and 1932. If, however, Blake had any contact with the Burney family, he could have known Traherne, for Charles Burney owned Traherne's book listed as follows in the *Burney Manuscripts:* "No. 393. Paper, small 8 vo., pp. 133. xvii Cent. 'Poems of Felicity, containing divine reflections on the native object of an infant ey, by Tho. Traheron B.D., Author of the Roman Forgeries and Christian Ethics,' with a dedication in verse by Philip Traheron." [*Catalogue of MS. in the B.M.* New Series. . . . MDCCCCXL. Part II. p. 140.] Two other minor links in this hypothesis may be mentioned. It was Charles Burney's brother-in-law, Samuel Rose, who was Blake's attorney when he was tried for treason in 1804. [Gilchrist, *op. cit.*, I, 174.] In October, 1788 Rose was living in Rathbone Place which was in the section in which the Mathews lived. [Wm. Cowper, *Poems*. London. p. lxxxiii.] It was one of Charles Burney's students at Hammersmith, T. C. Wainwright, who bought (c. 1820–1824) one of Blake's most handsomely colored copies of *Songs of Innocence and Experience*. [Keynes, *Bibliography*, pp. 123–124.]

43. Smith, *Nollekens and His Times*, II, 367.

44. Cunningham, *The Lives of the Most Eminent Painters and Sculptors*, p. 128.

45. W. G. Constable, *John Flaxman, 1755–1826*. London: University of London Press, Ltd., . . . 1927. p. 22. Permission to quote this text has been kindly granted by the publisher.

46. *Catalogue of an Exhibition of Original Drawings by John Flaxman, R. A.* New York: Scott & Fowles . . . 1918. p. 6.

47. *Fairfax Murray Collection of Flaxman MS.* in the Fitzwilliam Museum, Cambridge. (England) Cf. unpublished letters dated February 24, 1795; October 1, 1798; July 25, 1818. Permission to quote this collection of MS. has been graciously given by the Director of the Fitzwilliam Museum.

48. Blake, *Poetry and Prose*, pp. 1048–1049. Letter to John Flaxman, dated September 21, 1800.

49. *Ibid.*, p. 810.

50. It may be only a happy coincidence that Flaxman's titles, *The Four Seasons* and *Blindman's Buff*, reliefs of groups of children, suggest at once the early poems of Blake. The first most surely followed the poems (Constable, *op. cit.*, p. 84), and *Blindman's Buff* (reproduced in Church, *Josiah Wedgwood, Master Potter,* London. 1884. pp. 70–71), coming in 1782 (Smiles, *Josiah Wedgwood* . . . New York. 1895. p. 227), while preceding the publication of Blake's *Blindman's Buff*, could have followed a personal acquaintance with it.

51. Constable, *op. cit.*, p. 79.

52. *Lloyd's Evening Post*, XXVII, 573. (December 14, 1770.)

53. Smith, *Nollekens and His Times,* II, 353. Knight is wrongly referred to as Flaxman's first employer. Cf. Constable, *op. cit.*, pp. 6, 79.

54. Constable, *op. cit.*, facing p. 22.

55. Blake, *Poetry and Prose*, p. 1045.

56. *Ibid.*, p. 1046.

57. *Fairfax Murray Collection of Flaxman MS.* Unpublished letter, dated September 30, 1797.

58. Blake, *Poetry and Prose*, p. 1054.

59. *Ibid.*, p. 1084.

60. *Ibid.*, p. 1116.

61. *Ibid.*, p. 847.

62. *The Builder*, XXI, 60.

63. Blake, *Poetry and Prose*, p. 1110.

64. *Ibid.*, p. 1047.

65. *Ibid.*, p. 104.

66. This unique book was discovered when the Duke of Hamilton's palace was dismantled. *The London Times,* November 4, 1919, p. 15.

67. *Fairfax Murray Collection of Flaxman MS.* Unpublished letter, dated August 12, 1805.

68. Sotheby's *Sale Catalogue,* May 31–June 1, 1907. p. 56. No. 49.

69. *Fairfax Murray Collection of Flaxman MS.* Unpublished letter, dated August 19, 1800.

70. Blake, *Poetry and Prose*, p. 1049.

71. *Ibid.*, p. 1087.

72. Cf. *ibid.*, pp. 809, 810, 846, 847, 849, 850, 851, 1067.

73. *Ibid.*, pp. 1109–1110.

74. *Fairfax Murray Collection of Flaxman MS.* Unpublished letter, dated August 12, 1805.

75. Unpublished letter in the Library of the Historical Society of Pennsylvania. Privilege to quote this passage was kindly granted by Mr. Julian P. Boyd, Assistant Librarian.

76. Blake, *Poetry and Prose*, p. 1091.

77. *Ibid.*, pp. 1044–1045.

78. *Fairfax Murray Collection of Flaxman MS.* Unpublished letter, dated December 10, 1806.

79. *Ibid.* Unpublished letter, dated May 4, 1808. There is a suggestion that Gilchrist knew something of this quarrel in his account (I, 33): "In 1781, the sculptor [Flaxman] married, taking house and studio of his own at 27, Wardour Street, and becoming Blake's near neighbor. He proved—despite some passing clouds which for a time obscured their friendship at a later era—one of the best and firmest

218 *Windows of the Morning.*

friends Blake ever had; as great artists often prove to one another in youth."

80. *Ibid.* Unpublished letter, dated August 2, 1804.

81. Printed copy of the resolutions passed at a "General Meeting of the Master Paper-Makers, at the George and Vulture Tavern, Cornhill, London, the 13th day of June, 1803," on file at the London office of the Paper-maker's Association of Great Britain and Ireland, to whom the author is indebted for the information.

82. The author is indebted to Mr. A. Bone, Manager of the Nash Mills, Hemel Hempstead, for his courtesy in allowing her to examine the moulds and for his generous assistance in making impresses from the moulds.

83. This note is in the possession of Mr. Oliver R. Barrett, Chicago, Illinois. The author is greatly indebted to him for his invaluable assistance and for his permission to publish the MS.

Mr. Geoffrey Keynes questions whether Blake wrote this note. The author shared his question until her research produced evidence which convinced her that Blake wrote it.

84. Gilchrist, *op. cit.,* II, 256. It is worth noting that Blake referred to the twenty years previous to 1804 as being "dark, but very profitable years." (*Poetry and Prose,* p. 1109.)

85. Blake, *Poetry and Prose,* p. 1127.

86. Russell, *Letters,* pp. 51–52.

87. Margaret Ruth Lowery, *A Census of Copies of William Blake's "Poetical Sketches, 1783."* London: The Bibliographical Society. 1936. Since this census appeared in *The Library,* December, 1936, one more copy was located in the University of London Library.

88. John D. Ross, *The Story of the Kilmarnock Burns.* Stirling: Eneas Mackay. 1933. p. 21. Cf. *The Life and Works of Robert Burns,* edited by Robert Chambers. 1851 edition. I, 350.

89. a. *Lloyd's Evening Post,* XXXII, 384 (April 21, 1773); XXVI, 90 (January 24, 1770); XXX, 430 (May 4, 1772); XXXVIII, 344 (April 8, 1776); XL, 32 (January 8, 1777); XLII, 520 (June 1, 1778); XLIII, 408 (October 26, 1778); XLIII, 576 (December 14, 1778); XLV, 208 (August 30, 1779); XLV, 288 (September 22, 1779); XLVII, 390 (October 23, 1780); XLVIII, 79 (January 22, 1781); L, 358 (April 15, 1782); L, 239 (March 11, 1782); LI, 68 (July 18, 1782).

b. Brigadier-General Conyers Surtees, *The History of the Castle of Brancepeth* . . . [London: David Allen & Sons, Ltd.] 1920. p. 38.

c. *Repository of Arts, Literature, Commerce, Manufactures, Fashions, and Policies,* XXXII, 333. (May, 1810.)

d. *The History and Antiquities of Twickenham*: . . . London: Printed by and for John Nichols. 1797. In *Bibliotheca Topographica Britannica,* X, 20, 25, 143, 148.

e. *A List of the Members of the Society of Antiquaries of London, From Their Revival in 1717 to June 19, 1796.* London: Printed by and for John Nichols at Cicero's Head, Red Lion Passage, Fleet Street. MDCCXCVII. p. 28.

90. Blake, *Poetry and Prose,* p. 1130.

91. Gilchrist, *op. cit.,* I, 247.

92. Blake, *Poetry and Prose,* p. 847.

93. *Fairfax Murray Collection of Flaxman MS.* Unpublished letter, assigned to 1795.

94. On a print (the second state) called *The Accusers of Theft, Adultery, and Murder,* published June 5, 1793, Blake placed the quotation, "When the senses are shaken and the soul is driven to madness. Page 56." This is the page number of the *Poetical Sketches* where the sentence appears, showing that he must have had a copy of the *Poetical Sketches* in 1793. (Russell, *Engravings,* p. 67.)

95. Gilchrist, *op. cit.,* I, 23.

96. Sotheby's *Catalogue for July 16–20, 1886,* p. 183. No. 20.

97. Swinburne, *William Blake,* p. 8.

98. *The Harbinger* (N.Y.), VII, 73, No. 10 (July 8, 1848). This was first noted by T. O. Mabbott in *Notes and Queries.* Twelfth Series, X, 129. (February 18, 1922.)

99. *The Monthly Magazine, or British Register,* XXII, 633. (January 25, 1807.)

100. *The Monthly Review; or Literary Journal . . .,* LI, 216. (October, 1806.)

CHAPTER III

1. Blake, *Poetry and Prose,* p. 984.

2. Henry G. Hewlett in 1876 in *The Contemporary Review* (XXVIII, 756, 784) brought the charge that Blake was imitative by conscious effort "to a point of plagiarism." The investigations incident to this study do not sustain his statements.

3. Russell, *Letters,* p. 20.

4. Gilchrist, *Life of William Blake,* I, 7.

5. *Ibid.*

6. *Ibid.,* p. 18.

7. Oswald Crawfurd is the authority that this account was recorded in a letter from Blake to Butts which a friend of his bought at a sale in 1861. "William Blake: Artist, Poet, and Mystic." *New Quarterly Magazine.* MDCCCLXXIV. II, 475.

8. Blake, *Poetry and Prose,* p. 829.

9. S. Foster Damon, *William Blake, His Philosophy and Symbols.* London, Bombay, Sidney: Constable and Company Ltd. 1924. p. 255. Permission to quote this text has been kindly granted by the publisher.

10. Blake, *Poetry and Prose,* p. 800.

11. *Ibid.,* p. 1011.

12. Cf. Blake, *Poetry and Prose,* p. 622:
> . . . I have girded round my cloke, and on my feet
> Bound these black shoes of death, & on my hands,
>   death's iron gloves.

13. Ezekiel 7.8; 9.8; 14.9; 20.8, 13, 21; 22.22; 30.15.

14. Jeremiah 10.25; 42.18.

15. Lamentations 2.4.

16. Gilchrist, *op. cit.,* II, 208.

17. Cf. Jeremiah 25.32; 23.10; Nahum 1.3; Proverbs 1.27.

18. The description in the *Aeneid* of Mercury's flight from the heights of the sky to the sea is quoted in Dryden's translation in Bysshe's *Art*

of English Poetry (London. 1705. p. 259) which Blake owned, but it patently was not the description foremost in Blake's mind.

19. Cf. Exodus 3.20; 7.5, 19; 8.5; 9.22; 10.12, 21; 14.16, 26; I Samuel 11.23; 24.6; 26.9; II Samuel 1.14; Job 11.13; 30.24; Psalm 138.7; 143.6; Isaiah 31.3; Jeremiah 6.12; 15.6; 51.25; Ezekiel 6.14; 14.9; 3.5; St. Luke 6.10; St. John 21.18.

20. Cf. Ezekiel 21.7; Jeremiah 6.24; 50.43; II Samuel 4.1.

21. Cf. Psalm 2.1; 11.3.

22. Cf. Job 24.9: "They pluck the fatherless from the breast, and take a pledge of the poor."

23. Psalm 42.4; 86.6; Isaiah 65.19; 48.20; Jonah 2.9; Psalm 36.3; 50.19; 52.4.

24. Cf. Psalm 96.1, 12; 98.8; 69.34; 65.11–13.

25. Blake, *Poetry and Prose,* p. 829.

26. *Ibid.*

27. *Ibid.,* p. 844.

28. *Ibid.,* pp. 138–139.

29. *Ibid.,* p. 1040.

30. Cf. Psalm 27.5; 31.20.

31. Cf. Blake, *Poetry and Prose,* p. 349: "Then in my ivory pavilions I slumber'd in the noon . . ."

32. Milton's poem could have been further impressed upon his mind if he had heard at any Easter season during 1765–1780, either at Drury Lane or Covent Garden Theatres Handel's Oratorio "alter'd from Samson Agonistes of Milton." Cf. *Lloyd's Evening Post,* XX, 266. (March 19, 1767.)

33. Blake, *Poetry and Prose,* p. 1073.

34. *Ibid.,* p. 1038.

35. John Milton, *The Poetical Works.* London, New York, Toronto, Melbourne: Henry Frowde, Oxford University Press. 1908. (Edited by the Rev. H. C. Beeching.) *Samson Agonistes,* ll. 392–394. Permission to quote this text has been kindly granted by the publisher.

36. *Ibid.,* l. 712.

37. *Ibid.,* l. 51.

38. R. D. Havens calls attention to the likeness between Blake's phrase, "the form was manhood in the prime" and Milton's expression in *Paradise Lost,* XI, 245–246:

>His starrie Helme unbuckl'd shew'd him prime
>In Manhood where Youth ended; . . .

Richard Dexter Havens, *The Influence of Milton in English Poetry.* Cambridge: Harvard University Press; London: Humphrey Milford, Oxford University Press. 1922. p. 222. Permission to quote this text has been kindly granted by the publisher.

39. James Hastings, *A Dictionary of the Bible.* New York: Charles Scribner's Sons. 1902. IV, 607.

40. William Whiston (translator), *The Works of Flavius Josephus* . . . London: Printed for Lackington . . . 1820. I, 360. Bk. V, Ch. 8.

41. Cf. Blake's lines (p. 66, ll. 7–10) with *S. A.* l. 128; Blake's use of "tear" (p. 29, l. 7; p. 56, l. 11) with *S. A.* l. 128. The Bible uses "rent" in place of "tear." Cf. Blake's lines (p. 69, l. 27—p. 70, l. 4) with *Isaiah* 2.4.

42. Blake, *Poetry and Prose,* p. 468.

43. *Ibid.*, p. 1046.

44. Emily S. Hamblen, *On the Minor Prophecies of William Blake*. London and Toronto: J. M. Dent & Sons Ltd.; New York: E. P. Dutton & Co. Inc. [1930]. p. 6. Permission to quote this text has been kindly granted by Messrs. E. P. Dutton & Co.

45. Blake, *Poetry and Prose*, p. 797.

46. *Ibid.* Cf. John Milton, *The History of Britain, That part especially now call'd England* . . . London: Printed by J. M. for James Allestry . . . MDCLXX. pp. 4–5.

47. George Chapman, *The Iliads of Homer* . . . London: N. Butler. [1611]. Bk. XI, p. 149, ll. 6–7. Cf. Blake's "Jove weighs the counsel of futurity" (p. 25, l. 2) with *P. L.,* IV, 996–1002; with Chapman's *Iliad*, Bk. XXII, p. 303, ll. 8–12; and with Spenser's *The Faerie Queene*, V, ii, 30.3.

48. The Rev. R. Potter (translator), *Aeschylus.* New York: . . . Harper & Brothers . . . 1834. p. 211, ll. 922–927. (Classical Family Library. No. XIII. Stereotype Edition.)

49. A parallel between *L'Allegro,* ll. 28–29 and Blake (p. 17, l. 1) has been noted by S. Foster Damon, *op. cit.,* p. 258 and by R. D. Havens, *op. cit.,* p. 220.

50. Cf. Blake, *Poetry and Prose,* p. 173, ll. 21–22.

51. Cf. Milton's "One Talent which is death to hide" in *Sonnet XVI* with Blake's "that Talent which it is Death to Bury" in a letter to Hayley, December 11, 1805. (*Poetry and Prose,* p. 1120.)

52. [William Mason], *Musaeus: A Monody to the Memory of Mr. Pope, in Imitation of Milton's Lycidas.* London: . . . R. Dodsley . . . 1747. p. 22, ll. 5–12.

53. Reproduced on p. 9. *On the Morning of Christ's Nativity* . . . with a note by Geoffrey Keynes. Cambridge: At the University Press. 1923.

54. Havens, *op. cit.,* p. 217. Cf. Gilchrist, *op. cit.,* II, 202–261; *The Grolier Club Catalogue* of 1905; Milton's *Works.* Illustrations by William Blake. 2 vols. London: Nonesuch Press. 1926.

CHAPTER IV

1. Blake, *Poetry and Prose*, p. 232, l. 10.

2. Malkin, *A Father's Memoirs of His Child,* p. xxv.

3. *Ibid.*, p. xxxiv.

4. *The Monthly Miscellany,* III, 29 (January, 1775), announces a new octavo edition "complete and elegant" of Shakespeare's poems, sold by Evans for three shillings.

5. Cf. Young's remarks on genius and the power of the human mind to summon "shadowy beings from the vast void beyond real existence" in the edition by Edith Morley. (Manchester: At the University Press . . . 1918. pp. 13, 31.)

6. Samuel Johnson, *The Lives of the Most Eminent English Poets* . . . London: Printed for C. Bathurst . . . MDCCLXXXI. IV, 318–319.

7. Samuel Johnson, *The Rambler.* London: Printed for W. Strahan . . . MDCCLXXIX. III, 100. No. 121. (May 14, 1721.) Ninth edition.

8. Duncan C. Tovey (editor), *The Letters of Thomas Gray* . . . London: C. Bell and Sons Ltd. 1912. III, 305. Letter to James Beattie, March 8, 1771.

9. William Thompson, *An Hymn to May* . . . London: . . . R. Dodsley . . . [1740?]. pp. iii–iv.

10. Thomas Warton, *Observations on the Faerie Queene of Spenser.* London: Printed for R. and J. Dodsley . . . MDCCLIV. p. 181.

11. William Shenstone, *The Works in Verse and Prose.* London: Printed for R. and J. Dodsley . . . MDCCLXIV. I, 333.

12. Sampson, *The Poetical Works,* p. 21.

13. All references to Spenser throughout this study are made to the text of the Cambridge edition. *The Complete Poetical Works of Edmund Spenser.* Boston and New York: Houghton Mifflin Company . . . [1908]. (Edited by R. E. Neil Dodge.) Permission to quote this text has been kindly granted by the publisher.

14. Geoffrey Keynes (editor), *The Writings of William Blake.* London: The Nonesuch Press . . . MCMXXV. I, 350.

15. Sampson, *op. cit.,* p. 22.

16. For Spenser's further use of "leasing" in the sense of "lying" cf. *The Faerie Queene,* II, xi, 10.7; V, xii, 36.8; V, iii, 20.8; VI, i, 3.8; *The Shepheardes Calender, Maye,* l. 285; *Colin Clouts Come Home Againe,* ll. 102, 821; *Prosopopoia,* l. 699.

17. Cf. *The Faerie Queene,* I, viii, 8.7; I, xii, 9.9.

18. About 1810 Blake wrote: ". . . Bloated Gods, Mercury, Juno, Venus, & the rattle traps of mythology . . ." (*Poetry and Prose,* p. 818.)

19. *Ibid.,* p. 795.

20. Joseph Addison, *An Account of the Greatest English Poets. To Mr. H. S.* April 3, 1694. *Works.* London: Printed for Jacob Tonson . . . MDCCXXX. II, 35. (Second edition.)

21. Blake, *Poetry and Prose,* p. 1088. (January 27, 1804.)

22. *Ibid.,* pp. 857, 970, 979–980, 1106; and unpublished letter, October 7, 1803.

23. Milton, *op. cit.,* Preface to *Paradise Lost.*

24. Blake, *Poetry and Prose,* p. 551.

25. Cf. William Collins, *The Poetical Works.* London: Printed for T. Becket . . . MDCCLXV. p. 82, ll. 9–12:

> With woeful measures wan Despair—
>> Low sullen sounds his grief beguil'd,
> A solomn, strange, and mingled air,
>> 'Twas sad by fits, and starts 'twas wild.

26. Cf. *The Faerie Queene,* II, v, 27.4; II, xii, 49.9; II, xii, 44.5; VII, v, 13.4; IV, iii, 48.2; IV, iii, 42.6; IV, iii, 46.2.

27. Cf. *ibid.,* II, ii, 46.2.

28. E. H. W. Meyerstein, *A Life of Thomas Chatterton.* New York: Charles Scribner's Sons. 1930. p. 357. Permission to quote this text has been kindly granted by the publisher.

29. *The London Magazine or, Gentleman's Monthly Intelligencer,* XXXIX, 268. (May, 1770.) Cf. Thomas Chatterton, *The Complete Poetical Works.* London: George Routledge & Sons Limited; New York: E. P. Dutton & Co. 1906. I, 10. (Edited by Henry D. Roberts.

The Muses' Library.) Permission to quote this text has been kindly granted by the publisher.

30. Thomas Chatterton, *Miscellanies in Prose and Verse.* London: Printed for Fielding and Walker . . . MDCCLXXVIII. p. 59.

31. *The Works of Thomas Chatterton, Containing His Life by G. Gregory, and Miscellaneous Poems.* London: Printed by Biggs and Cottle . . . 1803. I, 15.

32. Henry Felton, *A Dissertation on Reading the Classics and Forming a Just Style* . . . London: Printed for Richard Baldwin . . . MDCCLIII. p. 168 ff. (Fifth edition.)

33. Cf. the use of "looked in," *The Faerie Queene,* I, i, 13.14 with the *Poetical Sketches,* p. 7, ll. 1–4; *The Faerie Queene,* I, ii, 1–8 with "Come o'er the eastern hill" in *To Spring* and "fervid car" in *To Summer; The Faerie Queene,* IV, x, 45.6–9 with the *Poetical Sketches,* p. 10, l. 10; and *The Faerie Queene,* I, i, 7.4 with the *Poetical Sketches,* p. 2, l. 13.

34. Cf. Collins, *op. cit., Eclogue the First,* p. 20, ll. 1–2:

> When sweet and blushing, like a virgin bride,
> The radiant morn resum'd her orient pride, . . .

Cf. also Alexander B. Grosart (editor), *The Complete Works of Joshuah Sylvester.* [London]: Printed for Private Circulation. 1880. I, 180, ll. 273–280:

> The sable Night dis-lodg'd, and now began
> Aurora's Usher with his windy Fan
> Gently to shake the Woods on every side,
> While his fair *Mistresse* (like a stately Bride)
> With Flowrs, and Gems, & *Indian* Gold, doth spangle
> Her lovely locks, her Lover's looks to tangle;
> When gliding through the Ayre in Mantle blew,
> With silver fring'd, she drops the pearly deaw.

35. Cf. *England's Helicon.* Reprinted from the edition of 1600. London: Printed for Frederick Etchella . . . p. 13: "Her mettall buskins deckt with flowers, as th' earth when frosts are gone."
Cf. also Collins, *op. cit.,* p. 85, ll. 2–5:

> When Chearfulness, a nymph of healthiest hue,
>> Her bow across her shoulder flung,
>> Her buskins gemm'd with morning dew,
> Blew an inspiring air, that dale and thicket
>> rung, . . .

36. Cf. Psalm 19.4–5: ". . . In them hath he set a tabernacle for the sun, Which is as a bridegroom coming out of his chamber and rejoiceth as a strong man to run a race."

37. Cf. Chatterton, *Ethelgar* (*T. and Co. Mag.,* I, 145): "The morn awoke the sun: who, stepping from the mountain's brow, shook his ruddy locks upon the shining dew; Aelgar arose from sleep; he seized his sword and spear, and issued to the chace."

38. For "dewy locks" cf. *The Faerie Queene,* IV, xi, 11.3; III, iv, 30.2. Cf. William Broome, *Poems on Several Occasions.* London: Printed for Henry Lintot . . . MDCCL. p. 19. (The second edition.)

> Till as a Giant strong, a Bridegroom gay,
> The Sun springs dancing thro' the Gates of Day:

> He shakes his dewy Locks, and hurls his Beams
> O'er the proud Hills, and down the glowing Streams: . . .

39. "Long-hu'd" is evidently a misprint for "long-liv'd."

40. J. William Hebel (editor), *The Works of Michael Drayton.* Oxford: Printed at the Shakespeare Head Press . . . 1931. I, 133, ll. 153–160. Permission to quote this text has been kindly granted by the publisher.

41. *Ibid.*, p. 137, ll. 331–334.

42. Cf. *The Faerie Queene,* III, iv, 51.6–9; I, x, 42.3; I, v, 19.2; III, ix, 53.5; *Paradise Lost,* VIII, 518–520.

43. Max Plowman would interpret *To Morning* symbolically. He says: "That visionary jewel, the little poem 'Morning,' which in a couple of stanzas epitomizes Blake's whole purpose, tells of the soul cleaving its way through the gates of night to meet the sun." (Max Plowman, *An Introduction to the Study of Blake.* London & Toronto: J. M. Dent & Sons, Ltd. 1927. p. 167.) This is a beautiful idea, but it does not take into account the relationship of the poem to Blake's youth and to the source of its inspiration. Permission to quote this text has been kindly granted by the publisher.

44. Mona Wilson, *The Life of William Blake,* p. 28.

45. Damon (*William Blake,* p. 256) refers to this poem as Blake's first protest against marriage, "playful enough now, but later to become quite bitter."

46. Alexander B. Grosart (editor), *The Complete Poems of Sir John Davies.* London: Chatto and Windus . . . 1876. II, 77. Cf. p. 65.

47. E. H. Fellowes (editor), *English Madrigal Verse, 1588–1632.* Oxford: At the Clarendon Press. MCMXXIX. p. 132. Permission to quote this text has been kindly granted by the publisher. Thomas Morley's *First Book of Ballets:*

> In nets of golden wires,
> In pearl and ruby spangled,
>   My heart entangled
> Cries and help requires.
> Sweet love, from out these briars
> But thou vouchsafe to free me,
> Ere long, alive, alas, thou shalt not see me.

[Thomas Lodge], *Rosalynde. Euphues golden Legacie, found after his death in his Cell at Silexedra* . . . London: Printed by Abel Ieffes . . . 1592:

> Ile shut mine eyes to keep you in,
> Ile make you fast it for your sinne,
> Ile count your power not worth a pinne,
> Alas what hereby shall I winne,
>   If he gainsay me?
> What if I beate the wanton boy with many a rod?
> He will repay me with annoy, because a God.
>   Then sit thou safely on my knee,
>   And let thy bower my bosome be;
>   O Cupid so thou pittie me,
>   Spare not but play thee.

Philip Sidney, *The Countess of Pembroke's Arcadia,* Cambridge: At the University Press. 1912. p. 139. Lib. I, Ch. 19. (Edited by A. Feuillerat):

> The house is made a very lothsome cage,
> Wherein the birdie doth never sing but cry;
> With such a will as nothing can asswage.
> Dearly the servants doo their wages buy,
> Revil'd for ech small fault, sometimes for none;
> They better live that in a gaile doo lie.
> Let other fowler spots away be blowne;
> For I seeke not their shame, but still me thinkes,
> A better life it is to lye alone.

Permission to quote this text has been kindly granted by the publisher. John Oldham, *Remains in Verse and Prose.* London: Printed for *Jo. Hindmarsh . . .* 1684. p. 83, ll. 1–13:

> That mighty Slave whom the proud Victor's Rage
> Shut Pris'ner in a golden Cage,
> Condemn'd to glorious Vassalage,
> Ne'er long'd for dear Enlargement more.
> Nor his gay Bondage with less Patience bore,
> Than this great Spirit brookt its tedious Stay,
> While fetter'd here in brittle Clay,
> And wish'd to disengage and fly away.
> It vext and chaf't and still desir'd to be
> Releas'd to the sweet Freedom of Eternity.

Dodsley, *op. cit.,* II, 308:

> Impatient of his iron cage
> The bird thus spends his little rage,
> And 'scapes with shatter'd wings:
> And soon with new-fledg'd pinions soars,
> And hast'ning to his native bow'rs,
> A joyful welcome sings.

48. Malkin, *op. cit.,* pp. xxiv–xxxvii.
49. One phrase, "crisped hair" (p. 66, l. 19), in Jonson's ninth lyric in *A Celebration of Choris* appears also in *The Faerie Queene,* II, iii, 30.1; *First Part of Henry the Fourth,* I, iii, 107. Blake could have read it in Potter's *Aeschylus,* p. 138, l. 908; p. 239, l. 7; p. 245, l. 192; or in Collins, *op. cit.,* p. 78, ll. 16–18.
50. Tovey, *op. cit.,* II, 1–2.
51. [Thomas Percy], *Reliques of Ancient English Poetry: Consisting of Old Heroic Ballads, Songs, and other Pieces of our earliest Poets . . .* London: Printed for J. Dodsley . . . MDCCLXV. This copy is now in the library at Wellesley College.
52. In *The Monthly Ledger* for May 1775 (II, 612–613) appear both *The Passionate Shepherd to His Love* (attributed to Shakespeare) and *The Nymph's Reply.*
53. *Mad Song* is in one point of style like much Elizabethan verse. It is the use of *lo* to introduce a sentence. Cf. Norman Ault, *Elizabethan Lyrics from the Original Texts.* London and New York: Longmans, Green and Co. . . . 1925.

Cf. also "my feet are winged" (p. 41, ll. 14–15), "winged with certain victory" (p. 39, ll. 3–4), and "wing their brows with hope and expectation" (p. 42, ll. 17–18) with "My thoughts are winged with hopes" and "winged with sweet hopes" in John Dowland's *First Book of Airs.* (Fellowes, *op. cit.,* pp. 409, 414, 499) Blake could have known these phrases as one knows any proverbial expression which is so familiar as to seem never to have been learned.

54. Mona Wilson, *op. cit.,* p. 326.

55. Gilchrist, *Life of William Blake,* I, 365.

56. *Ibid.,* II, 235. Cf. I, 365.

57. Sir Philip Sidney, *The Defence of Poesie* in *The Complete Works.* Cambridge: At the University Press. 1923. III, 8. (Edited by A. Feuillerat.) Permission to quote this text has been kindly granted by the publisher.

CHAPTER V

1. Blake, *Poetry and Prose,* pp. 856, 859, 970 ff.

2. *Ibid.,* p. 1024.

3. *Ibid.,* p. 1011.

4. *Ibid.*

5. *Ibid.,* p. 1060. Letter to Butts, Jan. 10, 1802: "One thing of real consequence I have accomplish'd by coming into this country . . . I have . . . resumed my primitive & original ways of Execution in both painting & engraving, . . ."

6. *Ibid.,* p. 1040.

7. *Ibid.,* p. 798.

8. Cf. Robert W. Babcock, *The Genesis of Shakespearean Idolatry, 1766–1799* . . . Chapel Hill: The University of North Carolina Press. 1931.

9. Blake, *Poetry and Prose,* p. 1116.

10. Gilchrist, *Life of William Blake,* I, 18–19.

11. A reproduction of the engraving of Edward the Third faces p. 13, Vol. I of Wright's *Life of Blake.*

12. Cf. *The Times Literary Supplement* (London), XXVI, 592. (September 1, 1927.)

13. Reproduced in Gilchrist, *op. cit.,* I, 254.

14. Wright in his *Life of Blake* (II, 97) quotes an anonymous writer in the *Monthly Review* for March 1833, who gave a conversation Blake is reported to have had in his last years with the "visionary" Edward the Third. The conversation becomes of interest through the striking resemblances between it and the lines about death and about the elation over entering battle in Scene V of Blake's early play, *King Edward the Third.*

The *Monthly Review,* however, for the date given does not record such an episode, nor was it found elsewhere. Mr. Wright was unable to cite the source of his information. Until its source is made authentic, this episode must be regarded as another apocryphal story. Even if the *Monthly Review* had recorded it and the writer been, as has been supposed, Crabb Robinson, one would still need to accept the report with caution because when Robinson went to Blake with intrusive, probing questions about the Spirit realm, Blake apparently played upon his credulity. Gilchrist stated (I, 327): "In society, people would disbelieve and exasperate him, would set upon the gentle yet fiery-hearted mystic, and stir him up into being extravagant, out of a mere spirit of opposition. Then he would say things on purpose to startle, and make people stare."

15. [Anon.], *King Edward III. An Historical Drama.* London: Printed by A. I. Valpy . . . 1814. *Preface.*

16. [W. Mountfort], *King Edward the Third, with the Fall of Mortimer, Earl of March. An Historical Play.* London: Printed for J. Hindmarsh . . . 1691. Blake's play shows no influence from Ch. F. Weiss's *Eduard der Dritte,* 1765 or Cresset's *Edoward III,* 1740.

17. [E. Capell], *Prolusions: or select Pieces of antient Poetry . . .* London: Printed for J. and R. Tonson . . . 1760. Hereafter this play will be referred to as *The Raigne* to distinguish it from other plays and to reduce the monotony of repeating the king's name. The text of *The Raigne* given here will be used since it is the only one Blake may have seen.

18. Swinburne (*William Blake,* p. 12) said: "Blake had probably never seen the praiseworthy but somewhat verbose historical drama on the same subject, generously bestowed upon Shakespeare by critics of that German acuteness which can accept as poetry the most meritorious powers of rhetoric. His own disjointed and stumbling fragment, deficient as it is in shape or plan or local colour, has far more of the sound and savour of Shakespeare's style in detached lines: more indeed than has ever been caught up by any poet except one . . . the author of 'Joseph and his Brethern'; . . ."

19. William Shirley, *Edward the Black Prince; or the Battle of Poictiers; An Historical Tragedy . . .* London: Printed for J. and R. Tonson . . . MDCCL. Cf. *Poetical Sketches,* p. 3, ll. 30–31; p. 61, ll. 27–28; p. 67, ll. 23–25; p. 22, ll. 20–21; p. 71, ll. 11–14.

20. Blake could have been interested in the presentation of Edward the Third's character by Gilbert West in *The Institution of the Order of the Garter.* (Dodsley, *op. cit.,* II, 107–166.)

21. Capell, *op. cit.,* III, iii, p. 56, ll. 16–25. Since the text of *The Raigne* in *Prolusions* is unlined, references will be given in terms of the page of the text and the number of the line on that particular page. Cf. *ibid.,* I, i, p. 8, ll. 12, 30.

22. A modern edition of Shakespeare has been selected for citation through this study: *The Complete Works* (Students' Cambridge Edition) Boston . . .: Houghton Mifflin Company . . . [1906]. (Edited by William A. Neilson.) Permission to quote this text has been kindly granted by the publisher.

23. Cf. *Poetical Sketches,* p. 36, ll. 4–10, 15, 23–27; p. 37, l. 5; p. 40, ll. 3–24.

24. For expression of fear cf. *Julius Caesar,* I, ii, 80, 196; iii, 60; II, i, 183; ii, 26, 35, 43; iv, 32; III, i, 102; IV, iii, 8–15; *Macbeth,* IV, ii, 4, 12–14; *First Part of Henry the Fourth,* IV, iii, 8–15; *Henry the Fifth,* IV, ii, 37.

25. *The Raigne,* IV, iv, p. 74, ll. 15–30:

> To die is all as common, as to live;
> The one in choice, the other holds in chace:
> For, from the instant we begin to live,
> We do pursue and hunt the time to die:

> First bud we, then we blow, and after seed;
> Then, presently, we fall; and, as a shade
> Follows the body, so we follow death.
> If then we hunt for death, why do we fear it?
> *Or,* if we fear it, why do we follow it?
> If we do fear, with fear we do but aid
> The thing we fear to seize on us the sooner:
> If we fear not, then no resolved proffer
> Can overthrow the limit of our fate:
> For, whether ripe, or rotten, drop we shall,
> As we do draw the lottery of our doom.

26. *Ibid.*, I, ii, p. 12, ll. 6–13.
27. Cf. *First Part of Henry the Fourth,* IV, i, ll. 1–11:

> *Hotspur* . . . If speaking truth
> In this fine age were not thought flattery,
> Such attribution should the Douglas have
> As not a soldier of this season's stamp
> Should go so general current through the world.
> By God, I cannot flatter.

28. Cf. *First Part of Henry the Fourth,* I, ii, ll. 220–226:

> Yet herein will I imitate the sun,
> Who doth permit the base contagious clouds
> To smother up his beauty from the world,
> That when he please again to be himself
> Being wanted, he may be more wonder'd at
> By breaking through the foul and ugly mists
> Of vapours that did seem to strangle him.

Cf. *Sonnet 33.*
29. Cf. *First Part of Henry the Sixth* (I, i, 8–14) regarding Henry the Fifth:

> England ne'er had a king until his time.
> Virtue he had, deserving to command.
> His brandish'd sword did blind men with his beams;
> His arms spread wider than a dragon's wings;
> His sparkling eyes, replete with wrathful fire,
> More dazzled and drove back his enemies
> Than mid-day sun fierce bent against their faces.

30. Cf. *The Raigne,* III, iii, p. 56, ll. 18–20; I, i, p. 8, l. 30–p. 9, l. 2.
31. *Ibid.,* I, i, p. 9, ll. 3–7.
32. Richard Garnett, "William Blake." *The Portfolio.* No. 22, p. 13. (October, 1895.)
33. Sir Walter Blunt in the *First Part of Henry the Fourth* may have given the surname for Blake's character. Lord Percy in the same play is one of the characters used by Blake.
34. *Henry the Fifth,* IV, vii, 14 ff.
35. *The Raigne,* II, i, p. 20, l. 18 has a similar idea: "But like a fading taper, dim and dead?"
36. Symons, *William Blake,* p. 66.
37. Cf. *Romeo and Juliet,* IV, i, 80–86; iv, 45–55; *Hamlet,* I, iv, 46–51; V, i, *passim; King John,* III, iv, 25–33; *Macbeth,* III, iv, 71.

Notes. 229

38. Blake, *Poetry and Prose*, p. 519.

39. *Ibid.*, p. 800.

40. Burke quoted this passage from Shakespeare in his second edition of the *Sublime and Beautiful* which Blake read as a child.

41. Blake, *Poetry and Prose*, p. 194.

42. Damon, *William Blake*, p. 322.

43. Blake, *Poetry and Prose*, p. 546.

44. Cf. Helen M. Williams, *An Ode on Peace*. London: Printed for T. Cadell. MDCCLXXXIII. pp. 5, 14; Beilby Porteus, *Death, A Poetical Essay*. Cambridge: Printed for J. Bentham . . . MDCCLXII. pp. 11–12.

45. Blake, *Poetry and Prose*, p. 120, ll. 31–34. Cf. *ibid.*, p. 968, *Annotations to Bacon's "Essays"*:

> "What do these knaves mean by virtue? Do they
> mean war and its horrors, and its heroic villains?"

46. Anna Bunston in "Blake's Songs of Battle," *Land and Water* . . . V, 15 (October 2, 1915), apparently considers all of Blake's statements sympathetic with war. She considers his interest to lie in the courage and mental elation of men as they face death which she thinks Blake always thought of as a "joyful translation," or as a "gate to life." Miss Bunston reconciles rather too easily the contradictory elements in Blake's depiction of war. Permission to quote this text has been kindly granted by the publisher.

47. Blake was always very patriotic. In *A Public Address* (*c*. 1810) he said: "Resentment for Personal Injuries has had some share in this Public Address, But Love to My Art & Zeal for my Country a much Greater." (*Poetry and Prose*, p. 813.)

48. Cf. Exeter's speech in *Henry Fifth* (II, iv, 104–109) with Blake's *Prologue to King John*. (p. 57, ll. 8–19.)

49. The writer is greatly indebted to Mrs. William Emerson of Cambridge, Massachusetts for the privilege of studying the *Rossetti MS.* in her possession.

50. Cf. Damon, *op. cit.*, p. 219.

51. Cf. Wright, *op. cit.*, p. 177; Mona Wilson, *op. cit.*, p. 201.

52. Garnett, *op. cit.*, p. 13.

53. *Ibid.*, p. 14. Paul Berger (*op. cit.*, p. 327) expressed much the same idea: ". . . l'imitation est shakespearienne, et ce seul fait, ce retour à la période d'Elizabeth, à un moment (1783) où la mode avait été si longtemps différente et commençait juste à changer, est caractéristique d'une tendance poétique nouvelle, dans laquelle l'imagination allait dominer."

54. Robert Lloyd, *Shakespeare: An Epistle to Mr Garrick* (1760) in *Poems*. London: Printed for the Author . . . MDCCLXII. p. 54, ll. 1–4.

55. Tovey, *Letters of Thomas Gray*, I, 100. (April, 1742.)

CHAPTER VI

1. The *Reliques* appeared in 1765.

2. Gilchrist, *Life of Blake*, I, 24.

3. E. de Selincourt, *Oxford Lectures on Poetry*. Oxford: At the

Clarendon Press. 1934. pp. 133, 135. Permission to quote this text has been kindly granted by the publisher.

4. Oswald Crawfurd, "William Blake: Artist, Poet, and Mystic." *New Quarterly Review*, II, 474–475.

5. Arthur Symons, *The Romantic Movement in English Poetry*. New York: E. P. Dutton and Company . . . 1909. pp. 38, 40. Permission to quote this text has been kindly granted by the publisher.

6. *Bulletin of The John Rylands Library, Manchester*. Manchester: At the University Press . . . 1928. XII, 33. (Edited by the librarian.)

7. Burlington Fine Arts Club, *Catalogue Blake Centenary Exhibition*. London: Privately printed . . . 1927. p. 12.

8. T. S. Eliot, *Selected Essays, 1917–1932*. New York: Harcourt, Brace and Company. [1932.] p. 276. Permission to quote this text has been kindly granted by the publisher.

9. [James Thomson and David Mallet], *Alfred: A Masque. . . .* London: Printed for A. Miller . . . MDCCXL. p. 43.

10. James Thomson, *The Complete Poetical Works*. London . . . . Henry Frowde, Oxford University Press. 1908. p. 38, ll. 931–935. (Edited by J. Logie Robertson.)

The Oxford edition has been chosen for all references to the poetical works because it has the "final text faithfully reproduced, word for word." The "final text" would have been the most complete text available to Blake. Collations with all earlier texts of the parallel passages have been made. Permission to quote this text has been kindly granted by the publisher.

11. Cf. Dodsley, *A Collection of Poems*, V, 156. The Honorable Sir C. H. Williams in *To Mrs. Bindon at Bath:*

> APOLLO of old on Britannia did smile,
> And Delphi forsook for the sake of this isle,
> Around him he lavishly scatter'd his lays,
> And in every wilderness planted his bays;
> Then Chaucer and Spenser harmonious were heard,
> Then Shakespear, and Milton, and Waller appear'd,
> And Dryden, whose brows by Apollo were crown'd
> As he sung in such strains as the God might
>   have own'd;
> But now, since the laurel is given of late
> To Cibber, to Eusden, to Shadwell and Tate,
> Apollo hath quitted the isle he once lov'd
> And his harp and his bays to Hibernia
>   remov'd;
> He vows and he swears he'll inspire us no more,
> And he puts out Pope's fires which he kindled
>   before; . . .

12. S. T. Coleridge, *Biographia Literaria; or Biographical Sketches of My Literary Life and Opinions*. London: Rest Fenner . . . 1817. I, 11–12: ". . . no models of past times, however perfect, can have the same vivid effect on the youthful mind, as the productions of contemporary genius. . . . But the writings of a contemporary, . . . surrounded by the same circumstances, and disciplined by the same manners, possess a *reality* for him, and inspire an actual friendship as of a man for a man . . ."

13. Thomson, *Complete Poetical Works,* p. 239.
14. Blake, *Poetry and Prose,* pp. 525, 529, 546, 561, 749.
15. *Ibid.,* p. 795 ff.
16. *Lloyd's Evening Post,* XXXIII, 350. (October 11, 1773.)
17. Thomson, *Alfred: A Masque,* p. 31, ll. 3–9, 16–25.
18. Russell, *Engravings,* pp. 26, 68.
19. Malkin, *A Father's Memoirs of His Child,* pp. xxi–xxii.
20. Keynes, *Bibliography,* pp. 32, 38. Cf. Russell, *Engravings,* p. 68.
21. Gilchrist, *op. cit.,* I, 32.
22. Blake, *Poetry and Prose,* p. 104.
23. James Macpherson, *The Works of Ossian, the Son of Fingal* . . . London: Printed for T. Becket . . . MDCCLXV. I, 18.
24. Edwin Ellis, *The Real Blake.* New York: McClure, Phillips & Co. MCMVII. p. 31.
25. Russell, *Engravings,* p. 54.
26. Mona Wilson, *Life of Blake,* p. 12. Also reproduced as a frontispiece in Ellis and Yeats, *Works* . . . London: Bernard Quaritch . . . 1893. III.
27. Cf. Blake, *Poetry and Prose,* p. 1108. Letter to Hayley (October 23, 1804): "I was a slave bound in a mill among beasts and devils; . . ."
28. Wright, *Life of Blake,* II, facing p. 80.
29. Keynes, *Bibliography,* facing p. 166.
30. Later Blake wrote (*Poetry and Prose,* p. 841): "The Greeks represent Chronos or Time as a very Aged Man; this is Fable, but the Real Vision of Time is in Eternal Youth. I have, however, somewhat accomodated my Figure of Time to the common opinion, . . . & I see Time aged, alas, too much so . . . But Time & Space as Real Beings, a Male & a Female. Time is a Man, Space is a Woman, . . ."
31. *Ibid.,* p. 127.
32. Russell, *Engravings,* p. 55.
33. Darrell Figgis, *The Paintings of William Blake.* London: Ernest Benn Limited . . . MCMXXV.
34. Binyon, *Engraved Designs,* p. 119.
35. Russell, *Engravings,* p. 54.
36. Blake, *Poetry and Prose,* p. 430.
37. Thomson may have been of further inspiration to Blake's later pictures if one considers the mood and manner as well as the imagery of the lines in *Liberty* (pp. 368–369, ll. 393–404):

'As o'er the wave—resounding deep
To my near reign, the happy isle, I steered
With easy wing—behold! from surge to surge
Stalked the tremendous Genius of the Deep.
Around him clouds in mingled tempest hung;
Thick flashing meteors crowned his starry head;
And ready thunder reddened in his hand,
Or from it streamed compressed the gloomy cloud.
Where'er he looked, the trembling waves recoiled.
He needs but strike the conscious flood, and shook
From shore to shore, in agitation dire,
It works his dreadful will.'

38. Samuel Johnson, *Lives of the Poets*. Oxford: At the Clarendon Press. MDCCCCV. II, 301. (Edited by George Birbeck Hill.)

39. Hannah More, *Slavery, a Poem*. London: Printed for T. Cadell . . . MDCCLXXXVIII.

40. Church, *Josiah Wedgwood*, p. 93.

41. Smiles, *Josiah Wedgwood*, p. 64.

42. Blake, *Poetical Sketches*, pp. 31–32, 40, 42, 43, 52, *passim*.

43. Cf. the ideas in Seally's *January, An Ode. The Lady's Magazine*, II, 280 (January, 1771):

> Shall Commerce ever sacred be
> Blest offspring sprung from *Liberty:*
> > While circling time renews the strain.
> Beneath a Monarch's fost'ring care,
> See! ships unnumber'd ride in air,
> > Like lordly forests flow the trembling main.

44. Thomson, *Alfred, A Masque*, p. 43, ll. 25–28.

45. Blake, *Poetry and Prose*, p. 857.

46. Thomson, *Complete Poetical Works*, p. 398, l. 204; p. 312, ll. 21–22. Cf. "unfettered thought" in p. 330, l. 212; p. 412, l. 687; "enthralled the mind," p. 338, l. 388.

47. There are numerous other reminiscences of *Liberty* in *King Edward the Third*. Cf. the passages on war: its glory (p. 325, l. 38), its desolating effect (p. 249, ll. 332, 337), the ecstasy of soldiers about to enter battle (p. 348, l. 282). Cf. also Thomson, *Complete Poetical Works*, p. 321, l. 321 and p. 325, l. 34 with Blake, *Poetical Sketches*, p. 30, ll. 13–15; Thomson, *Complete Poetical Works*, p. 379, ll. 778–781 with Blake, *Poetical Sketches*, p. 29, l. 9.

48. Thomson, *Complete Poetical Works*. Cf. p. 45, l. 1143: "Truth, goodness, honour, harmony and love, . . ."

49. It will be remembered that in certain copies of the *Poetical Sketches*, Blake changed *her* to *his*, p. 12, l. 6.

50. Cf. Thomson's *Spring* (*Complete Poetical Works*, p. 12, ll. 249–251):

> "Meantime the song went round; and dance and sport,
> Wisdom and friendly talk successive stole
> Their hours away; . . ."

51. Eusebius, *Winter, a Poem* in *The Monthly Ledger, or Literary Repository*, I, 267. (November, 1773.)

52. Joseph Warton, *Odes on Various Subjects*. London: Printed for R. Dodsley . . . MDCCXLVI. p. 9, ll. 19–20. Cf. Spenser's *The Faerie Queene*, VII, vii, 31.

53. Samuel Ashby, *Miscellaneous Poems* . . . London: Printed for W. Miller . . . 1794. p. 141, ll. 107–110. Cf. Dodsley, *op. cit.*, III, 228.

54. Thomson, *Complete Poetical Works*, p. 190 ff.

55. Blake, *Poetry and Prose*, p. 562.

56. William Wordsworth, *Poems* . . . London: Printed for Longman, Hurst, Rees, Orme, and Brown . . . 1815. I, 44.

57. Blake, *Poetry and Prose*, p. 1025. The sonnet to which Blake referred contained the following lines which must have impressed him:

Heaven-born, the Soul a heaven-ward course
  must hold;
Beyond the visible world She soars to seek,
(For what delights the sense is false and weak)
Ideal Form, the universal mould.
  (Wordsworth, *op. cit.*, II, 179, ll. 55–58.)

58. Blake, *Poetry and Prose*, p. 1067.

59. A number of parallels not elaborated in the text merit a brief report:

"Hecla" in *To Winter,* a volcano in southwestern Iceland, is mentioned by Thomson first in the 1744 edition (*Complete Poetical Works,* p. 218, l. 888) and by Percy (*Reliques,* I, 314 and II, 170). Thomson's phrase "vegetable soul" (p. 211, l. 707) is to be compared with Blake's "vegetative man," "vegetable world," "vegetable eyes" of *Poetry and Prose,* pp. 514, 573, 618, 830, and a score of others.

Thomson's description of the robin (p. 195, ll. 245–251) should be compared with Blake's description, pp. 296–297. The episode in Blake's "When early morn walks forth" should be compared with Thomson's description of adolescent love and rivalry and consequent despair in p. 43, ll. 1074–1080; p. 44, ll. 1092–1098.

Blake's unusual piece of realism, *Blind-man's Buff,* is but an episode from such scenes as described by Thomson in p. 208, ll. 617; p. 209, l. 5.

60. [Mark Akenside], *The Pleasures of Imagination. A Poem.* London: Printed for R. Dodsley . . . MDCCXLIV. p. 4, ll. 56–59.

61. *Ibid.,* p. 15, ll. 288 ff.

62. *Ibid.,* p. 31, ll. 9–11.

63. *Ibid.,* p. 16, ll. 312–319.

64. Meyerstein, *Life of Chatterton*, p. 82.

65. *Lloyd's Evening Post*, LII, 451. (May 10, 1783.)

66. Austin Lane Poole (editor), *The Poetical Works of Gray and Collins.* London: Humphrey Milford . . . 1926. p. 311, ll. 5–6; p. 312, ll. 15–16, 19–20. (Second edition.) Permission to quote this text has been kindly granted by the publisher.

67. *Ibid.,* p. 98, ll. 3–6.

68. *Ibid.,* p. 55, ll. 3–4.

69. Thomas Gray, *Poems. A New Edition.* London: Printed for J. Dodsley. MDCCLXVIII. p. 30, ll. 1–4.

70. Blake, *Poetry and Prose,* p. 118, ll. 5–6.

71. Gray, *op. cit.,* p. 4, l. 5; p. 5, l. 2.

72. Joseph Warton, *op. cit.,* A. 2.

73. Damon, *William Blake,* p. 259.

74. The period in l. 28 is obviously a misprint.

75. Blake, *Poetry and Prose,* pp. 77, 90.

76. Saintsbury, *History of English Prosody,* III, 11–13.

77. E. de Selincourt, *op. cit.,* pp. 133–134.

78. *The Distracted Lover* uses the phrase "meridian glories" (II, 355, ll. 9–10) as Blake used it in *To Mrs. Ann Flaxman. (Poetry and Prose,* p. 104.) Cf. Blake's "Bring me an axe and spade, Bring me a winding

sheet" with Percy, *Reliques,* I, 162, ll. 29–32 and with *Hamlet,* V, i, 101.

79. Gilchrist, *op. cit.,* I, 294.

80. Cf. Percy, *op. cit.,* I, 226, ll. 13–16; 288, ll. 61–62 with *Poetical Sketches,* p. 11, ll. 7–8.

81. The rhythm of "My silks and fine array" is strikingly like that of "The earth, late choakt with showers" of Lodge in *Scillaes Metamorphosis* (1589) in *The Complete Works.* [Glasgow] : Printed for the Hunterian Club. MDCCCLXXXIII. I, 46.

82. Cf. *Night, An Ode,* by T. H. in *Lloyd's Evening Post,* XIX, 628. (December 30, 1766.)

83. Horace Walpole, *The Castle of Otranto and the Mysterious Mother.* London: Printed at the Chiswick Press . . . 1924. (Edited by Montague Summers. Text of the first edition) : (*) p. 32; (†) p. 34; (‡) p. 35; (§) p. 36; (‖) p. 37; (¶) p. 137. Permission to quote this text has been kindly granted by the publisher.

84. Blake, *Poetry and Prose,* p. 864.

85. Cf. Elenor's lament (p. 8, l. 18—p. 9, l. 10) with the lament of Comala in Macpherson, *op. cit.,* I, 129.

CHAPTER VII

1. Gilchrist, *Life of Blake,* I, 25.

2. Symons, *William Blake,* p. 37.

3. Damon, *William Blake,* p. 31.

4. Mona Wilson, *Life of Blake,* pp. 6–7.

5. E. de Selincourt, *Lectures,* p. 135.

6. Horace Walpole wrote to the Rev. Wm. Mason, February 17, 1777 [Mrs. Paget Toynbee (editor), *The Letters of Horace Walpole.* Oxford: At the Clarendon Press. MCMIV. X, 15] : "Mr. Tyrrwhit has at last published the Bristol poems. He does not give up the antiquity, yet fairly leaves everybody to ascribe them to Chatterton, if they please, which I think the internal evidence must force everyone to do, unless the amazing prodigy of Chatterton's producing them should not seem a larger miracle than Rowley's and Canning's anticipation of the style of modern poetry."

Walpole's allusion is to the statement in the preface: "Whether the Poems be really antient or modern; the compositions of Rowley, or the forgeries of Chatterton; they must always be considered as a most singular literary curiosity."

Permission to quote this text has been kindly granted by the publisher.

7. Blake's copy of Chatterton, with the later owner's name, Samuel Palmer, written on the inside of the front cover, is in the private library of Sir Sidney Cockerell, Director of the Fitzwilliam Museum in Cambridge, England, to whom gratitude is expressed for the privilege of examining it.

8. Meyerstein (*Life of Chatterton,* p. 109) says that the pseudonym was evolved from the "Durham Man of Bristol"—Turgot—whose signature appeared in some source books used by Chatterton.

9. *The Town and Country Magazine,* I, 616. (November, 1769.)

10. *The Gentleman's Magazine,* XLII, 285. (June, 1772.)

The London Chronicle, XXXI, 589. (June 19, 1772.)

Cf. reviews in *The Monthly Review; or Literary Journal,* XLVII, 150 (August, 1772) and *The Critical Review; or Annals of Literature,* XXXIV, 234–236. (September, 1772.)

11. Meyerstein, *op. cit.,* p. 451.

12. *Ibid.*

13. *The Town and Country Magazine,* I, (1) 40–41; (2) 94–95; (3) 152–153; (4) 202–203; (5) 245; (6) 312; (7) 343; (8) 413–414; (9) 482–483; (10) 535–536; (11) 584–585; (12) 628–629.

14. Blake, *Poetry and Prose,* p. 636.

15. *The European Magazine and London Review,* IV, 390. (November, 1783):

> "All think Chatterton is dead,
> His works are worth preserving!
> Yet no one when he was alive,
> Would keep the bard from starving."

16. Blake, *Poetry and Prose,* p. 633.

17. *Ibid.,* pp. 796–797. Blake said, "Mr. B. has in his hands poems of the highest antiquity." This could not refer to any of his own works. Could this be an allusion to some of Chatterton's poems?

18. Blake's indebtedness to Bryant's *New System, or, An Analysis of Ancient Mythology* (London: Printed for T. Payne . . . MDCCL-XXIV [Vol. III, MDCCLXXVI]. *Preface*) has not been previously described. It appears in the ideas in Blake's *Descriptive Catalogue* (*Poetry and Prose,* pp. 796–797); in the use of "Har" in *Tiriel* (Bryant, *op. cit.,* I, 94); and in the use of names altered to make Thamuz, Thamas, Themis, Ethothion, and Thermodon (*Ibid.,* II, 346, 447). The plates in Bryant's three volumes are mainly signed by Basire. It is Russell's opinion (*Engravings,* p. 191) that these are "either wholly or at least in part from the hand of Blake."

19. Blake, *Poetry and Prose,* pp. 869, 871, 872.

20. [Thomas Bridges], *The Battle of the Bonnets, a Political Poem, from the Erse.* London: Printed for W. Bingley . . . 1768.

21. [Anon.], *Gisbal, an Hyperborean Tale: Translated from the Fragments of Ossian, the Son of Fingal.* London: Printed for the Author . . . MDCCLXII. p. 43.

22. Toynbee, *op. cit.,* XIII, 216.

23. One recognizes one of Ossian's sources when he reads Isaiah 9.5 and 17.12–13. Cf. Ossian, I, 76 and I, 57.

24. Chatterton's *Ethelgar* shows his keener realization of scene and more poetic rendering of it than was ever in Ossian. It begins: "'Tis not for thee, O man! to murmur at the will of the Almighty. When the thunders roar, the lightnings shine on the rising waves, and the black clouds sit on the brow of the lofty hill; who then protects the flying deer, swift as a sable cloud, tost by the whistling winds, leaping over the rolling floods, to gain the hoary wood: whilst the lightnings shine on his chest, and the wind rides over his horns." (*T. and Co. Mag.,* I, 144.)

25. The phrase, "sea of blood," was used by Thomson in *Liberty.* (*Complete Poetical Works,* pp. 319, l. 252; 328, l. 1079.) Cf. *ibid.,* p. 325, ll. 32–33 with *Poetical Sketches,* p. 52, l. 28; 22, l. 5.

26. Cf. with the passage in *Hardyknute* (Percy, *Reliques,* II, 97, ll. 205–206) :

> "Another arrow weil he markd
> It persit his neck in twain."

27. "Barrathon" recalls the name "Berrathon" which was the name of one of the Ossianic pieces in which also other names like "Tarthoma" and "Uthal" may have suggested some of Blake's later coinages in his prophetic books.

28. Cf. Blake's lines (p. 36, l. 18) :

> ". . . and lightning flashed
> From his eyes across the field . . ."

with Macpherson's lines in *Fingal* (I, 7) : "Their eyes are like flames of fire and roll in search of foes of the land," or in *Sul-malla of Lumon* (II, 231) : "His eyes were wandering flames, . . ." and in *Carricthura* (I, 277) : "His eyes appear like flames in his dark face."

29. II Samuel 1.6: "Saul leaned upon his spear."

Cf. Ossian, I, 237, 318: II, 32, 82.

30. Cf. *Tiriel* (*Prose and Poetry,* p. 156) :

> " 'Madness & deep dismay possess
>   the heart of the blind man,
> " 'The wanderer who seeks the woods,
>   leaning upon his staff?' "

Cf. *First Part of Henry the Fourth,* I, iii, 32: Hotspur—"leaning upon my sword."

31. Blake, *Poetry and Prose,* p. 104.

32. Macpherson, *The Works of Ossian,* I, 309, 329, 312.

33. Miss Elizabeth Carter once wrote Mrs. Montague:
"I have lately been reading some of the Poems of Ossian, and was struck by a singularity which I never remarked before, that among such innumerable multitude of similies [*sic*], there are scarcely any that are taken from animals. I think, in what I have been reading, absolutely none, except from the eagle." (The Rev. Montague Pennington (editor), *Letters from Mrs. Elizabeth Carter, to Mrs. Montague* . . . London: Printed for F. C. and J. Rivington . . . 1817. III, 17).

34. Chatterton used "lions of war" thrice in the *T. and Co. Mag.,* I, 427. Cf. his use in *Ælla:* "Ælla was chafed, as lyons madded bee." [Thomas Chatterton], *Poems, Supposed to have been written at Bristol by Thomas Rowley* . . . London: Printed for T. Payne and Son . . . MDCCLXXVII. p. 130.

35. Chatterton makes other references to wolves in *T. and Co. Mag.,* I, 425, 426, 427.

36. *The Court and City Magazine,* I, 86. (February, 1770.)

37. Thomas Chatterton, *The Complete Poetical Works* (Roberts edition), I, 81.

38. *The Town and Country Magazine,* I, 711.

Cf. Blake, *Poetry and Prose,* p. 73:

> "What immortal hand or eye
> Could frame thy fearful symmetry?"

Cf. Collins's *Ode to Fear* (*The Poetical Works,* p. 44) :

> "What mortal eye can fix'd behold?"

Cf. Thomas Traherne, *The Rapture* (*Poetical Works.* London: P. J. & A. E. Dobell. 1932. p. 111) : "What hand divine . . ."

39. Blake's "Gordred" is surely formed from Chatterton's "Godred" which Chatterton used again in *Craishes Heraultry* and in *The Unknown Knyght.* Chatterton added a footnote to "Hel" in *Gorthmund* to explain "Hela," a god of the Danes, whose symbol was the black raven. In Blake's *Tiriel* a woman character is named "Hela."

40. Chatterton, *Poems . . . By Thomas Rowley,* p. 47, ll. 57–60.

41. *Ibid.,* p. 45, ll. 21–24.

42. *Ibid.,* pp. 61, ll. 341–344; 62, ll. 359–360.

43. *Ibid.,* pp. 60, ll. 315–330; 54, ll. 205–214; 59, ll. 303–304; 61, ll. 337–340.

44. *Ibid.,* p. 60, ll. 521–522.

45. Blake, *Poetry and Prose,* p. 897.

46. Chatterton, *Complete Poetical Works* (Roberts edition), I, 135, ll. 13–14.

47. Blake, *Poetry and Prose,* p. 873.

48. *Ibid.,* p. 878.

49. Chatterton, *Complete Poetical Works* (Roberts edition), I, 93, ll. 157–158.

50. *Ibid.,* I, 68, ll. 31–33.

51. Cf. *ibid.,* I, 98, l. 295; 99, ll. 332–337; 97, ll. 285–290 with Blake, *Poetry and Prose,* pp. 866, 867, 878.

52. Chatterton, *Complete Poetical Works* (Roberts edition), I, 171, ll. 23–28.

> For had I never known the antique lore,
> I ne'er had ventured from my peaceful shore
> To be the wreck of promises and hopes,
> A Boy of Learning, and a Bard of Trophes;
> But happy in my humble sphere had moved,
> Untroubled, unrespected, unbeloved.

CHAPTER VIII

1. Leonard Welsted, *The Works, in Verse and Prose . . .* London: Printed by and for the Editor . . . MDCCLXXXVII. p. 141. (Edited by John Nichols.)

2. Meyerstein, *Life of Chatterton,* p. 216.

3. T. S. Eliot, *Selected Essays,* p. 4.

4. Cf. *A Description of Morning* in *The Monthly Ledger, or Literary Repository,* I, 152 (September, 1773) for an example of the prevalent mode.

5. Cf. William Woty, *An Ode* in *The Poetical Calendar . . .* London: Printed by Dryden Leach . . . MDCCLXIII. IV, 5–6. (Edited by Francis Fawkes and William Woty.)

6. Charles Churchill, *Gotham. A Poem.* London: Printed for the Author . . . MDCCLXIV. II, 1, 3:

> Verse is with them a knack, an idle toy,
> A rattle gilded o'er, on which a boy
> May play untaught, whilst, without art or force,
> Make it but jingle, Musick comes of course.

. . . .

Let *liquid* Gold emblaze the Sun at noon,
With *borrow'd* beams let Silver *pale* the Moon,
Let surges *hoarse* lash the resounding shore,
Let Streams *Maeander,* and let Torrents *roar,*
Let them breed up the melancholy breeze
To *sigh with sighing, sob with sobbing* trees,
Let Vales embroid'ry wear; let Flow'rs be ting'd
With various tints, let Clouds be lac'd or fring'd,
They have their wish; . . .

7. Lucy Allen Paton, "A Phase of William Blake's Romanticism." *Poet Lore* . . . V, 483. (No. 10, 1893.) Permission to quote this text has been kindly granted by the publisher.

8. Osbert Burdett, *William Blake.* New York: The Macmillan Company. 1926. p. 12. (English Men of Letters.) Permission to quote this text has been kindly granted by the publisher.

9. R. B. Adam and R. B. Adam, Jr., *A Letter of William Blake.* Privately printed.

10. Plowman, *An Introduction to the Study of Blake,* p. 23.

11. Blake, *Poetry and Prose,* p. 1050. Cf. *ibid.,* p. 1066.

12. Wicksteed, *Blake's Innocence and Experience,* p. 35.

13. Hamblen, *On the Minor Prophecies of William Blake,* p. 4.

14. Blake, *Poetry and Prose,* p. 551.

15. Adequate exposition of Blake's prosody has been given in: Saintsbury, *The History of English Prosody,* III, 4–30; Damon, *William Blake,* pp. 45–60; and Eric Partridge (editor), *Poetical Sketches by William Blake with an Essay on Blake's Metrics by Jack Lindsay.* London: The Scholartis Press . . . 1927. pp. 1–20.

16. T. Sturge Moore, "William Blake." *The Quarterly Review,* CCVIII, 33. (January, 1908.) Permission to quote this text has been kindly granted by the publisher.

17. Charles Gardner, *William Blake the Man.* London: J. M. Dent & Sons, Limited . . . MCMXIX. p. 16. Permission to quote this text has been kindly granted by the publisher.

18. Symons, *The Romantic Movement in English Poetry,* p. 41.

19. James Thomson ("B.V."), *Shelley, a Poem . . . to which is added an Essay on the Poems of William Blake* . . . [London]: Printed for Private Circulation . . . 1884. p. 102.

20. Blake, *Poetry and Prose,* p. 794.

21. Harold Bruce, *William Blake in This World.* New York: Harcourt, Brace and Company. [1925.] p. 42. Permission to quote this text has been kindly granted by the publisher.

22. Blake, *Poetry and Prose,* p. 554.

23. *Ibid.,* pp. 1108–1109.

24. Swinburne, *William Blake,* p. 14.

25. Shepherd, *The Poetical Sketches,* p. xii.

26. A. E. Housman, *The Name and Nature of Poetry.* New York: The Macmillan Company . . . 1933. p. 39. Permission to quote this text has been kindly granted by the publisher.

INDEX